L. Keiser

CAMBRIDGE PAPERS IN SOCIAL ANTHROPOLOGY

General Editor: Jack Goody

No 9 Caste Ideology and Interaction

CAMBRIDGE PAPERS IN SOCIAL ANTHROPOLOGY

1 *The Developmental Cycle in Domestic Groups*, edited by Jack Goody

2 *Aspects of Caste in South India, Ceylon and North-west Pakistan*, edited by E.R. Leach

3 *Marriage in Tribal Societies*, edited by Meyer Fortes

4 *Succession to High Office*, edited by Jack Goody

5 *Dialectic in Practical Religion*, edited by E.R. Leach

6 *Councils in Action*, edited by Audrey Richards and Adam Kuper

7 *Bridewealth and Dowry*, by Jack Goody and S.J. Tambiah

8 *Questions and Politeness*, edited by Esther N. Goody

Caste Ideology and Interaction

Edited by Dennis B. McGilvray
University of Colorado, Boulder

CAMBRIDGE UNIVERSITY PRESS
CAMBRIDGE
LONDON NEW YORK NEW ROCHELLE
MELBOURNE SYDNEY

Published by the Press Syndicate of the University of Cambridge
The Pitt Building, Trumpington Street, Cambridge CB2 1RP
32 East 57th Street, New York, NY 10022, USA
296 Beaconsfield Parade, Middle Park, Melbourne 3206, Australia

First published 1982

Printed in Great Britain at
the University Press, Cambridge

Library of Congress catalogue card number: 81-18037

British Library Cataloguing in Publication Data

Caste ideology and interaction
(Cambridge papers in social anthropology; 9)
1. Caste – India 2. Caste – Sri Lanka
I. McGilvray, Dennis B.
305.5′0954 DS422.C3

ISBN 0 521 24145 6

CONTENTS

FIGURES, MATRICES AND TABLES

FIGURES

MATRICES

TABLES

CONTRIBUTORS TO THIS VOLUME

DENNIS B. McGILVRAY received a Ph.D. in anthropology from the University of Chicago in 1974. He has taught at the University of Santa Clara and at Cambridge University, where he was a University Assistant Lecturer in the Department of Social Anthropology from 1973 to 1978. He later spent two years at Cornell University as an Andrew W. Mellon Postdoctoral Fellow before becoming an Associate Professor of Anthropology at the University of Colorado, Boulder. His publications include papers on ritual, ethnomedicine, and Eurasian ethnicity in Sri Lanka, and he is preparing a monograph on social organization in eastern Sri Lanka.

R.L. STIRRAT completed a Ph.D. in social anthropology at Cambridge University in 1973. He has taught at the University of Aberdeen, and he is now a Lecturer in the School of African and Asian Studies at the University of Sussex. He has published papers on kinship, demonic possession, compadrazgo, and the trading networks of fishermen in Sri Lanka.

STEPHEN C. LEVINSON has done sociolinguistic fieldwork in the Koṅku region of western Tamilnadu, South India. He received a Ph.D. in anthropology from the University of California at Berkeley in 1977, and he is presently a Lecturer in the Department of Linguistics at Cambridge University. During 1980–81 he was a member of the Working Group on Language and Cultural Context at the Australian National University. He is the co-author, with Penelope Brown, of a paper on politeness phenomena in vol. 8 of this series, and he has written a book in the Cambridge Textbooks in Linguistics series, *Pragmatics*.

GEOFFREY HAWTHORN studied at Oxford and the London School of Economics and taught at the University of Essex before becoming a Lecturer in Sociology at Cambridge University. He was a Visiting Professor at Harvard University in 1973–74 and a Visiting Member at the Institute for Advanced Study at Princeton in 1979–80. He is the author of *The*

Sociology of Fertility and *Enlightenment and Despair: A History of Sociology*, and he is the editor of *Population and Development: High and Low Fertility in Poor Countries.*

NOTE ON ORTHOGRAPHY

Except where English spellings are already well established, the Tamil words in this volume are rendered in accordance with the transliteration scheme of the University of Madras *Tamil Lexicon*, and the Sinhalese words follow the conventions of modern Sri Lankan scholarship.

Introduction

It has been two decades since the publication in this series of *Aspects of Caste in South India, Ceylon, and North-West Pakistan* (E.R. Leach, ed., 1960), a collection of important ethnographic and analytical papers which provided an impetus for further study of South Asian systems of caste organization. In the intervening years both the ethnographic record and the range of theoretical frameworks to interpret data on caste systems have so greatly expanded that it would be quite possible today to convene a collection of papers dealing with any one of many specialized 'aspects of caste' currently under investigation. The unit of study has continued to diversify over the period, so that reports of localized village caste hierarchies have been supplemented by studies of regional caste organization and longitudinal studies of caste mobility through time. Yet, despite the increasing diversity of empirical work, the compelling patterns of similarity and variation in caste systems throughout the region continue to nourish efforts to discover a single pan-Indic rationale, or cultural logic, which could be seen to underly all manifestations of caste organization.

Broadly speaking, the essays in this volume challenge the uniformity and consistency of indigenous 'caste ideologies' in different South Asian fieldwork settings, while at the same time seeking to trace how these ideologies impinge upon the actual patterns of group interaction observable in South Asian life. The term 'ideology' in this context has entered South Asian anthropology through the work of Louis Dumont, and it is used here to refer to a coherent and systematic set of indigenous ideas, assumptions, and values which inform, shape, and give meaning to a broad range of social institutions. In the papers which follow, 'caste ideology' should be understood to include, but not necessarily be limited to, the specific ideology of purity and varnaic hierarchy which uniquely defines the Hindu caste system for Dumont. The second theme of this volume is 'interaction', by which is meant communicative behaviour in the broadest sense. It would refer to social interaction which is either direct or indirect, private or public, although in real-life situations such distinctions tend to be blurred. However, the term interaction is particularly meant to suggest the behaviourally-situated aspects of caste and the competitive nature of actual caste systems in operation.

At the moment, there appear to be two major approaches to the global interpretation of South Asian society from the point of view of the South Asian cultural heritage itself, the first being that of Louis Dumont. His insightful and synoptic work has consistently enjoined anthropologists to recognize a unity of structural principles in South Asian society: namely, a presumption of universal group hierarchy and a strict separation of secular authority (power) from religious status (purity), of which caste is said to be the most pervasive and telling expression (Dumont 1970). More recently, McKim Marriott and others have proposed a new 'ethnosociological' or 'monistic' interpretation of South Asian society which is said to have greater cultural validity and more general applicability throughout the region. This approach detects a deeper and more universalizing mode of South Asian thought which views castes as part of a unified hierarchy of natural and social 'species', each caste mutually defined and sustained through the asymmetric exchange of morally-encoded substances (Marriott 1976a; Marriott and Inden 1977; for a further explanation of this theory see also McGilvray *infra*, section 2.1).

A critical assessment of the methodological and empirical foundations of these particular theories is taken up to some extent in each of the four papers in this volume, together with a critique by Hawthorn of the assumption, typified in the approach of the political scientist Rajni Kothari, that caste identity is a major motivating factor in modern Indian politics. Despite an acknowledgement of the need for the study of local variation, both the Dumontian and the 'ethnosociological' approaches pursue a hypothesis of Indic unity, a single uniquely South Asian formulation of reality, an ideology which is *the* essence of India. While these attempts seek the important goal of sociological generalization, they both adopt special criteria of 'authenticity' in their assessment of the empirical evidence. Dumont sees the ideology of textually orthodox dualistic Brahman/Kshatriya varna systems as genuine, while variant or incomplete systems are merely 'quasi-caste'. The ethnosociologists link their interpretation of the ideology of 'coded substance' to specific textual sources of medical and legal theory whose impact on social thought may be partial or uneven in some areas of South Asia. None of this precludes further research, but the tendency to emphasize the study of atemporal pan-Indic caste ideology does detract from the study of regionally-defined and historically-grounded caste systems as functioning sociological entities, regardless of whether, from an *a priori* definitional point of view, they exhibit caste or merely quasi-caste, a belief in 'bio-moral substance' or nothing of the kind.

It was the wish to re-establish a degree of methodological contact with human actors situated in local caste systems, interacting with others and seeking to make sense of their own social institutions, which provided the initial focus of interest around which this volume developed. All four of the contributors participated in the research seminar on 'Hierarchy and Interaction' held during 1976–7 in the Department of Social Anthropology at Cambridge, out of which grew the final versions of the papers they have presented here. One of the more important intellectual starting points for this seminar was the transactional analysis of inter-caste food prestations developed by Marriott (1959; 1968a). Thus the 'interactional' slant and the emphasis on caste hierarchies rather than on class relations were intentionally chosen as major foci of our papers from the start, although Geoffrey Hawthorn's essay, with its analysis of rural 'political class' alliances, is an exception. Two of the contributors conducted fieldwork in ethnic or religious minority communities in Sri Lanka – Stirrat in the west coast Sinhalese Catholic settlements near Chilaw, McGilvray in the east coast Tamil Hindu and Moorish (Muslim) region of Batticaloa – and their papers follow the precedent for Sri Lankan research established by Leach, Yalman, and Banks in the 1960 *Aspects of Caste* volume. Levinson's data were collected in the well-documented Hindu hamlet of Ōlappāḷaiyam in the Koṅku region of western Tamilnadu, South India (Beck 1972), while Hawthorn's discussion is taken from the perspective of modern Indian political processes as a whole.

The papers in this volume assess some of the existing work on the theory of caste, and several of them present considerable new data. At the same time, it is possible to detect some general findings which emerge from the book as a whole.

1. *The polyvocal aspects of caste rank.* The constellation of behavioural traits commonly identified with the operation of local caste hierarchies, including asymmetrical inter-caste transactions in food and drink, asymmetrical removal of wastes, caste endogamy or hypergamy, differential access to domestic and ritual space, order of precedence or seating in public events, display of honorific or stigmatizing symbols of office or profession, sumptuary rules, expressions of honour and deference in verbal interaction, and so forth, can be surprisingly versatile and polyvocal markers of social rank. While they unambiguously convey assertions of relative superiority and inferiority – and this is clearly their intent – they do not unambiguously express the dimension or aspect of social rank

which is being claimed. Honour, after all, can be deserved in many ways. Several of the papers in this volume show that some classic South Asian tactics for asserting and maintaining caste rank are compatible with different indigenous views of what that rank *represents*. Levinson's detailed measurement of the highly systematic patterns of inter-caste verbal politeness (or lack thereof) reveals a uniform language of rank which is highly effective in defining the local caste hierarchy, but he notes that the precise significance of the ranks – the ideology which renders it meaningful in local terms – is contentious, probably split between the ideals of the 'left-hand' and the 'right-hand' caste divisions, and in any case, unnecessary to an understanding of how the ranks in general are established behaviourally. McGilvray's paper, which explores the variety of conscious justifications for caste in a regional system which lacks Brahmans, reveals that the 'orthodox' ideology of collective purity and pollution which is so often said to rationalize caste hierarchies in other Hindu areas is, in eastern Sri Lanka, replaced by a 'secular' ideology of kingly honour, feudal division of labour, and matrilineal law. And yet, within the limitations of a distinctive social structure, the outward manifestations of inter-caste behaviour here are indistinguishable from patterns reported from South Indian regions where caste purity seems more to dominate popular consciousness.

On the other hand, Stirrat's account of ideas about caste in a Sinhalese Catholic fishing village seems to illustrate a movement away from a firmly centred caste ideology of any kind, allowing people to invoke a variety of poorly integrated themes in discussions of caste, including the antiquity of caste settlements, the relative prestige of caste occupations (farming vs. fishing), the aristocratic cachet of certain caste-linked *vasagama* names, and the 'metaphorical' purity of caste blood. The interpretation of caste membership in Stirrat's Wellagoda is a matter of considerable personal discretion, and the overall level of concern with such matters is low. Yet the elements of a caste debate can be mustered when needed, as at the time of a controversial marriage. It is also interesting to note that both Stirrat and McGilvray have detected strongly unilineal ideas of caste membership, patrilineal on the west coast and matrilineal on the east coast, which deviate from the usual belief in bilateral caste descent.

Empirically it seems that the two major themes around which South Asian caste-rank symbolism is organized are those of religious status (purity, priestly descent, sacred knowledge, etc.) and of feudal-style patronage and service (kingship, allocated division of labour, hereditary servitude, etc.), although these two motifs may be linked, as in the ideal of kingly supervision of religious institutions which McGilvray notes in eastern Sri Lanka. What is striking is how often the same rank-generating caste interactions can be validated in terms of *both* of these ideologies. Downward distribution of food and refusal to accept food upward makes sense as a tactic to protect and enhance bodily purity, but it can also be seen as a gesture of *noblesse oblige* and a statement of position as patron and protector. Caste endogamy conserves the purity of the group, if you care to see it that way, but it can also symbolize notions of inherited honour and the limits to intimacy which uphold the dignity of political authority. Sumptuary rules can be seen as enforcing an outward indexical display of the gradations of inward spiritual status of ranked castes, or they can be justified as a chartered form of privilege, a prerogative of feudal office. Even Hindu priestly castes, whose privileged access to the innermost temple sanctum proclaims their unequivocal superiority in religious status, may find their role denigrated as one of humble 'service' or subordination in relation to the authority of the non-priestly groups who control the management of a temple. Further examples might be adduced, but the point is to suggest that the perceived meaning of caste interaction in actual South Asian settings is capable of a great deal of pragmatic and historically contingent polyvocality, making a unitary ideology of caste difficult to establish on a pan-Indic ethnographic basis and illustrating instead the scope for dynamic variation in symbolic emphasis between regional caste systems and even between the perspectives of different groups within a local caste hierarchy.

2. *Some insights from the interaction perspective.* Careful attention to the patterns of interaction in ongoing caste systems reveals some of the psychological reality of caste-ranking manoeuvres and of the categories of meaning with which they are associated, but it also brings out some of the more subtle and unnoticed patterns of individual motivation and group alliance which a formal ideology of caste rank would not predict. Levinson's paper exploits the methodological advantages of aggregate interaction research by choosing to monitor one medium of social exchange, the use of honorific and dishonorific forms of address, which helps to confirm and to sustain the local ranking of castes on a day-to-day basis. As Levinson notes, linguistic interaction is highly public, its meaning is independently testable, and it is 'the most frequent form of exchange', all of which make it an extremely sensitive indicator, not of people's private aspirations, but of their publicly ratified achievements in asserting caste rank. Levinson carefully sifts his data on pronouns and honorifics through a sequence of separate matrices to reveal a pattern of caste hierarchy more complex and more subtle than traditional ethnographic

techniques would be likely to reveal. Verbal deference on the basis of the relative age of the interacting individuals is itself shown to be an important and systematic marker of caste-bloc solidarity and rank. Furthermore, the existence of allied caste-blocs within the overall hierarchy of castes is demonstrated by Levinson's matrices to be a significant aspect of local caste systems, one which may permit a group to offer alliance in one interactional medium in order to gain rank in another.

The nature and degree of solidarity among allied castes is a phenomenon which merits comparative study across regions of South Asia. In some parts of eastern Sri Lanka, as McGilvray reports, the alliance between two dominant landowning castes is given explicit mythic justification and is publicly ratified by reciprocal cross-caste marriage. Yet in the same region there is also a highly ritualized interactional display of caste and matriclan rank in terms of unequal 'shares' (specialized participation rights) in communal temple and mosque ceremonies. In Wellagoda, Stirrat's fieldwork site on the west coast of the island, the salient arenas of caste interaction are much more personal and informal; in fact, one must examine the day-to-day content of gossip and the language of petty dispute in order to discover what the recurring themes of local caste ideology actually are.

Both Stirrat and McGilvray emphasize the importance of acquiring more complete data on the range of ethnosemantic categories, the relevant social contexts, and the actual expressions of speech encountered in the ethnographic search for evidence of such anthropological concepts as 'purity' or 'bio-moral substance', or even local oral recensions of such textual themes as *karma* and *dharma*. In the cases reported here, the vocabulary of ordinary village discourse on such matters, even in the specialized domain of ethnomedical knowledge, proved to be more disjunctive and equivocal than the prevailing theories of Indic rationality would have suggested. At the same time, both Levinson and McGilvray agree that the two-dimensional model of inter-caste transaction strategies which accompanies Marriott's 'ethnosociological' theory of Hindu thought is both insightful and productive.

Approaching caste interaction not from the perspective of fieldwork observation but instead 'from above', from the standpoint of the long-term imposition of specific rules and conditions on local political behaviour, Hawthorn argues that caste loyalty within local and regional political alliances is less a primordial sentiment grounded in traditional Indian social structure than a byproduct of colonial idealizations and rigidifications of the caste system introduced with the British Raj. Indeed, given this colonial penchant for legitimizing caste rights and caste boundaries where formerly there had been a more fluid and holistic Dumontian system of structural relations between castes, Hawthorn finds it surprising to observe how *relatively free* of caste sentiment post-Independence Indian politics has been, the dire predictions of some eminent political scientists notwithstanding. The one-party structure of the Indian system during most of the Independence period so defined and constituted the setting within which political interaction took place that pursuit of interests on the exclusive basis of caste identity was largely unproductive. Hawthorn says the system did create a 'political class' of dominant landlord caste members who proceeded to reinforce their traditional sources of caste authority both politically and economically. Thus, dominant caste identity was often enhanced and became linked to the fortunes of the Congress machine, but this was the inadvertent result of an agrarian-based one-party political system, not a product of caste as an underlying motive for political action. If Hawthorn's reading of the evidence is valid, it provides an important perspective on caste ideology and interaction, one which demonstrates again the 'compartmentalization' effect and which suggests that the extension of caste sentiment into different realms of life can be greatly reduced by the prevailing rules governing culturally distinct domains of interaction.

Altogether, the emphasis in these essays is upon matters of localized variation and contextual detail, linked to broader criticism of contemporary theory and method. They seek to widen the field of comparison in the study of caste, not to promote a sterile *empiricisme atomisant* (Dumont 1979: xxxi). While each of the four papers must be judged independently, this broader intent is shared among them all.

Caste conundrums: Views of caste in a Sinhalese Catholic fishing village

R.L. Stirrat

1. INTRODUCTION

Once, when I was talking about caste with one of the last Italian missionary priests in Sri Lanka, Father Rastoldo,[1] he mentioned to me that caste was only important for the rich and for the low castes. For most Catholics in the country who are neither very rich nor of very low caste, such matters are of relatively minor importance. In my own experience of Catholicism in Sinhalese Sri Lanka, I have found Father Rastoldo's comments to be generally correct. Sometimes people are willing and even eager to talk about caste. Sometimes, no one displays the least interest in an institution which many observers see as being central to South Asian society.

1.1. Aims

In this paper I am concerned with one village which I have christened 'Wellagoda' and which lies on the coast about 50 miles north of Colombo. The village is entirely Catholic, most of the households depend directly on fishing, and people claim to belong either to the Karāva or the Goyigama castes. But for most villagers most of the time, caste is an unimportant matter. In contrast with the impression one often gets when reading descriptions of caste in South Asian villages, caste is not something which affects Wellagoda people on a day-to-day basis. The unimportance of caste in this village seems to me to make the Wellagoda material of some interest in itself, and of some more general interest for the light it may throw on our understanding of caste.

In the present context I cannot hope to explain or account for caste, the peculiarities of caste, or the relative absence of caste in Wellagoda. Such an enterprise would appear to me to require a persuasive general analysis of caste in Sri Lanka including the impact of Catholicism. These as yet do not exist. So what I shall do here is to produce an account of caste as it is seen by the people of Wellagoda. Straight away I must point out that their notions of caste are somewhat confusing and thus at times this paper may appear somewhat confused. Yet this confusion is in itself crucial to caste in Wellagoda and any attempt to avoid it would, I think, amount to a bowdlerization of the data and a misrepresentation of the actual situation.

In summary, I shall argue that, in Wellagoda, caste is divorced from notions of purity, impurity, pollution and so on. Rather, the notion of caste in an extremely simple form exists in itself as part of a segmentary and holistic notion of society. This in turn is related to ideas about the past and stands in contrast to the flux, fluidity and essentially individualistic nature of actual social relations today. But before developing the argument, let me make a few general comments relevant to Wellagoda.

1.2. The background

Today, Catholics form around 8% of the total population of Sri Lanka. The greatest concentration of Catholics is found in a narrow coastal strip, never more than three or four miles wide, running north from Colombo for about 50 miles. Further north Catholics still form a major proportion of the population but in absolute terms are less numerous.

Catholicism was introduced into Sri Lanka in the sixteenth century by the Portuguese. It would appear that most of the early conversions were based on converting the leaders of the local population, the masses following in their wake (Abeyasinghe 1966: 200 *passim*; De Silva 1972; Tennent 1850). And it would also appear that many of the conversions were made on a caste basis. This seems especially true for the Karāva caste who today form the largest caste category among the west-coast Catholic population (Ryan 1953). In all, at least fourteen different castes are represented amongst the Catholics in this area.

Wellagoda is situated towards the northern end of this Catholic strip. Historically, the village appears to have grown up in the late nineteenth century. Writers earlier in the century refer to the area around Wellagoda as being particularly wild, infested with elephants and other dangerous creatures (e.g. Percival 1805: 108). But this picture changed rapidly with the spread of commercial coconut production northwards along the coast, and the necessary influx of a labouring population. The foundation of Wellagoda seems to have been the result of a growing market for fish among the local population. The first historical mention of the village I have found is in 1888 when the Government Agent wrote in his diary that he was having difficulty in collecting the '*wadiya* tax' from migrant fishers using the beach at Wellagoda.

At some point, probably in the 1890s, some of these migrant fishermen who camped on Wellagoda beach for a few months each year began to settle down, buy land and build houses. These people were mainly members of the Karāva caste from Negombo who spoke Tamil although claiming to be Sinhalese. Whether or not there were already other settlers in Wellagoda is unclear. Today, besides those villages who claim a Negombo ancestry and sometimes still refer to Negombo as *ūr* (Tamil: 'home village'), there are others, both Karāva and Goyigama, who claim either to be descended from autochthonous inhabitants of Wellagoda, or to have originated in other areas of the coastal belt. In general those who do not claim a Negombo ancestry claim to have always been Sinhalese speakers.

In 1971, the population of Wellagoda was something over 700, forming around 140 households, although today (1979) there must be well over 160 households in the village. Of the 140 households in 1971, 100 depended directly on fishing whilst the remainder of the population was involved in a motley collection of jobs: teachers, clerks, labourers, a few boutique keepers, and a few who had no visible means of support.

Elsewhere (Stirrat 1975b) I have discussed at length the social organization of fishing in Wellagoda. What is significant in the present context is that economic activity in this village is highly individualistic. The techniques of production and the nature of the productive enterprise are such that all fishing households own the fishing gear that they use. The household is the basic unit of economic activity and relations between households are generally highly competitive. Fortunes rapidly change, the rich of one generation producing the paupers of the next. There is no fixed economic ranking system, and villagers view wealth as being, unfortunately, a transient quality.

In caste terms, everyone in Wellagoda claims to be either Karāva or Goyigama although, as I shall show later, these claims are not always acknowledged by others in the village. The Karāva form the majority of the population, 83.4% (593 out of 711) in 1971. Despite the residential absence of other castes in the village, Wellagoda people do come into contact with such people. The men either frequent the Barbers' (*Panikki*) saloons or use the barber who comes every Saturday to the village. There are a couple of Washermen (*Radā*) families who come to the village, particularly for the girls' puberty rituals (*kotahala gedera*) and occasionally to supply white cloths at weddings. And finally Wellagoda people obtain arrack from Limeburners (*Hunu*) who live across the lagoon from the village.

1.3. Concepts of caste

It is perhaps worthwhile saying a little about the linguistic concept, 'caste', before going any further. As Pitt-Rivers (1972) has shown at length, 'caste' is originally a Portuguese term. In South Asian languages there is no verbal concept semantically identical with 'caste'. In Wellagoda, a number of Sinhala terms are used to talk about what I have labelled as 'caste'. Some of these, such as *kattiya*, simply mean 'group'. But three are more directly related to the English term 'caste': *jātiya*, *vargaya* and *kulaya*.

The most commonly used term in Wellagoda is *jātiya*, a term which has a fairly wide field of reference (see Béteille 1964, Hocart 1950, Leach 1961). Sociologically, it can be used in a number of ways, e.g.

(1) for a 'national' group, e.g. Ceylonese, Indian, British;
(2) for a racio-linguistic group, e.g. Sinhalese, Tamil, English;
(3) for a religious group, e.g. Hindu, Buddhist, Catholic;
(4) for named, hereditary groups of the type recognized in English as 'caste', e.g. Goyigama, Karāva, Salāgama.

The important thing to notice is that *jātiya* does not simply mean 'caste'. Rather, it is related to the idea of 'kind' or 'species' or 'variety'. It is a classificatory concept stressing identity and non-identity. And if one asks about a person's *jātiya* one tends to be given an answer stressing either racio-linguistic identity (e.g. Sinhalese or Tamil) or religious identity (e.g. Catholic or Buddhist). *Vargaya*, rarely used in Wellagoda, appears to have the same sort of semantic field as *jātiya*.

Kulaya more closely approximates to the English notion of caste. According to Geiger's etymological dictionary, it can be glossed as 'family, caste, rank or tribe'. Normally it is used along with *bhēdaya* (division) and thus is used to talk about the caste divisions between people. But in Wellagoda, *kulaya* and *kula bhēdaya* are rarely used, and I was told that *kulaya* could only be used to refer to the Karāva and the Goyigama.

But of course, rather than use any of these terms, the most frequently used term in Wellagoda is *minissu* which simply means 'people'. Thus they talk about the Goyigama *minissu* or the Karāva *minissu* rather than use any specific term. In sum, then, there is no precise equivalent to the English term 'caste', a word which, itself, has been imposed from without.[2]

2. CONCEPTIONS OF CASTE

The basic problem in discussing caste in Wellagoda is knowing where to start. It is not as if there is a set of cosmic polarities, a well worked-out theology into which the empirical data can be neatly slotted. So perhaps the easiest and most suitable place to start this account is through examining what caste is *not* about in Wellagoda.

2.1. Purity, pollution, etcetera

Readers of theorists such as Dumont and Yalman will be familiar with the notion that caste is in some sense or other related to problems of purity or pollution. For Dumont, one of the basic strands in his argument is the complementary opposition (and hierarchical relationship) of purity and impurity. Indeed for Dumont, this opposition is the basic structural principle of Indian society and culture, caste being little more than a working-out of this principle on the substantive level.[3] Yalman's argument, although primarily concerned with Sri Lanka rather than with India, is similar in certain respects and shares some elements in common with Dumont's. For Yalman, caste is crucially concerned with the avoidance of pollution and with the protection of female purity (Yalman 1960; 1963; 1967). For both Dumont and Yalman a direct link is predicated between the purity and impurity of caste, and the pollution of the person involved in the processes of life: events such as birth, death and menstruation. Similar claims are also made by writers such as Marriott and Inden (Marriott 1976b; Marriott and Inden 1974).

Obviously in this paper I cannot enter into a prolonged discussion of various writers' usage of terms such as 'pure', 'impure', 'polluted' and so on. But whatever the case may be in India, and despite Yalman's claims, it is very difficult in Sinhalese Sri Lanka to bring together notions concerning personal pollution and notions concerning caste. In the case of Wellagoda, it is a downright impossibility.

In Wellagoda, and indeed, throughout low-country Sri Lanka, there is a large vocabulary used to describe states which can loosely be translated into English as 'impure', 'polluted', 'dirty', and so on. For instance, perhaps the closest equivalent to the English term 'pure' is *pirisidu* which can be translated as, 'clean, pure or chaste'. Thus the Virgin Mary is *pirisidu*; so are virgins and children in general. To engage in certain types of Catholic exorcism rites one must be *pirisidu* – i.e., one must abstain (at least on a temporary basis) from sex and from the consumption of alcohol and meat, in particular of pork. And the opposite of *pirisidu* is *apirisdu* which can be glossed as 'unclean, unchaste, impure'.

Closely related to the term *pirisidu* is *suda* which as well as meaning 'pure' also means 'clean' and 'white'. Although it can be used to talk of, say, the Virgin Mary or of children (where it tends to be synonymous with *nirdōsa*: 'innocent') it tends to have the connotation of physical cleanliness (e.g. newly washed clothes) or of honesty. In the context of clothes, the opposite of *suda* is usually *kilutu*, which simply means 'dirty' in the sense of 'soiled'.

From *kilutu* we can move on to two other terms, *pili* and *jarava*. *Pili* refers, for instance, to the dirt of latrines, urine, and faeces. It is obnoxious, odorous, disgusting, attractive only to demons. And *jarava* as well as referring to 'dirt' also is used to talk about 'dirty behaviour', children playing with shit for instance.

All these terms tend to be used in rather different contexts than the last term I wish to mention, *killa*. In Wellagoda, as elsewhere in Sinhalese Sri Lanka, *killa* refers to 'personal pollution' and is perhaps best translated as 'pollution' or 'polluted'. *Killa* refers to a certain noxious and infectious state of being of a person in certain situations. Menstruating women have *killa*; childbirth and death involve *killa*; infectious diseases involve *killa*. Obviously, because women menstruate and bear children, women are more susceptible to *killa* than are men. But in no way are they permanently imbued with *killa*. Furthermore, *killa* is a temporary phenomenon. Give it time and it goes away.[4]

To discuss fully the various dimensions along which notions of purity and impurity, cleanliness and non-cleanliness, pollution and non-pollution are organized in Wellagoda would obviously be far outside the scope of this paper. But what is crucial and what I want to stress in the present context is that no matter what may be the case elsewhere, none of these terms is used in Wellagoda to talk about caste. At no time have I heard people either implicitly or explicitly conceptualize caste or caste differences in terms of, or as the result of, any of the concepts mentioned above. And in response to direct questions, people would deny that lower castes are somehow more 'polluted' or 'less pure' than the higher castes. Rather, the terms which are used include 'good' and 'not-good' (*honda* and *honda naeae*) or 'high' and 'low' (*ihala* and *pahala*).

This disjunction between caste on the one hand and notions of pollution, purity and impurity on the other is crucial in comprehending caste in Wellagoda. For if Dumont is right for India, and if Yalman is correct for Kandyan Sri Lanka (although both analyses, particularly Yalman's, are questionable), then caste in Wellagoda is somewhat unusual in the South Asian context.[5] Besides Barth's data from the Swat Pathans (Barth 1960), the only similar case which comes readily to mind is Fuller's discussion of the Kerala Christians (Fuller 1977). Fuller claims not only that caste is divorced from ideas of personal pollution, but that the Christians of Kerala have no concept of personal pollution, a claim which has been ethnographically challenged (see Ferro-Luzzi 1976).

2.2. The organizational principles of caste

Besides the divorce of questions concerning purity and pollution from caste in Wellagoda, there are two other features which caste in Wellagoda shares in common with the Swat Pathans and the inhabitants of Kerala. First of all, membership of caste categories is strictly defined by unilateral criteria, and secondly, a person's caste position is fixed once and for all by birth.

Returning to caste as it is generally portrayed in the literature, membership of castes is usually seen as being in some sense or other bilaterally determined. Admittedly, from India and Sri Lanka, there are signs of 'unilateral drift'. So Dumont when talking of North India considers cross-caste unions in which the child takes the caste of the father. In a somewhat tautological aside he goes on to state that such unions and such a mode of caste ascription are only possible when the partners are 'within permitted degrees' (Dumont 1970: 117). Similarly, Yalman claims that in parts of Sri Lanka there is a tendency towards unilineal pedigrees, towards cumulative filiation which demarcates, conceptually at least, categories of people within castes (Yalman 1967: 140–5, 271–81). But even so, Yalman claims that both partners in such unions must be of the correct caste and all that is created are caste-like divisions within generally bilaterally defined castes (Yalman 1967).

Besides these cases where patrifiliation is stressed, there are also situations where matrifiliation becomes equally important. From India there are the famous Nayars (Gough 1961; Fuller 1976); from Sri Lanka there are the cases described by McGilvray (1973, and this volume). But in general, even when there is such a unilineal bias, the husband must be superior to the wife in 'caste' terms, and the union must be 'within permitted degrees'.

In Wellagoda, the situation is radically different. Here, no matter what the caste of the mother, the offspring of any union (including illegitimate unions) always take the caste of the father (i.e. genitor). This is true no matter whether the father is of higher or lower caste than the mother. And this is not simply a statement concerning hypothetical possibilities. I know of instances where Karāva women have married Potter (*Baedahala*) or Washer caste (*Radā*) men, the offspring of these marriages belonging to those lower castes. And similarly, I know of cases where Karāva men have married lower caste women, and again there has been no uncertainty as to the caste of the children, the latter being just as much Karāva as their fathers.

This rule that patrifiliation alone determines a person's caste position is linked to another peculiarity of caste in Wellagoda: that one's caste is fixed once and for all at birth. No matter what activities a person may engage in, these activities can in no way affect their inherited caste status. Thus a woman can marry and have sex with men of any caste without putting at risk her caste position. There is no way, unlike in India, in which a person can 'lose caste'. Indeed, when I suggested that marriage or sex might reduce a woman's caste position, my remarks were greeted with bafflement and amazement.

These three features (i.e., the separation of caste from problems of purity, pollution etc.; the permanence of caste position ascribed at birth; and the principle of patrifiliation) appear to me to form a coherent set of principles which stand in marked contrast to those which are frequently stated to underlie caste in the interior of Sri Lanka, let alone those found on the Indian mainland.[6] And they have obvious implications for marriage. In terms of a woman's (or a man's) caste position, it is immaterial who is married, and when there are inter-caste marriages, there is no uncertainty as to the caste of the children.

2.3. Caste and biology

So far, I have tried to show what caste in Wellagoda is *not* about, and what are the basic organizational principles which determine a person's caste position. In this and the next few sections I want to talk about what caste *is* about, to put some 'body' onto these rather abstract principles.

The importance of patrifiliation and the fixed nature of a person's caste position are both in some ways related to the processes of conception and birth. In a certain sense, caste is a matter of 'nature': caste is thought to be a matter of 'blood' – *le*. In this context, the 'blood' is said to come from the child's actual father, the genitor. So members of different castes have different 'blood', Karāva 'blood' being different from Goyigama 'blood'. Thus caste becomes a matter of natural differences and castes become analogous with species, each caste being a biologically defined entity and differences between castes being seen as biological differences.[7] At times, it is even claimed that the personal characteristics of members of different castes differ, and that psychological differences are genetically inherited through patrifiliation. Thus the Karāva are fierce and strong: it's in their blood. The Goyigama are more stable, less arrogant, less uncouth.[8]

Yet we must exercise extreme caution in considering the status of such remarks. Here, I am not trying to delineate a primitive version of those intellectual schemas reported by Marriott and Inden (Marriott 1976b; Marriott and Inden 1974). The comments made by Wellagoda people concerning biological relatedness and differentiation are not capable of bearing sustained systematization unless decontextualized to an alarming degree.

As I have described elsewhere (Stirrat 1975a), notions of blood relatedness in the context of caste conflict with notions of blood relatedness in the field of marriage restrictions. If the former stress patrifiliation, then the latter stress bilateral relatedness. One way of talking about the differences between castes and about the nature of caste is to use a biological idiom: castes are *like* species. But when challenged, informants would deny this was anything more than a metaphor. And at all times, children are 'blood relations' (*le naedaeyo*) of both their parents.

'Blood' and 'biology' are thus used as metaphors in Wellagoda. To say that Karāva 'blood' is different from Goyigama 'blood' is a statement similar to those which impute 'blue blood' to the British aristocracy. In both cases there is a vague, unformalized, set of ideas that there is (somehow) some sort of difference between categories of people. But to raise such metaphorical statements to the level of an ethnosociology or, rather, an ethnobiology, is to go too far.

So 'blood' is simply a metaphor, used to talk about the unilateral nature of caste and the fixity of caste from birth. But the unilateral principle is what is important. Not only is it used to demarcate castes in a (theoretically) unequivocal fashion, but it is also used to demarcate divisions within a caste. And here we move from biology to names.

2.4. Caste as 'social descent'

In Wellagoda, as is general throughout this area of Sri Lanka, personal names consist of three elements: the *vasagama* name; the *avassa* name; the *pelantiya* name.[9] Thus a man's full name might be, 'Warunakulasuriya Antony Fernando'. 'Antony' is his *avassa* name. It is the personal name given to him at his christening, and may have in front of it his father's *avassa* name. The *vasagama* name, 'Warunakulasuriya', and the *pelantiya* name, 'Fernando', are both inherited through patrifiliation. And these names, particularly the *vasagama* name, are directly related to caste and to distinctions within castes.[10]

For instance, in this part of Sri Lanka most Karāva possess one of three *vasagama* names: Warunakulasuriya, Mihindakulasuriya or Kurukulasuriya. In Wellagoda, about 58% of the total population (66% of all Karāva) are Warunakulasuriyas. There seems to be some evidence that in the past these names were quite distinctly ranked, and that marriage between these names was frowned upon. Even today in Negombo, the major Karāva centre on the northwest coast, separate areas of the town are loosely associated with different *vasagama* names. At present, even though there is no clear ranking system, the point remains: all these names are associated with claims to honour and status. Not only are they caste linked and embody claims to caste status, but they also represent claims to a position within the caste. Thus names like 'Warunakulasuriya' are said in Wellagoda to be evidence of a 'warrior' past. And although people in Wellagoda cannot elaborate beyond this point, there are others who can.[11] Even in Wellagoda, the Warunakulasuriyas are confident that somehow their name represents a more glorious ancestry than do other *vasagama* names.

Even if only for the ethnographic record, there is a further system of intra-caste subdivisions also involving the patrilineal inheritance of names. Unlike the naming system mentioned above, this system is restricted to those villagers who claim descent from Negombo and who generally use Tamil. These subdivisions are vague, shadowy categories known in Tamil as *kulams* (I found no Sinhala equivalent term) and in formal terms represent shallow patrilineages. They have an odd – indeed, exotic – collection of names: 'the people of the ghost house', 'elephant buttocks', even 'dog shit', but beyond that have no social existence.[12] Frequently people were unsure as to which *kulam* they belonged; there was no hint that *kulams* were ranked or that they were ever exogamous. All that can be said is that the *kulams* are part of a general system of social classification or categorization which relies on patrifiliation as its organizing principle.[13]

Throughout the naming system there was a continual undertone in informants' comments that somehow inherited names were related to blood-lines; that Warunakulasuriyas had different 'blood' from other Karāva. But this was an undertone; again it was a metaphor or an analogy rather than a worked out system. What is apparent is the *possibility* of a segmentary structure consisting of castes; of names within castes associated with intra-caste differentiation (*vasagama* names), and of further subdivisions (*kulams*).

Yet despite the fact that these segmentary potentialities are never realized in the form of substantive 'groups', this does not mean that these names have no sociological significance. For these inherited names of the type found in Wellagoda are effectively titles. They are claims to a certain social position by virtue of descent through cumulative patrifiliation from illustrious ancestors. They represent claims to a certain 'social honour' (*tattvaya*) which is an inheritable commodity. So despite the fact that most people in Wellagoda may today be fishermen, through these names they can (and occasionally do) claim an identity with supposedly illustrious forebears who were soldiers, headmen and even kings. Thus 'truly' these people who are fishers are in their 'inner essence' something very different.[14]

2.5. Caste as occupation

But if caste is something to do with 'social honour', with claims to aristocratic pedigrees, then it is also something very closely tied up with occupation. Each caste is seen as having a particular occupational speciality: Hunu are limeburners, Goyigama are farmers. When they are not claiming to be aristocrats, Karāva are fishermen. In this context, caste is nothing to do with 'blood' nor directly with the social pretensions of various people, but both with a vision of the social division of labour as it existed in the past, and with the actual division of labour as it exists in the present.

When people talk about the origins of caste, they say it is a creation of the ancient Sinhalese kings. The latter created castes so that certain services essential to society would be provided. Thus there are potters, washers, goldsmiths, blacksmiths, etc. A few villagers even talk about caste being the creation of King Mahasammata, a myth which crops up elsewhere in Sri Lanka (see Hocart 1950: 51; Pieris 1956: 169; Yalman 1967: 89).[15] This view of caste sees the institution simply as a matter of the division of labour: it has nothing to do with purity, impurity, pollution or whatever.

This interpretation of caste obviously relates back to what I have said about caste and social honour, but it also points in another direction, not to the past but to the present, for in this view of caste, caste is simply a matter of occupation. Thus in Wellagoda, 16% of the population claim to be Goyigama whose caste occupation is cultivation. Of these Goyigama, over half are today fishermen. Frequently, even Goyigama informants have told me that, 'Now we are all Karāva because we all fish'. And it seems that other Goyigama not resident in Wellagoda are unwilling to accept Wellagoda Goyigama as 'true' Goyigama because their occupation puts their claim to Goyigama status in question.

Furthermore, this notion that caste is a matter of occupation is related to the 'lowness' of certain castes who are seen, either historically or in the present, as being servants of the higher castes. Superiority and inferiority in this context are defined in terms of independence and dependence.[16] This idea which purports to explain the lowness of certain castes is difficult to maintain for some supposedly 'low' groups, e.g. the Salāgama and the Hunu. It is, however, clearer for two castes which do come into close contact with the people of Wellagoda, the Barbers and the Washers. They do carry out personal services for the Wellagoda population just as servants do for their superiors.

Once again this raises the problem of caste and pollution. Both Washers and Barbers do come into contact with *killa* through their caste occupation. In a general sense, all castes who are concerned with bodily effluent and *killa* are low, but this does not mean that they absorb the *killa* or that their lowness is dependent on their relationship with *killa*. For in actual fact, Washers are not very low in the caste hierarchy and no one I talked to said that their lowness was a matter of association with *killa*. I was told that if a Karāva or a Goyigama took to being a professional washer, then no one would like to associate with them. But whether they would cease to be 'true Karāva', whether their 'Karāva-ness' would be put at risk, was as usual a matter of some confusion.

In sum then, caste is seen as being related to the question of occupation, in particular of a 'traditional' occupation. I must stress 'occupation' for it is nothing to do with economic success. How these occupations are ranked, and how castes are ranked, seems a purely arbitrary matter as far as Wellagoda people are concerned. 'That's just the way it is', was the usual answer.

2.6. Caste as the past

The picture which I hope has emerged is that 'caste' in Wellagoda can mean or can be talked about in a number of ways. At one extreme it is a matter of 'nature'. Castes are different because of certain genetic properties. At another extreme, caste is an invention of man, nothing to do with inherent differences between people but to do with an artificially created division of labour: a sort of 'social contract' theory of society. In between, caste is something to do with social honour, in part a product of the kings of the past who have given honours to illustrious ancestors, honours which have somehow become an 'inheritable commodity'.

I think two points are worth stressing about caste as it is seen in Wellagoda. The first is that caste exists in itself; it cannot be reduced to anything else, either economics or purity/pollution or whatever. Occupation, 'blood', 'social honour' are all ways of talking *about* caste, but they are not caste. Secondly, what brings together the various contexts in which caste is mentioned are that they are all, in some way or other, connected with the past rather than the present.

Thus 'blood' depends on inheritance from the past. 'Social honour' refers to rules the ancestors are supposed to have had. And 'occupation' refers to the actions of past kings. In a sense, what caste is about is an idealized past where social order existed. The past, through caste, becomes a moral construct used to pass judgement on the present. Thus the contexts in which caste was mentioned were those in which some aspect of the present was being criticized, and in particular the way in which in Wellagoda, money becomes the supreme arbiter of social position. Thus informants would frequently contrast those names which they considered to have developed through the ages by patrifiliation, and which represent 'true' claims to status, with those names which have been 'usurped', which people have obtained 'by money'. When caste is stressed, what is stressed is the old, the stable, the constant, and true. And such values stand in opposition to the new, unstable, false, shallow, fickle and transient values of economic success and politics, of the *nouveau riche* and 'filthy lucre'.[17]

In sum, what caste does seem to be about is a view of society which is holistic, which denies change. It is a highly conservative, anti-individualistic ideology.

Now of course, this 'traditionalist' view of the true nature of society is only one possibility. Another, totally opposed view of society is one in which caste is seen as irrelevant and unreal. Again it is seen as something to do with the past, but the idealized past becomes something irrelevant for the present. And today, what is important is economic worth and success. Instead of a holistic, timeless, static view of what society should be, individualistic notions become predominant. In the extreme cases, people would say that whilst caste may have been important in the past, today the supreme arbiter of reputations is money.[18]

These two positions, 'traditionalist' and 'modernist', 'holistic' and 'individualistic', caste as 'correct order' and caste as 'outmoded past' do not, I must stress, denote separate categories of people in the village. Rather, they denote two extreme sets of statements about caste which an individual might support on different occasions in the same discussion. And given the economic structure of the village with its stress on the household economy and economic competition between households, caste as anything more than a picture of the past would be untenable.

2.7. Inequality and overlapping

As I mentioned earlier, the most frequent Sinhalese term used in Wellagoda to talk about 'caste' is *jātiya*, and this term primarily refers to the notion of categories, either of people or things. It connotes differentiation rather than hierarchialization and in no way is there any inherent notion of inequality in the concept of *jātiya*. Yet at the same time, when *jātiya* is used to refer to people, it is associated with ideas of inequality. And perhaps this is inevitable: that once categories of people are separated out, there is a tendency to rank the categories.

This tendency to invest social categories with inequality is evident not only in those contexts we label as 'caste' but also in those we describe as 'ethnic' or 'religious' categories.

Thus Wellagoda people see Tamil and Sinhalese as separate and opposed types of humanity. To Wellagoda people, and purely in the local geographical context, Sinhalese as a category of humanity are superior to Tamils. This does not mean that all Sinhalese are superior to all Tamils. Indeed, the Goyigama as a caste are equivalent to the Tamil Veḷaḷar, the Karāva are equivalent to the Tamil Karaiyār, and so on. Rather, what is being said is that Sinhalese-ness is superior to Tamil-ness. Furthermore, this relative ranking is viewed as a matter of power. Informants freely admitted that in Jaffna, Tamils are superior to Sinhalese for there the Tamils have power.

Rather different is the case of religion. Here there is a gradation, a hierarchy if you like, which is phrased not in terms of power but in terms of proximity to the ideals of Catholicism. Thus at the bottom of the ladder are the Hindus. Then come the Buddhists who are, to the Catholics, at least monotheistic! Above them are the Muslims who are considered to follow the religion of the Old Testament, and finally come the Catholics. But again, caste divisions run across these religiously defined boundaries. The context of inequality has to be defined, and in different contexts the same people end up in very different positions.

When we come to caste, the notion of inequality becomes somewhat opaque, and as should already have become clear, the criteria available for ranking castes are not simple and unambivalent. At base, what is central to the whole notion of caste in Wellagoda is that castes are unequal: everyone agrees on that. For some, to ask why castes are ranked is a non-question; for others various myths and statements are produced but in a *post hoc* fashion.

In general, people in Wellagoda are not interested in the niceties of caste ranking. The most general distinction is that between the 'good castes', the Karāva and the Goyigama who live in the village, and the rest – barbers, potters and so on, who do not live in Wellagoda. The ranking of these lower castes was seen as a problem for the lower castes, not for the superior Karāva. In a sense, Wellagoda people are quite correct, for sociologically speaking the relative caste positions of the lower castes are irrelevant.

There are, however, certain ideas on what can and cannot be done with members of the lower castes. People claim that one should not eat with them: in some cases not even accept water from them. If they are invited to formal occasions such as weddings or funerals, they should eat apart from the 'good' people. If a low caste person does sit down to eat with members of a higher caste at such an occasion, then the latter have the right (almost a duty) to overturn the table. Yet all this was told me in the context of hypothetical situations.[19] Furthermore, there was no question of the lower castes somehow polluting the higher castes. It was rather a matter of an extreme code of manners than a set of ritual injunctions designed to protect the persons involved.

Now, although I have talked as if everyone in Wellagoda was Karāva or Goyigama, and that in the village there are no members of the lower castes, in practice the situation was not as simple as this. Firstly, there is little general agreement as to who has or has not usurped their names or their caste status. Secondly, people do not agree over the relative ranking of the Karāva or the Goyigama and of names within castes. And finally, people do not agree as to the relative importance of caste as a ranking system in relation to other ranking systems, notably wealth. In a later section I shall say more about some of these problems in the context of marriage choices. Here, I shall limit my comments to the problem of relative ranking.

Both Karāva and Goyigama claim to be superior to each other. At the national level this conflict is of long standing and is perhaps best represented by the famous 'Kara-Goi' conflict of the late nineteenth and early twentieth centuries (Roberts 1969). In the village it is only an ever-present undertone. The debate (or what there is of it) is couched in terms of the superior 'blood' of each caste or the glorious ancestry of each caste. Thus the Karāva at times claim to be the descendants of warriors. Occasionally they even use the term 'Kshatriya', more usually saying that the term Karāva derives from 'shoulder', where the King appointed them his soldiers. Thus they deride the Goyigama who, they claim, have always been simple peasants. Of course the Goyigama deny such tales.

Alternatively, the argument over status is couched in economic terms.

It is said that 'a long time ago' a Karāva and a Goyigama had an argument as to their relative status. The Goyigama claimed superiority because he produced rice and man had to have rice to live. The Karāva countered by saying that man could not live on rice alone; he had to have a fish curry to make it palatable. But, said the Goyigama, the rice goes on the plate first. To this the Karāva answered that the fish went on top. Of course this is simply a childish story, and my informant viewed it as such. Yet, being a Karāva, he made it very clear to me who had won the argument.

This story introduces occupation. In this context, any Goyigama claim to superiority can be countered by Karāva pointing out that whatever their traditional role they are now fishers like the Karāva. Depending upon which line one cares to follow, either the Karāva are superior or the two castes are equal. About all they do agree about is that the gap between them is not all that great, and that they are superior to other castes.

Turning to names, if the relative ranking of castes is unclear, then so is the ranking of names within castes. Probably the most general statement one can make is that any person will tend to claim that his or her *vasagama* name is at least as good as any other *vasagama* name. As Warunakulasuriya is the most common name then, not surprisingly, Warunakulasuriya is frequently thought to be the 'best' name one can have.

Perhaps more interesting is that in terms of ranking, the Karāva and the Goyigama tend to overlap in the context of *vasagama* names. Thus most Karāva would put certain *vasagama* names which they recognize as Karāva below other *vasagama* names they recognize as being Goyigama. On the one hand it is true to say that castes are considered as discrete, hierarchically arranged categories. Just as Sinhalese-ness is in certain senses superior to Tamil-ness, so Karāva-ness is superior (or inferior) to Goyigama-ness. But just as individual Tamil castes are superior to individual Sinhalese castes, so some Goyigama are considered superior to some Karāva – even by the Karāva. What is constant is the idea that there is inequality of some sort. But there is no system of caste inequality.

In sum then, it seems to me that caste and the caste hierarchy in Wellagoda can be seen either as a system of great flexibility – or of total disorder. All that is constant is that people are unequal, that in certain situations this inequality is thought to be concerned with birth, blood or occupation, and to be related in some way connected with the past.

2.8. Caste and Catholicism

This paper is not about caste and Catholicism but about caste in Wellagoda.

As I indicated in the Introduction, the importance of caste varies greatly through the Catholic areas of Sri Lanka, and the situation I am describing here is not general among Catholics along the coast of Sri Lanka. Rather it is one extreme situation.

Yet it would be difficult to ignore religion altogether, and the problem remains of the relationship between caste and religion. For Dumont, caste is intrinsically linked with Hinduism and without the latter there can be no caste. Thus in Sri Lanka there is no caste, only quasi-caste (Dumont 1970: Ch. 10). Similarly, the Pathans of the Swat valley have no 'true' caste (see Parry 1974). But this formulation leads to all sorts of problems. For instance, Fuller in his work on Kerala Christians has found it necessary to distinguish between caste as theology and caste as ideology (Fuller 1977). Thus although these Christians do not share a theology of caste with their Hindu neighbours, they do share an ideology! This appears to be an ancient argument: de Nobili was using it in the seventeenth century in Madurai where he attempted, rather unsuccessfully, to reconcile castes with Catholicism through defining caste as, in effect, being a matter of 'secular' ideology (Cronin 1959). Furthermore, Dumont's limitations on the use of caste are somewhat presumptuous in the case of Sri Lanka where the indigenous peoples see their institutions of caste as being of the same order as those of the Hindus. Admittedly, this is not the place to launch an attack on Dumont's ideas of what caste is and is not, but it has to be borne in mind that he has in effect ruled out of court many of the more interesting problems concerning caste, i.e., what happens in the margins of the Hindu heartland.

In Sri Lanka, the Church used caste as a means of conversion and as a means of organizing the converted. Throughout the coastal belt there are caste-based churches, in places only a few yards apart. Furthermore, even where churches cater for a mixed caste population, the internal organization of the congregation is often caste based, different castes having different lay leaders (*annāvis*) and separate *novenas* during the church feast. Finally, the clergy is overwhelmingly drawn from the Karāva and the Goyigama castes, lower caste priests being very rare indeed.[20]

On the ideological level, Catholicism is no more antithetical to caste than is – say – Buddhism. In Wellagoda, caste is usually seen as something outside religion. All agree that caste is an institution of the world, concerned with profane society rather than the spiritual life. There is no caste in heaven; the important personages of Catholicism such as Christ and the Virgin Mary are not thought of as belonging to castes.[21] Yet even if caste is not to do with the spiritual life, it is felt by some (in their more 'traditional' moments) that the Church should protect the clarity of castes. Some say that the Church should stop people from changing their names; some say that the Church should prevent cross-caste marriages. And these sentiments are not restricted to the villagers. They crop up, often in stronger terms, amongst priests whose interest in caste is expressed (or disguised) as an interest in the 'true history', the 'facts of the past'.

But this is only one expression of the relationship between caste and religion, for there are also occasions when it is claimed that caste is not simply outside religion, but opposed to religion. In recent years the Church has begun to attack caste, and sermons are being given which deny its validity. Thus after such a sermon villagers would occasionally announce that caste was a 'mistake' of their ancestors, that it had no place in the world of today and that there were only two *jātiya*, male and female.[22]

3. CONTEXTS OF CASTE REALITY

So far, I have written about caste in what amounts to a vacuum. I am only too aware that the picture I have given of caste in Wellagoda must appear somewhat disordered and confused, but I must stress that the situation itself is disordered and confused. In an effort to make the situation clearer I shall now examine the situations in which caste does become a matter of some interest for the people of Wellagoda.

3.1. Questions and gossip

Not surprisingly, the most frequent context in which caste became a topic for conversation was when I asked about it. And this is an important point. I must stress once more that caste is not an all-pervading topic of conversation in Wellagoda. It is not something which intervenes in villagers' day-to-day existence, and I was once told, 'You're the only person who ever talks about things like this.' Admittedly it was very rarely that caste as a fact-of-life was denied in Wellagoda, but in comparison with topics such as wealth, it was of relatively minor importance.

Thus what I have written in the previous section is a product in large measure of direct questioning. The discussion does not arise out of actual social situations, social dramas or whatever, and caste infrequently came up in undirected conversations.

This lack of interest in caste is associated with a lack of knowledge of caste. People were frequently unsure of the caste affiliation of their neighbours. In the parliamentary elections of 1970, many voters were unclear as to the caste of the candidates.

But this is not to say that caste was never a matter to be brought up in gossip and slander. The point here is simply that given the uncertainty over the ranking of castes and names, plus the uncertainty over who has or has not usurped names and caste status, then the caste claims of any person in the village are at risk and can be brought into question very easily. And given that caste is mixed up with notions of a correct and a true order of society, then to attack a person's caste pretensions is at base to attack their respectability and their good faith. This fragility of caste status is a peculiarly marked problem for those who claim Goyigama status, and for those who in economic, political or kinship terms are marginal to the mainstream of village life. Thus individuals who have political aspirations in the village context are frequently subjected to attack as to their caste position.

Closely linked with this fluidity and uncertainty, and related to the way in which this uncertainty is used in attacking the pretensions of people, is the problem of marriage. And it is here that caste is of most immediate importance in Wellagoda life.

3.2. Caste and marriage

To start off with, let us look at what appears to be a paradox in the relationship of caste to marriage. In terms of the principles of caste allocation to which all in Wellagoda subscribe and which I have outlined earlier, who one marries is unimportant in caste terms. Caste is a fixed quality given at birth and determined by patrifiliation. There is no doubt over the caste of the offspring; a marriage in no way affects the caste status of the partners involved. Yet in actuality, considerations of caste are of central importance in marriage choices and negotiations, and affinal ties between people are crucially related to problems of caste status.

In Wellagoda, besides setting up the nuclear family, marriage is also considered to set up affinal relations (*vivāha naekaema*) between the nuclear families of bride and groom. Furthermore, this relationship between families is inherently asymmetrical. Thus it should not be reciprocated, it involves an unequal relationship between wife's brother and sister's husband; it involves dowry payments which in extreme cases approximate to 'groom price'; and it involves a series of rituals in the marriage which stress the inferiority of the wife givers (Stirrat 1975a).

The principle of asymmetric or hypergamous marriage is common throughout South Asia (see Parry 1974; Pocock 1972; Yalman 1963 etc.). For Dumont, hypergamy is directly related to the hierarchical relationship of purity and pollution and the concept of *kanyā dān*, the 'gift of a virgin'. Indeed, Dumont goes so far as to argue that caste endogamy is logically secondary to hypergamy, and that the latter is more in harmony with the logic of the caste system (Dumont 1970).

In Wellagoda (and I suspect elsewhere) there is an ambiguity at the heart of this notion of asymmetry. Is the inequality of affinal partners fixed prior to marriage, i.e., does the marriage choice reflect previous inequality? Or is it the result of marriage, i.e., does marriage produce inequality between the affinally related families? In a sense, this asymmetry works at both levels, but the picture is obscure. First of all, caste inequalities are only one of a series of factors which enter into the scheme of things, and secondly, as I have continually stressed, such is the confusion as to ranking that no one knows, or at least can be sure of persuading others, what the ranking scheme is between and within castes.

Caste is only one of a series of factors involved in marriage. Personal characteristics such as character and physical appearance are important, but wealth and caste are probably the most basic – at least to the parents. The ideal is to find one's child a spouse who is both rich and has good claims to being of good caste. This latter factor tends to imply either some sort of distant relationship or a close personal knowledge of the persons involved.

But given this, we can recognize two extreme situations. The first is where money is all important. 'I would give my daughter to a Rodiya if he was rich enough,' one man told me, although I doubt if in fact he would.[23] At the other extreme, caste is all important and people would look shocked and disgusted at the thought of marrying their children to lower caste partners.

It seems to me that the importance of caste in this context does not centre about the problem of female purity. Rather it is through marriage that one can validate one's own pretensions to a certain caste status. But although the marriages of both sexes are important in this context, the marriage of women, of daughters and sisters, is the more significant in that these marriages determine to whom one is inferior.

Whilst I lived in the village, all the marriages which took place were between people whose claims to caste status were generally similar, and in those caste in itself was not an important issue. But, given the rather confusing nature of caste in Wellagoda and the existence of contradictions between caste status and economic status, there have been cases where wealth has overcome considerations of caste status. These marriages have resulted in a series of affinal relations which have implications for the caste aspirations of a number of village households.

One example of the interplay between caste and marriage is shown in Figure 1. Peter, who claims to be a Goyigama, was a successful fisherman who married Anne, a Warunakulasuriya . . . Fernando, of a family generally accepted as 'true' Karāva. Peter's daughter Maria married Thomas, who claims to be Karāva. Thomas, in common with people like Joseph and Norbert, claim that Peter is not 'really' Goyigama but some lower caste, and that Anne was only married to him for financial reasons. But there the agreement ends, for Joseph and Norbert, along with Peter and Antony, all consider Thomas not to be a 'true' Karāva, claiming him to be descended from low caste Indian Tamil immigrants. So when Norbert's daughter married Xavier, Thomas and his children were not invited to the wedding because of their caste. And when Joseph's daughter married Vincent, Thomas was invited out of politeness but, as all expected, did not attend. Yet Maria went to both weddings as she was considered of 'good' caste.

The Xavier of this story belongs to a rather interesting group known as the *lokuru minissu*. They all have Warunakulasuriya . . . Fernando names and all claim to be Karāva, but everyone else tends to view them as being very low in the caste hierarchy. I have even heard it said that 'good' people should not accept water from them.

It is not very clear who or what *lokuru* means. Village theory maintains that *lokuru* means 'greedy' and that their ancestors used to steal food from other people's households and eat until they were sick! But this does not explain why they are treated as low caste and why others tend not to interdine or marry with them, even though some *lokuru* are fairly well off. In one *lokuru* household there are two brothers and a sister, all middle-aged and all unmarried, presumably because they are *lokuru*. An examination of Figure 2 will serve to show how caste and marriage interplay in the *lokuru* case. Whilst the *lokuru* people's case is quite clear, the status of others is more problematic. Thus the children of Eusebius and of Alphonsu bear little taint of their mother's low status. In part, this is a direct result of caste being patrilineally inherited, but it is also related to the dogma that wife-givers are inferior to wife-receivers. For if we look at Andrew's descendants we find their status is suspect because Andrew gave his daughter Elizabeth in marriage to Martin, thus implying their inferiority to the *lokuru* people. And this kind of taint spreads. Veronica, Elizabeth's sister, married John, and they had a son, Marcel. In one sense, Marcel's caste status depends on that of his father John. But Marcel's

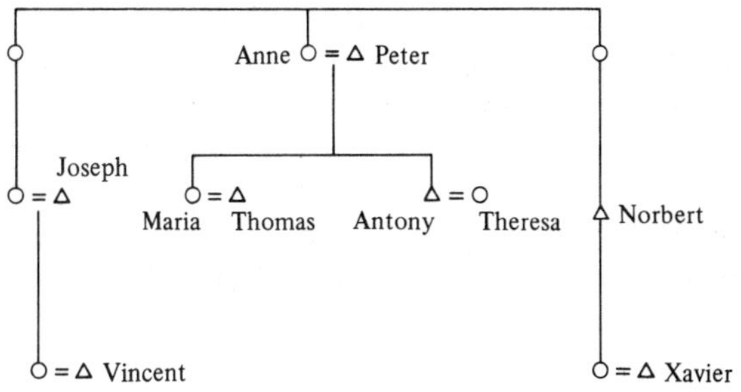

Figure 1. The genealogical background of a dispute over 'true' Karāva caste identity

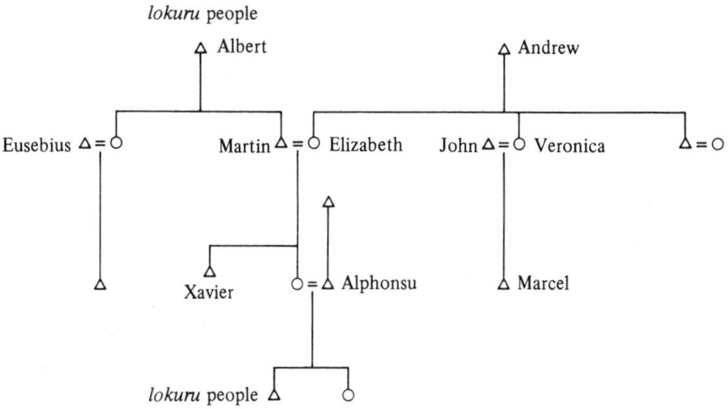

Figure 2. The spread of inferior *lokuru* status through marriage

enemies refer to him as a *lokuru* man, and his rather odd behaviour is rationalized in these terms. In a way, he is in the same position as the 'real' *lokuru* because, like them, his father married one of Andrew's daughters. Of course, all this is relative. Whilst this appears to be the logic behind the claims that Marcel is 'really' *lokuru*, his friends would deny such arguments.

One way around this sort of problem is to deny that one's affines are really low, each family persuading the other that both are of good status. Thus returning to Figure 1, Norbert had to marry his daughter to Xavier as Xavier had already got the girl pregnant. Norbert now claims that his daughter's affines are *honda minissu*, 'good people' of respectable caste. But unfortunately no one believes him.

Another way of dealing with the caste implications of marriage is to reverse the asymmetry of the marriage rituals. In Wellagoda there is a group of families who claim to be Goyigama but whom others consider to be Potters by caste. Thus all the descendants of Lawrence shown in Figure 3 are Potters. Antony and Albert both married women from families which claimed Karāva status but which were willing to marry their daughters to lower caste men for economic reasons. In both cases during the wedding ceremonies the grooms had to go down on their knees before the bride's brother and formally ask for their brides, behaviour unheard of in normal marriages. Their close relations such as Moses, Matthias and Lucas avoided such indignities by marrying outside the village.

So, although marriage may be divorced from caste on a theoretical level, in practice the two are closely related. In this context, given the uncertainty as to the true nature of claims to caste status, the problem is to validate one's own claims and avoid a 'credibility gap'. The cases I have described here are, perhaps, the more extreme ones, and normally there is not the same degree of inequality between affines. Yet to a greater or lesser extent, any marriage in Wellagoda has implications for the caste aspirations of those involved. Furthermore, it is really only in marriage that caste becomes an important issue in Wellagoda social life. Thus a certain circularity sets in. Affinal relationships are important in the definition of caste status. Yet caste status is really only important in determining the marriage choices which create affinal relations.

4. CONCLUSION

I have tried to present an account of caste as it exists in Wellagoda. The account may seem confused, but ideas about and behaviour concerned with caste in Wellagoda are confused. It is not the core (or template) of Wellagoda social life; it is not at the forefront of peoples' minds except where marriage is concerned. I am tempted to abdicate intellectually at this point and claim that caste is simply an 'idiom', a language borrowed from elsewhere to talk about social relationships. But this would be a false representation. Ideas and notions concerning caste have a reality *sui generis* in Wellagoda.

The normal alternative to such an abdication is to produce in the conclusion of a paper such as this a 'with one bound he was free' type of solution. The seeming confusion is suddenly reduced to order in a feat of intellectual gymnastics. This too, I am afraid, is not possible for me at

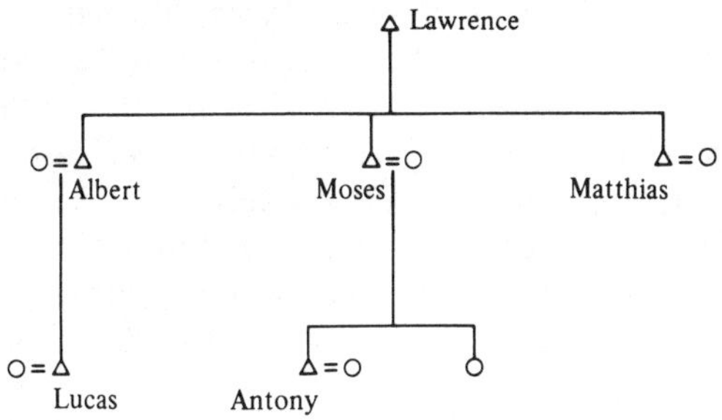

Figure 3. Reversing the ritualized inferiority of wife-givers in order to equalize Potter/Karāva marriages

least. Rather, all that I shall and can do is to make some tentative remarks which may make some semblance of sense.

A number of points stand out when one compares caste in Wellagoda with the reports on caste elsewhere in South Asia. The first is that the principles of caste in Wellagoda are highly simplified in comparison with those described from other ethnographic contexts. Here, caste is fixed at birth and is unalterable. It is not associated with a series of complex notions of purity or pollution, nor with an elaboration of ritual roles and duties. Caste is simply a matter of patrifiliation.

Secondly, here in Wellagoda, caste exists in itself. In an odd way, in India and elsewhere in South Asia, caste does not exist in itself. Rather, it is part of, and is implied by, higher (or more elementary) levels of reality. Thus Dumont sees caste as being the result of and implied by a particular theology which is logically prior to the institutions of caste. Marriott and Inden see caste as the working out of a series of notions concerning bodily substances and inter-personal exchanges. And in Sri Lanka, caste is seen either as an elaboration of close kin marriage which in turn is the logical result of an almost paranoid interest in female sexuality (Yalman) or is a moment in a complex politico-economic-religious liturgy (Hocart). In other words, caste does not, or rather is not seen to, exist in itself.

In Wellagoda, however, caste is not tied up with religion, sex, or what Hocart would call a 'liturgy'.[24] Caste exists here in itself, divorced from politics, economics or religion. It ceases to be a totalistic and holistic model of society. Rather, it becomes marginal and secondary to social life. But it becomes 'pure' caste, existing only in itself, an attenuated and simplified form of caste elsewhere.

Yet whilst the principles of caste in Wellagoda may be simple, the empirical manifestations of caste and the ideas concerning the content of caste have become complicated and confused. There is little agreement as to the relative importance of caste, to the relative ranking of castes, and to who is or is not in any particular caste. And it seems to me that this simplification of principles, the divorce of caste from other areas of social life, and the complexity of the empirical situation are all related features and are significant as a totality in how we go about understanding caste in Wellagoda.

I am reminded here of some of Bloch's comments in his recent Malinowski Lecture (Bloch 1977). He remarks in this lecture how some societies, such as India, appear to have a 'lot' of social structure whilst others do not. Furthermore, he points out how this thing called 'social structure' is something which appears primarily in ritual and symbolism and he suggests that it is closely related to what he labels, rather obscurely, 'institutionalised hierarchy'. 'Social structure' then becomes a 'mode of discourse' which is a mystification of the true world. Furthermore, given his approach, we would expect that the less the amount of 'institutionalised hierarchy', the less the amount of 'social structure'.

Bloch's comments are in many ways remarkably apposite for Wellagoda. What struck me, and worried me, when I first did fieldwork there was the lack of what I had been led to expect from reading South Asian ethnographies. There was no immediately apparent 'institutionalised hierarchy'. 'Social structure' seemed to be absent. Rather, the village consists of individualized households related by dyadic ties rather than any holistic social model represented in ritual and symbolism. In other words, the 'confusion' or 'complexity' I have mentioned throughout this paper is, in Bloch's terms simply a lack of social structure, a lack of institutionalized hierarchy. Whilst elsewhere in India the complex system of caste is directly associated with a complex institutionalized hierarchy, here in Wellagoda, because there is little in the way of institutionalized hierarchy, the principles of caste become simplified and attenuated.

But there is something more to Bloch's comments on 'social structure' – or the lack of it. In his lecture, he stresses how 'social structure' is essentially a series of ritual statements, a part of a 'discourse, dominated by the past in the present'. In the context of caste, here is the idea of a timeless, changeless order, where 'inequality takes on the appearance of an inevitable part of an ordered system', a picture which appears to fit the classic ethnographic (and analytic) pictures of caste in South Asia.

Furthermore, in Wellagoda, the split between what I have labelled 'modernist' and 'traditionalist' views of caste are similarly concerned with the past and its relation to the present. The modernist position is that caste is to do with the past and with an old and outmoded hierarchical order of society. But now, caste is outmoded: it is something of little relevance to a present dominated by economics, politics – by, if you like, an individualistic ethos. But the traditionalist stance stresses not what is but what should be. Caste represents the morally correct, true order of society in a timeless vacuum. It represents an anti-individualist stance in which the realities of the present are hidden behind a caricature of the past.

One final point: marriage. Why is it that only in the context of marriage should caste retain a relevance and an importance for all? On the matrimonial level, the answer, I suppose, is simply that here one's claims to a caste status can be validated. But on a more general level, the point about marriage appears to be that marriage is seen in Wellagoda (and indeed in Catholic thought) as the key basis of society (see Stirrat 1975a). And if so, then it must be related to the 'traditionalist' position which stresses the idea of society, for the modernist one stresses not society but individualism.

Mukkuvar vannimai: Tamil caste and matriclan ideology in Batticaloa, Sri Lanka

Dennis B. McGilvray

1. INTRODUCTION

Hence it is true that the ideology in which we see the conscious centre of caste can be lacking here or there *within the Indian world*, and observation of these cases is of the greatest interest, to show us to what extent and in what conditions institutions of this kind can survive the weakening or disappearance of their ideological aspect.

(Louis Dumont, *Homo Hierarchicus*, 1970: 46)

The question of caste ideology, that is, how caste systems are conceived and understood by the people who live their lives within them, is the focus of this essay. It is a tribute to Louis Dumont, and to his determined advocacy of a Hindu ideology of purity and pollution as the superordinate or 'encompassing' criterion of Indian caste society, that his work serves today as the standard reference point against which his colleagues in South Asian anthropology feel obliged to measure their own theoretical positions. However, at least one theoretical school now advocates a more radical interpretive framework based upon distinctive South Asian 'coded bodily substance' concepts said to be more ideological and culturally authentic than any proposed by Dumont (Marriott and Inden 1974; 1977; Marriott 1976a). While the work of Dumont, on the one hand, and the formulations of Marriott and Inden, on the other, represent the most clearly contrasting interpretations of caste as seen 'from the inside', mention will be made of a number of other writers who employ elements of both approaches. What is generally lacking, however, is sufficient attention to what Dumont himself, in the rare passage quoted above, admits to be an urgent research priority: the documentation and analysis of local caste systems in which the salient ideologies of rank are, from a South Asian comparative standpoint, atypical, disjunctive, or attenuated.

This essay describes a search for indigenous theories of caste and matriclan rank in the Tamil-speaking settlements of the Batticaloa region on the east coast of Sri Lanka. Contrary to expectation, the findings of this research throw doubt upon *both* the major theories. The ideology of caste and matriclan rank here shows far less evidence of the Dumontian 'purity' symbolism, or of the post-Dumontian 'coded bodily substance' concepts, than one would expect, given the alleged ubiquity of these indigenous ideas throughout the Hindu world. Instead, one finds that a strong ideology of chiefly conquest, a system of matrilineal clan rights, and a traditional array of 'marks of honour' – all associated with ideals of the *Mukkuvar vannimai*, the regional chiefship of the Mukkuvar caste – pervade local thinking about social status and marriage alliance. Ideas of ritual purity, on the other hand, emerge mainly within domestic life-crisis contexts and are not articulated as a rationale for the collective status of caste groups. Theories of bodily substance are highly developed, but in the view of local people they clearly belong to the cultural domain of medicine and health, not to an 'ethnosociological' metaphysic of caste identity.

These findings are of some ethnographic interest in themselves, but they also serve to underwrite the strong critique of 'purity' and 'bio-moral substance' theories of caste with which this essay concludes. Rather than pursue single-mindedly a unique vision of the 'essence' of caste in all its manifestations, we should instead view South Asian symbols and theories of society in the light of the specific historical factors which gave rise to regional caste systems in the first place and which subsequently conditioned the tone and content of indigenous thinking about local caste hierarchies. In the Batticaloa area, as no doubt in other South Asian subregions, the 'symbolic language' of the caste system was shaped by the historical circumstances surrounding the establishment of the dominant caste, its ideological resources, and its specialist groups. Here, in fact, a heritage of warrior conquest by a formerly low-ranking Malabar fishing caste, combined with a distinctive non-Brahman Vīracaiva (Lingāyat) priestly tradition, has produced a regional caste system with a markedly 'political' (or Hocartian) ideology of caste rank and caste honour. If we would give more recognition to historical discontinuities in the propagation, cultural transmission, and social reception of allegedly pan-Indic social and cosmological ideas, as well as to the precise ethnographic contexts in which these ideas are invoked, the usefulness of such concepts in comprehending specific caste systems would be considerably enhanced.

2. AN OVERVIEW OF CURRENT THEORY

2.1. Dumont and the 'substance and code' approach

A recent trend in the study of South Asian caste, kinship, and marriage systems has been a greater attempt to utilize traditional Indic theories of society and indigenous beliefs about the unitary bio-moral quality of action and bodily substance in the analysis of fieldwork data. Dumont's insistence upon the ideological supremacy of status (purity) over power in Hindu caste systems (Dumont 1970: Chs. 2–3) must be taken as the most important stimulus to this renewed interest in what has been termed the 'ethnosociology of Hindu caste systems' (Marriott & Inden 1977). Dumont's position is by now well known: it can be summarized as the assertion that Hindu caste society is a reality *sui generis* built upon the ancient ideological foundation of a radical split between contingent secular power (embodied in the ideal of the Kshatriya *varna*) and absolute ritual purity or status (embodied in the ideal of the Brahman *varna*). Dumont insists upon a structuralist or holistic view of caste as an ideologically-governed system in which the ritual superiority of the Brahman subordinates or 'encompasses' secular power at the most general or abstract level of Hindu society, although particular social contingencies may temporarily reverse this relationship in certain regional and historical settings ('interstitial levels', 1970: 197). This hierarchical relationship between the priest and the king is the essential criterion of caste in the Dumontian sense of the term. On these grounds he has argued that society in Sri Lanka is built upon 'quasi-caste rather than caste proper', since Brahmans have never been numerous in Sri Lanka and the Buddhist concept of kingship rejects the Brahman–Kshatriya duality (Dumont 1970: 215–16; S.J. Tambiah 1976).

A number of 'post-Dumontian' formulations and reformulations have now emerged, seeking to trace intrinsically Indian patterns of thought more deeply and rigorously than Dumont himself had done. An additional inspiration for this trend has been the work of David Schneider, whose book on American kinship (1968) succinctly suggests that a 'cultural account' of American kinship, that is, an account of the defining features of kinship relationships from an indigenous actor's point of view, would stress the dual concepts of shared natural bodily substance, e.g. 'blood' ('relationship in nature'), and normative code for conduct ('relationship in law'). Kinship in this perspective is a fundamentally cultural construct which may include symbols of 'hard' biogenetic reality as well as moral injunctions or 'codes for conduct' specifying kinship relationships. Marriott and Inden (1974; 1977), following Barnett (1970), detect a striking contrast between this dualism which Schneider notes in American kinship ideology and what they interpret to be a universal monism in Hindu taxonomic thought, a philosophic tradition which does not distinguish two separate realms of 'natural' versus 'moral' phenomena. Instead, all substances, all actions, and all intangible influences are assumed to embody and convey essential qualities; they are all 'code-substances' or 'substance-codes', continuously interacting upon one another within a single transformative plasm or matrix of atom-like quality-particles which, in various combinations, are felt to constitute the ranked natural genera of inanimate, animate, and divine beings, including *varnas*, castes, clans, and other ranked human genera (Marriott 1976a; Inden 1976: 11–48).

Particular attention is thus directed toward indigenous views of the creation, composition, and behaviour of the human body, seen in this perspective as a locus of 'bio-moral substances' (e.g. blood) which embody both physiological properties pertaining to bodily states as well as moral properties pertaining to social rights and duties. A Hindu caste, from this point of view, is a group sharing a distinctive type of bio-moral substance which caste members preserve, even occasionally improve, through strict observance of caste rules governing key social transactions, such as marriage, food exchange, and occupational performance. Perhaps the most important aspect of this 'ethnosociological' interpretation for fieldwork in South Asia is the manner in which it bridges the gap between claims of intrinsic or attributional caste superiority on the one hand (Stevenson 1954), and the equally visible role which competitive inter-caste transactions play in generating and changing local caste rankings on the other (Marriott 1959; 1968a). By virtue of this highly developed Hindu metaphysical system, all types of inter-caste transactions and relationships, including withdrawal from interaction itself, can be seen to affect the coded-substance (and the rank) of the castes involved. This interpretation argues that 'purity' and 'power', the categories so assiduously separated by Dumont,[1] are in reality aspects of the same thing: 'a unitary Indian concept of superior value – power understood as vital energy, substance-code of subtle, homogeneous quality, and high, consistent transactional status or rank' (Marriott 1976a: 137).

Some of these concepts have recently been applied to ethnographic material from Bengal and Tamilnadu. Inden and Nicholas (1977) have sought to elucidate Bengali concepts of 'blood' and 'love' as linked elements which constitute the core symbols in the Bengali kinship system, and thus they consider their analysis to be a 'cultural account' of Bengali kinship in David Schneider's sense of the term. Inden (1976) has also produced a historical study of marriage transactions between the highest Bengali Brahman and Kayastha clans and clan grades ca. 1500–1850 A.D.

which relies heavily upon caste genealogical records (*kulajī*) as well as upon textual commentaries and published formulations of 'marriage theory' from the period. These documents are treated as authentic indigenous codifications of the ethnosociological perspective outlined by Marriott and Inden (1974; 1977).

Fruzzetti and Östör have also produced their own 'cultural account' of Bengali kinship, inspired by Schneider and Dumont, which they consider to be 'totally different in theory and method' from the approach of Marriott and Inden (Fruzzetti & Östör 1976: 100). One aspect of this difference is their rather greater concern with the categories of thought revealed in the actual statements Bengali villagers make about blood-linked kinsmen and about blood-transforming marriages, as opposed to Marriott and Inden's more textual or esoteric theory of monistic coded substance. A second aspect is their desire to retain the Dumontian concept of purity versus power, which they feel avoids the cultural solipsism of the Marriott and Inden approach (Barnett, Fruzzetti & Östör 1976: 631–6). However, additional Bengali evidence of the existence of a widespread transformational 'philosophy of rank' based upon combinations of three elemental 'qualities' (*guṇ*) has been provided by Davis, and this has been taken in support of Marriott and Inden's position (Davis 1976: 6, Marriott 1976b; 190n.).

Several other recent studies using natural substance as an explanatory tool have utilized data from Tamilnadu and Sri Lanka. Barnett's work on the high-ranking Koṇṭaikkaṭṭi Vēḷāḷar (KV) caste in the Chingleput District of Tamilnadu (Barnett 1970; 1973a; 1973b; 1975; 1976), like that of Fruzzetti and Östör in Bengal, places great emphasis upon a local ideology of caste and kin-group 'purity' which is believed to reside in the blood. In the KV example, ranked endogamous kindreds (*vakaiyara*) within the caste preserve distinctions of blood purity, but this purity is susceptible to refinement or degradation as a result of conformity or non-conformity with the transactional rules of the caste or kindred with respect to such things as marriage choice, diet, and exchange of food. A further set of KV ideas deals with exogamous patrilineal *kōttiram* memberships and a bilateral theory of conception in which the father contributes the 'body' (*utampu*) and the mother the 'spirit' (*uyir*) of the foetus. Accounts of Tamil caste and kinship in the northern Jaffna peninsula of Sri Lanka (Banks 1957; 1960; David 1972; 1973b; Pfaffenberger 1977) differ in many respects from the Tamilnadu KV material, but the idea of blood purity and a version of the *utampu/uyir* distinction are said to be present there as well (David 1973a: 523; 1974: 53; 1977: 182).[2] Batticaloa is located southeast of Jaffna, separated from it by 175 miles of sparsely populated Dry-Zone jungle. With regard to these and many other ideas, I hope to show how Batticaloa is quite distinct from Jaffna.

2.2. Yalman's Kandyan studies

Although anthropological interest in the exploration of indigenous theories of purity and bodily substance in South Asia has expanded greatly over the past ten years with the publication of major theoretical formulations by Dumont, Schneider, Marriott and Inden, and others, one of the most important contributions came earlier in the work of Nur Yalman on caste, kinship, and marriage in the Kandyan highlands of Sri Lanka (Yalman 1960; 1962; 1963; 1967; 1969). It was Yalman's work, above all else, which provided the suggestion and stimulus for my own research in eastern Sri Lanka, and so it is necessary to discuss some of his major findings in greater detail.

Yalman noted that Buddhist Sinhalese villagers in the Kandyan area discuss differences between castes, ideally endogamous bilateral kindreds (*pavula*), and aristocratic patrilines (*wamsa*) all with reference to a common theory of 'good' (*honda*) and 'bad' (*naraka*) blood, and he interpreted the Kandyan tendency to maintain (at least in fiction, if not always in fact) the principle of endogamous boundaries as a functional correlate of the bilateral nature of caste and kindred ('micro-caste') affiliation. Such groups seek to protect their purity by restricting, or claiming to restrict, the source of reproductive fluids (distillations of the blood) to members of the group itself. Hypergamous marriage patterns, such as those of the Nayars and Nambudiri Brahmans of Kerala, are seen by Yalman as 'variants' on the basic bilateral endogamous caste model under the influence of strong unilineal descent principles. Unilineal descent ideas in the form of patrilineal 'aristocratic pedigrees' (*wamsa*) in certain elite Kandyan families are maintained despite the fact that they contradict the generally accepted Kandyan theories of bilateral purity of caste blood, and the principle of hypergamy is recognized between such *wamsa* (Yalman 1967: 138–49, 172–80). In general, argues Yalman, unilineal descent principles provide alternative ways to delineate social groups and, as such, they tend to reduce the need for caste endogamy. If one assumes that group status in South Asia is centred on the idea of ritual purity, and that purity is always protected and preserved through the women of the group (Yalman 1963; 1967: 177–80), hypergamy is the logical alternative to endogamy when unilineal descent rivals bilateral caste as a basic feature of the social order (Yalman 1967: Chs. 12, 15, 16). Yalman's aim is to show that there is a 'general structure' of caste and kinship in South India and Sri Lanka which has at its core a Dravidian kinship classification with bilateral cross-cousin marriage, bilateral descent and inheritance, and certain South Asian cultural axioms about group hierarchy as a manifestation of ritual purity. Purity is conveyed in the blood and is preserved through special restrictions on the sexuality of women. This general structure is capable of many different empirical transformations in different areas under the influence of different descent principles. One of the empirical variants which Yalman tried to generate from this general structure is what he called 'the matrilineal hypergamous variant', which he identified among the Tamils and Muslims of the Batticaloa region and which is the ethnographic focus of this essay (Yalman 1967: Ch. 15).

3. AN ETHNOGRAPHIC SKETCH OF BATTICALOA

3.1. Castes and communities

Batticaloa, or *Maṭṭakkaḷappu* as it is known to the inhabitants, constitutes a distinctive region of Sri Lanka by all the major criteria: historical, linguistic, cultural, and social structural. For geographical and historical reasons, it must also be seen as a zone of relative isolation (Cohn 1967; 1971: 26–8). The first anthropological interpretation of this part of the island is contained in Yalman's monograph, *Under the Bo Tree* (1967: Chs. 14–15), and many of the ethnographic peculiarities noted by Yalman served equally well as starting points for my own research (McGilvray 1973; 1974; 1976). The data presented here were gathered primarily in two locations during two fieldwork trips to the east coast. These two locations, the town and vicinity of Akkaraipattu (Amparai District) and the village and vicinity of Kokkaṭṭiccōlai (Batticaloa District), typify respectively the two characteristic types of settlement patterns found along the east coast as a whole: densely packed semi-urban coastal settlements of Hindu and Muslim wet-rice cultivators and fishermen, on the one hand, and dispersed, mainly Hindu, villages situated inland and separated from the coastal settlements by extensive semi-saline lagoons, on the other (Ryan 1950: 10–12). Both the Hindus, who are officially termed Ceylon Tamils, and the Muslims, who are termed Ceylon Moors,[3] speak Tamil (with minor dialectical variation) and live in adjacent ethnically compartmentalized villages (*kirāmam*) and government Headmen's Divisions (*kuṟicci*) along the coast. Neither the small groups of Tamil Christians scattered throughout the region[4] nor the Sinhalese Buddhists who occupy the lands further inland[5] play any direct role in the situation I wish to describe. The local Eurasian 'Burghers' are discussed elsewhere (McGilvray, 1982b).

The Hindu Tamiḻs in the town of Akkaraipattu provided an opinion-ranking of the main locally recognized Hindu castes which is summarized in Table 1. There are some other local groups which, for various reasons, Tamil informants insisted were incommensurate and impossible to rank alongside the Hindu castes. The Moors, constituting more than 60% of the population of the town, were the most important such exception: they consider themselves, and are considered by the Tamils, to be a separate 'race-cum-ethnic group' (*inam*), not merely adherents of a separate religion.[6] It is difficult to know precisely where the Moors fitted into the social hierarchy, say, a hundred years ago, but there is no doubt that the high caste Tamils treated them as inferiors. They were once given a recognized place in regional Hindu temple festivals and were accorded the right to have the lowest castes serve them, but communal hostility and separatism between Tamils and Moors is now quite strong. In fact, the Moorish population in this region is largely the product of marriages with, and conversions from, the Hindu castes. They consequently share the kinship patterns, matrilineal clan organization, matrilocal marriage system, and many other customary practices of the Hindu Tamils, with the exception of the fact that they are not themselves divided into what could truly be called a Muslim caste system. There is a tiny, markedly inferior, and strictly endogamous group of Muslim Barber-Circumcisers (*Ostā*), a small semi-endogamous set of persons with the title of *maulānā* claiming patrilineal descent from the Prophet's family, and a small group of Sufi mystics (*Pāvā*, 'Bawa'; *Pakīr*, 'Fakir') whose recruitment is based upon a mixture of patrilineal descent and discipleship. The vast majority of Moors have no connection with these groups and are internally differentiated only by their matrilineal clan and mosque affiliations as well as by the standard socio-economic criteria of wealth, education, and occupational status. Aside from employing some Tamil agricultural labour, the Moorish community is primarily linked to the Tamils through its domestic reliance upon Tamil Washermen and its commercial relationships with Tamil Barbers, Smiths, and, until recently, Paṟaiyar Drummers.[7]

Four other groups were excluded by the informants who provided the caste ranking in Table 1, and again, their reasoning was based upon the claim that these groups were anomalous and incommensurate because of their race, religion, or recent origin.[8] However, from the standpoint of this

Table 1. *Tamil opinion-ranking of eight castes traditionally associated with the Hindu caste system in Akkaraipattu*

	K	M	T	C	VN	N	P
V	28/18	35½/11½	46/0	45/1	46/0	46/0	43/3
K		30/16	45/1	45/1	45/1	46/0	44/2
M			45/1	43/3	46/0	46/0	42/4
T				35½/10½	45/1	45/1	39/7
C					39/7	38/8	40/6
VN						26/20	35/11
N							35/11

High castes: 'Tamils' or 'Good/high/big people' (V, K, M)

Artisan & professional castes (T, C)

Kuṭimai Service Castes (VN, N, P)

Caste affiliation of respondents (N = 46)

V Vēḷāḷar Cultivator (15)
K Vīracaiva Kurukkaḷ Priest (3)
M Mukkuvar Cultivator (14)
T Taṭṭār Smith (1)
C Cāṇṭār Climber (4)
VN Vaṇṇār Washerman (3)
N Nāvitar Barber (1)
P Paṟaiyar Drummer (5)

Note: The procedures follow those developed by Freed (1963), Marriott (1968a), Hiebert (1969; 1973) and others, but no statistical test of significance was applied. The matrix has been tilted upright for ease of viewing. To illustrate how the table is read, note that in the cell farthest to the right, 43 respondents ranked the Vēḷāḷar caste above the Paṟaiyar caste, but three respondents expressed the opposite opinion, i.e., that Paṟaiyars rank above Vēḷāḷars. In the event of an equal ranking of two castes, each caste was awarded a score of ½. Castes and blocs of castes differentiated and ranked by a consensus of at least 2:1 are delineated by a heavy black line.

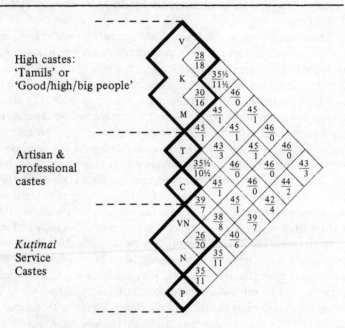

essay, the most central questions concern neither the Moors nor the secondary Hindu and Christian groups but the traditional Hindu castes in Table 1. These are the castes which are seen to have an acknowledged position in the local social order historically instituted by ancient kings.

The basic features of caste rank in Akkaraipattu reveal a high-caste stratum of 'good (*nalla*)/big (*periya*)/high (*uyarnta*) people' incorporating three partially and equivocally ranked castes. This stratum is very often referred to simply as 'Tamils', in contrast to the clearly ranked inferior castes who are referred to by their caste names. The middle castes are generally producers of specialized goods and commodities, such as metalwork (here, Blacksmiths and Goldsmiths are one caste) or products of the coconut and palmyra palm (Climbers were formerly producers of fermented toddy and jaggary sugar). At the bottom are the three domestic service castes, the Washerman, Barber, and Drummer, who are termed collectively the *kuṭimai*, or hereditary household servants. There is no distinct set of agricultural serf (*aṭimai*) castes, such as the Paḷḷar of Jaffna and Tanjore (Banks 1960; Béteille 1965), and, although the behavioural reality is probably quite similar, there is no verbal stress on the metaphor of the low castes being 'bound' (*kaṭṭuppāṭu*) as David reports from Jaffna (1973b and *passim*).[9] However, the ritual services of some or all of the *kuṭimai* castes at both temple festivals and domestic life-crisis ceremonies is a highly coveted mark of honour (*varicai*) which the highest castes have traditionally guarded with jealousy (McGilvray, in press).

3.2. Matrilineal organization

Marital residence for all Hindu and Muslim groups in the Batticaloa region follows a sort of shifting matri-uxorilocal pattern. The wedding takes place in the bride's natal house, and the married couple continue to reside for a period (typically between 6 months and 2 years) with the bride's parents and unmarried siblings. After this, the married daughter takes full possession of the natal house in fulfilment of her dowry, while her parents and some or all of her unmarried siblings move to another house, which is usually new and smaller and is preferably situated in the same or an adjacent compound (*vaḷavu*). Virtually all wealth and immovable property is transferred, or at least pledged, as dowry, which thereby acts as a sort of pre-mortem matrilineal inheritance (Goody 1973) tending to provide greater shares for the elder daughters. Brothers must work to help dower their sisters before they are allowed to marry and leave the household. The kinship pattern is identical for both Tamils and Moors, with some lexical substitutions. Both sets of terminology conform to the symmetrical Dravidian 'general structure' described by Yalman (1967: 216–21 and *passim*). Equal preference for matrilateral and patrilateral cross-cousin marriage is the stated norm, but statistically, MBD marriage seems to be more common than FZD marriage.[10]

From the point of view of social organization, no doubt the most distinctive feature of the entire east coast region, extending from Kottiyar Bay (Trincomalee) in the north to Arugam Bay (Pottuvil) in the south, is the system of dispersed named matriclans which are known individually as *kuṭi*. With the exception of Christian groups in some places, notably the Portuguese Burghers and other Catholic inhabitants of the town of Batticaloa itself, some pattern of matriclan affiliations is recognized within every Hindu caste and in every Moorish community in the region. The first feature of the kuṭi which local people cite is usually the rule of matriliny: *tāy vaḻi* or *peṇ vaḻi*, literally 'mother way' or 'woman way'. The kuṭi is also readily seen as exogamous by informants, and statistical evidence shows this to be remarkably true, except among some *kuṭimai* castes, particularly the Nāvitar Barbers.[11] The rule of kuṭi exogamy is coextensive with the logic of the Dravidian kinship structure which entails that no real or classificatory cross-cousin will ever belong to Ego's matriclan. Members of a kuṭi are not likely to have any awareness of, or interest in, segmentary genealogical links between themselves and shared apical ancestors, and only occasionally is there evidence of explicit and rather shallow sub-lineages (known variously as *vairruvār*, *vakuttuvār*, *kūṭṭam*, *kattarai*). Some matriclans are limited to specific localities while others, larger and usually more prestigious, are distributed here and there over a 60-mile length of the coast.

Among the Tamils, each caste is subdivided among a set of distinctively named constituent matriclans, so that, apart from a few recurring kuṭi names and the anthropologically-elicited residue of unheard-of clans, it is usually possible to identify a person's caste indirectly by first ascertaining the name of his kuṭi. There is a widespread ideal model of seven kuṭis within every Tamil caste and of eighteen kuṭis amongst the Moors, but in fact their local number varies a great deal. In each locality, a certain number of Moorish kuṭis carry the same names as high caste Tamil kuṭis, but the majority are distinctively Moorish. The kuṭi names themselves are quite diverse and some of them are nearly inscrutable: among the high castes they range from the conspicuously kingly and martial kuṭi names found among the Mukkuvars (e.g. Kāliṅkā, an Orissan dynasty; Paṭaiyāṇṭa, leader of armies) to the more heterogeneous but more priestly kuṭi names of the Vēḷāḷars (e.g. Kaṇṭan, Lord, one who saw; Attiyā or Attiyāyan, reader of scripture) and the clear sectarian markings of the Vīrasaiva Kurukkaḷ kuṭis also sometimes referred to as *kōttiram*-s (e.g. Caṅkamar, cognate with the Lingāyat Jangama priest of Mysore; Tēcāntira kurukkaḷ, foreign kurukkaḷ). In the middle of the caste hierarchy (Smiths, Fishermen, Climbers) kuṭi names occasionally borrow elements from those of higher castes, but they commonly show a wide mixture of vague honorifics (e.g. Cūriyaṭappan, solar chief; Vīramaṇikkan, heroic gem) and much more folksy names (e.g. Kaṟuttakkanni, dark virgin; Cummāṭukkaṭṭu, wearing a head-pad for carrying loads). Among the service castes, kuṭi names are generally regional place-names which are said to designate the geographical origins of local sub-groups (e.g. Tāḷaṅkuṭā Vaṇṇān, Paṭṭimēṭu Paṟaiyan). Moorish kuṭi names may range from the kingly (e.g. Rācāmpiḷḷai, royal descent), to the geographical (e.g. Vaṭakkanā, northerner), to the occupational (e.g. Ōṭāvi, carpenter, not related to actual occupation), to the kintyped (e.g. māmanāppiḷḷai, 'MB's or FZH's child', i.e., cross-cousin) to the personal (e.g. Ammanācci, granny).

A detailed account of kuṭi names cannot be undertaken here (see McGilvray 1974), but despite their richness and diversity, it is evident that relatively few have any clear reference to ancestral females. There are no matrilineal personal names,[12] no revered clan origin-places, no jointly held houses or lands,[13] no tutelary clan deities, and no ancestral cults. In these and other respects the contrasts with Nayar society in central Kerala are quite marked, while there are greater resemblances to northern Kerala Nayars, Tiyyars, and Mappillas (Gough 1961; Aiyappan 1944).

Today, kuṭi affiliation continues to have relevance in marriage choice and in the management of Hindu temples and Muslim mosques. Each kuṭi selects one or more representative elders, an office termed *Vaṇṇakkar* by the Tamils and *Maraikkār* by the Moors, to sit on the management committee of the caste temple or neighbourhood mosque. Frequently one or more kuṭis may assert traditional pre-eminence in temple or mosque affairs, a status typically dramatized and validated by some conspicuous prerogative of ritual or ceremonial which is denied to other kuṭis, such as the right to receive the first offerings from the deity or the right to erect a feasting enclosure (*kantūri pantal*) in front, rather than to the side, of the mosque. Yalman correctly saw evidence of this tendency in his brief visit to the east coast (Yalman 1967: 326), but my own research has revealed that considerable attention has also been traditionally paid to elaborately graded marks of honour (*varicai*) in the conduct of Tamil domestic rituals. The higher castes and their kuṭis were allotted specific numbers of symbolic household decorations, such as decorated pots arrayed on the roof and cloths hung beside the doorway, as well as prescribed services from the *kuṭimai* service castes.

3.3. Ambiguities of caste and matriclan

Some striking contrasts with our standard picture of South Indian, particularly Tamil, caste systems are evident in this region. What Yalman first noted (1967: 329) in the statements of his informants from the Tamil village of Tambiluvil six miles south of Akkaraipattu, and what I quickly encountered in the initial stages of my own fieldwork, was the relative looseness and flexibility of statements about the conceptual boundary between a caste (*cāti*) and a matriclan (kuṭi). Both terms are, of course, highly polysemic and contextual: *cāti* (jāti) in the most general sense means 'genera, kind, type', and kuṭi can be traced back to the root-meanings of 'hut, house, household, family dependents' (Winslow 1862: 314). As Yalman reports, people may refer one moment to 'Mukkuvar kuṭi' or 'Vēḷāḷar kuṭi' and refer a moment later to specific matriclans within these categories. Yalman's tentative finding was that, among the higher groups, the expected clear endogamous boundaries between ranked bilaterally-constituted castes were absent on the east coast. Instead, the emphasis seemed to be on a ranked set of kuṭis, some sharing caste names, some having distinct names of their own, which blurred the lines between presumptive caste categories such as 'Vēḷāḷar', 'Kurukkaḷ', and 'Mukkuvar'. Yalman also reported that local informants described the marriage arrangements between the exogamous kuṭis as being explicitly hypergamous, with women of certain lower clans having enduring hypergamous marriage links with men of certain higher clans.

Given these assumptions, and noting his experience in the Kandyan highlands where villagers spoke clearly of endogamous and hypergamous marriage strategies which would ensure the protection and possible enhancement of 'good blood', Yalman suggested that social organization on the east coast could be interpreted as a further instance of how a unilineal descent principle coupled with hypergamy could render the principle of bilateral caste endogamy 'unnecessary'. The matrilineal kuṭi could be seen to carry all, or at least the largest share of, ritual status for its members, whose hierarchical resource was further protected by hypergamy, the 'second line of defense' (Yalman 1967: 179) even in bilateral caste situations. The model was applicable to the Malabar Coast as well. It even seemed to account for the fuzziness of local statements about social groups, '. . . since the status-bearing unit can be a single lineage with hypergamous connections and it may be difficult in the continuous descending steps of status to say exactly where one "caste" category ends and the next begins' (1967: 366).

Yalman's interpretation was quite ingenious, and it naturally served as a starting framework for my own research in the region. At the same time, too, some of the writers discussed earlier were beginning to argue their case for 'coded natural substance' symbolism as the indigenous underlying rationale for all South Asian caste systems. There seemed good reason to think that Yalman's 'hypergamous-unilineal-purity' thesis would form the basis of a more detailed ethnographic analysis which would also detect a theory of coded natural substance, probably 'blood', as the carrier of intrinsic ritual status or purity. Ultimately, however, *neither* of these frameworks provided a satisfactory account of the data which emerged from fieldwork.

The first theory to be discarded was Yalman's, with its crucial postulate of hypergamy. It is inscrutable why his informants spoke of hypergamy, as no such pattern of hypergamous marriage, ideal or actual, was found to exist between castes or kuṭis. This finding is corroborated by Hiatt (1973: 235) and was cross-checked statistically against marriage samples (McGilvray 1974: 272) to eliminate the possibility of bias in informants' statements. Instead of hypergamy, one finds reciprocal marriage exchange (or 'alliance') between pairs of high-ranking matriclans in particular localities. The relationship between matriclans strongly linked by marriage is sometimes described as *maccān maccinan* (cross-cousins, i.e., brothers-in-law), *koṇṭān koṭuttān* (receiving and giving), or *cōṭi cōṭi* (paired up), just as the ensuing terminological restrictions on marriage between certain clans are expressed as *aṇṇan tampi* (elder and younger brother) or *akkā taṅkaicci* (elder and younger sister) relationships.[14]

Yet, despite the empirical inadequacy of Yalman's account of hypergamy, there was still reason to suppose that the observed symmetrical marriage exchange between prestigious local matriclans might reflect some underlying ideology of the conservation of purity or natural substance, as suggested by the work of Yalman, Dumont, and the 'substance-code' theorists, which would provide a key to some of the unusual aspects of culture and social structure in the Batticaloa region. The evidence from fieldwork in Akkaraipattu, reinforced by briefer visits to other parts of the region, pointed in particular to five seemingly anomalous, but interrelated, features. First, it was necessary to account for the fact that Tamils of the high caste stratum in Akkaraipattu unabashedly contracted marriages, indeed even major kuṭi marriage exchange alliances, across putative caste boundaries, thus violating the expected rule of caste endogamy. The prevalence of this practice was found to vary significantly in different areas of the Batticaloa region, but when it occurred, it did not seem to diminish the sense of caste identity of the spouses or their offspring in the eyes of the local people. Second, informants consistently asserted that caste affiliation, like matriclan membership, descended strictly in the female line (*tāy vaḻi*, *peṇ vaḻi*), rather than bilaterally as one commonly finds in other South Asian caste systems. Third, there were vague and contradictory statements from local informants as to the genealogical 'path' or spread of ritual pollution following a death, in striking contrast to the role of the unilineal kin group as a community of mourners in many parts of South Asia. Fourth, it appeared that Hindu purity and pollution ideas were generally less pervasive and unitary, more varied and context-linked, than a reading of the South Asian ethnographic literature might lead one to expect. This fact helped to frame the fifth and final problem: namely, that despite considerable historical and ethnographic evidence of closely regulated symbols and privileges of caste and kuṭi hierarchy in domestic life, in marriage alliance, and in temple ritual, there seemed relatively few clearly defined caste and kuṭi 'interests' which could account for this concern.

4. BELIEFS ABOUT PURITY AND BODILY SUBSTANCE

4.1. Blood, sex and reproduction

In the hope of finding some indigenous conceptual basis for these atypical patterns, I turned, particularly in my second fieldwork trip, to the investigation of beliefs about bodily substances, ideologies of caste and matriclan descent, and theories of purity and pollution. Some of the information which follows was gleaned from casual remarks, but much of it comes from discussions with members of a non-random sample of 35 informants selected for their previously proven reliability and their likely familiarity with, and interest in, local ethnophysiological and medical theories.[15] Judging from Yalman's data on the Kandyan Sinhalese, and from the recent 'cultural accounts' of caste and kinship in Bengal, Tamilnadu, and Jaffna mentioned previously, it seemed reasonable to expect that a theory and a symbolism of blood, more than that of any other natural substance, would dominate local discussions of descent and group status. However, when I attempted to raise this topic in conversations I found people were both apathetic and embarrassed. The Tamil words for blood (*irattam*, *utaram*) in the Batticaloa region would appear to invite stronger initial cognitive associations with menstrual pollution and the butcher's shop than with descent and purity. It later became evident that blood played an important role in thinking about bodily health and vitality but that 'purity of blood' was *not* a basic symbol of social hierarchy in this region. Indeed, comments about blood and ethnophysiology were uniform in some ways, but strikingly varied in other respects (see also McGilvray 1982a).

Elements of the Ayurvedic medical tradition (e.g. Caraka 1949) continue to exert a strong effect upon common belief and curing practices here but, as in other areas of the island, some of these ideas have been subjected to local reinterpretation (Obeyesekere 1976). Blood is recognized to be the primary transformation of food within the body, the source of all bodily substance and strength. The basic understanding of this process can be outlined as follows: food, which in Sri Lanka is epitomized by boiled rice, is taken into the alimentary tract and converted to *annaracam* or chyle, which in turn is converted partially into blood and partially into waste (*malam*). It is the strength and quantity of the blood which accounts for the strength (*pelan*, *sakti*) and growth (*vaḷarcci*) of the body. The English word 'force' (*pōs*) has crept into the local Tamil vocabulary, and one often finds it used to characterize the state of the blood. In this context, the term *pōs* connotes the energy, the amount, and the pressure of the blood present in the body. The process of physiological maturation from infancy to adulthood is a concomitant of the increasing 'force' of the blood in the body, and the process of ageing and senescence is believed to be the direct consequence of the declining energy/quantity/pressure of the blood.[16]

Both the nature of one's diet and of one's physical environment have recognized effects upon the internal state of the body, and both are related, with varying degrees of sophistication by different informants, to the influence of the three Ayurvedic humours (*muppiṇi*): namely, *vātam* or *vāyvu* (wind, the source of motion), *pittam* (bile, the source of heat), and *cilērpanam* (phlegm, the connective or aqueous humour). One's daily regimen, the environment of one's work, and the components of one's diet all convey different proportions of the three humours, which are imperfectly associated in most ordinary thinking with heating (*cūṭu*), cooling (*kuḷir*), and dermatologically eruptive (*kiranti*) qualities. As one might expect, the ideal of bodily health is based upon an elusive equilibrium of such qualities: not too much heat, not too much coolness, not too much eruptive quality.

Theories of conception in this region contend that a woman is fertilized when male semen (*cukkilam*, *intiriyam*, *vintu*, *kāmappāl*, etc.) mixes in the womb with female semen (*curōnitam*, *nātam*, but frequently unnamed). In accord with a widespread South Asian belief, male semen is described as a refined form, or distillation (*vaṭippu*), of the blood, following some traditional ratio, e.g. blood : semen = 40 : 1 or 60 : 1. There seems to be no specific organ of seminal production, except, perhaps, the brain itself, which is also the place where male semen is stored and conserved. Thick, white, unexpended semen, like the blood from which it is made, has 'force' (*pōs*) which makes for healthy children, and the loss of semen drains the body of blood, i.e., strength and substance. If semen can be retained, particularly during adolescence and young manhood, its vital qualities can be redirected internally toward greater physical, and ultimately spiritual, development. Informants were less certain about the nature of female semen; it was generally connected with blood and sometimes assumed to be quite similar to male semen. Some informants considered it to come from the chest or the womb; some felt it was less important in conception than male semen; and a few were unfamiliar with the concept altogether.

Conception occurs with the combination of the sexual fluids during that part of her monthly cycle when the woman's uterine 'flower' is open to admit them. In the man, the heat of sexual desire 'melts' the semi-solid reservoir of semen at the top of the head, and it then flows, in some accounts via an intermediate storage sac in the navel, to the penis. The testicles, although recognized as related to sexuality in some way (e.g. in the gelding of bullocks by crushing the testes), were never connected by informants with the sexual act.[17] There was no corresponding account of the internal flow of female semen or of its physical properties. During orgasm, both the man and the woman ejaculate their sexual fluids into the womb, where they mix to produce the beginnings of an embryo in the form of a bubble (*kumiḻi*), a lump (*kaṭṭi*), or a sprout (*muḷai*). A few informants, mostly curing specialists, added that the three Ayurvedic humours, and particularly the *pirāṇa vāyvu* (wind of life), were also present at conception. If a specific source of *uyir* (life, spirit) was known, it was always said to be the *pirāṇa vāyvu*, an element which pervades the womb from the surrounding universe, not from either parent. Only four informants out of the sample of 35 denied any knowledge of a female substance involved in conception, and only one informant mentioned the idea of the male 'seed' implanted in the female 'field' as recorded in

Bengal and as described in the Laws of Manu (Manu IX, 31–56; Fruzzetti & Östör 1976; Dube 1978).

Some informants also cited an interesting assortment of additional factors which were conducive to successful impregnation, ranging from unity of mind, to simultaneous orgasm, to forceful seminal ejaculation. However, the important point is that conception is seen as fundamentally bilateral, involving substances from both parents. Few characteristics of the child are felt to be entirely determined by the conception itself, except for the sex of the child. Informants mentioned four different theories of how the sex of the child is determined at conception: whether intercourse takes place on even (male) versus odd (female) days following the end of menstrual pollution, whether the parents are breathing through the right (male) versus left (female) nostril at the moment of conception, whether the first sexual fluid to enter the womb is male or female, and whether relatively greater amounts of male or female semen is deposited in the womb. All subsequent gestation and development of the embryo draws solely upon the resources and bodily substance (blood) of the mother. Subsequent intercourse during the first part of the pregnancy is allowed, but it has no effect of nourishing or contributing to the embryo.[18] The momentary quality of the paternal connection, as contrasted with the mother's intimate burden of carrying and nourishing the child through pregnancy, is recognized in the well-known proberb: *Aiyāvukku aintu nimisham, ammāvukkup pattu mātam*, 'Five minutes for the father, ten months for the mother.'

Within the womb, the child receives a continuous, direct blood transfusion from the mother via the opening (*tuvāram*) all foetuses are believed to have at the top of the head.[19] By the time the pregnancy is approaching term, the child is felt to be receiving liquified food (*annaracam*) via the umbilical cord, which is thought to develop late. Many informants identified the blood which assists and nourishes the foetus as the mother's menstrual blood, seen as clean and beneficial blood accumulating in her womb during the pregnancy, rather than flowing out as a notoriously polluting substance during normal menstruation. After childbirth, the mother nurses the infant with breast milk, another transformation of her own blood, and later she prepares and feeds the child solid food with her own hands.[20]

As the child grows toward adulthood, nutrition from food supports the constant production of blood, from which all other bodily substances are produced. It is only when the body is nearing its adult size and form that the production of blood begins to surpass the body's need for natural building material, and it is at this point that sexual maturation occurs. The onset of a girl's first menstruation is both a result and a proof of the fact that her body now has excess or waste blood (*kaḷivirattam*) to dispose of. A boy's seminal emissions are likewise a sign of nearing maturity and vitality of the blood, but he is strongly enjoined to conserve this blood (semen) and transmute it into greater bodily, intellectual, and spiritual power. This women cannot do, and for good (indigenous) reasons. While few informants were able to offer a complete explanation of the menstrual cycle, there was considerable agreement that, without it, women would have a dangerously high level of blood in their bodies, much higher than that of men. The monthly flow of menstrual blood from women is said to be a mechanism, instituted by Lord Civa, which insures that women's natural surplus of blood (and hence physical strength and vitality, including sexual desire) is regularly drained away, allowing males to retain control and mastery over women. 'If it were not for her monthly period,' said one local Hindu Ayurvedic practitioner, 'five men could not hold one woman down.'

In later life, the decline in the quantity, vitality, and 'force' of the blood begins to have deleterious effects upon health and sexual vigour. The menopause occurs when the female blood supply is no longer in excess, and the early death of some men is attributed to their reckless expenditure of semen in middle and old age. Age is also felt to be accompanied by changes in bodily heat, a factor which limits the acceptable age of marriage partners. Local thinking on this matter is not altogether uniform, but a five- to ten-year superiority in age is considered essential for the husband. A man between the ages of 20 and 30 is considered to be at the peak of his natural powers, and this enables him to exercise proper control over his bride, who will be between the ages of 15 and 20. Greater age in marriage also works to the advantage of the man, it is felt, because he benefits from the sexual relations he has with a strong-blooded young woman.[21] Sexual relations with a woman who is older than her partner will prove extremely deleterious, even fatal, to the man. One explanation offered for this is that individuals, as they lose blood in ageing, simultaneously gain in bodily heat, 'just as a pressure-lamp becomes hotter and hotter as the fuel is used up'. A severe imbalance in bodily heat between sex partners is harmful to both, but a younger man is felt to be particularly vulnerable, it seems.

In an attempt to crystallize some of the ideas which had been put forth, I asked, 'Whose blood, the father's or the mother's, flows in the veins of the child?' Opinion was sharply and fairly evenly divided three ways, and in retrospect it seems that the question in this form had scarcely occurred to many informants. Some, who had earlier stressed the potency of male semen in conception, said that semen was a concentrated form of the father's blood, hence the child shared the father's blood (see Banks 1957: 115, and David 1973a: 523, for the same view in Jaffna). But others vehemently opposed this view, saying that the tiny amount of father's semen was insignificant in comparison with the mother's massive transference of blood during pregnancy and lactation. The child's blood was definitely that of the mother, according to this second view. The third viewpoint was that both parents had contributed elements of bodily substance, making the blood of the child a bilateral composite of the mother's and the father's blood. Even in the latter case, no theory of paired paternal *utampu* (body) and maternal *uyir* (life, spirit) was articulated, although one person said that the father's semen governed the *uruvam* (form, shape) of the child.

My question about the child's blood was seen by some as rather obsessive and academic, for it left out of consideration the whole dimension of maternal emotional attachments (*anpu*, love; *pācam*, ties; *paṟṟu*, attachment). The maternal connection is actually paramount in all discussion of childhood attachments, it recurs in discussion of dowry and matrilocal residence, and it again emerges in discussion of the spread of death pollution. Although I never recorded the statement that the matrilocal residence rule made the in-marrying fathers and sons-in-law 'strangers' to the household (cf. Yalman 1967: 286–7),[22] the obverse point of view, that the women in their natal/dowry houses in their natal villages form the stable conceptual core of the household, was frequently voiced by informants. The expression *tāy pācam* (maternal bonds) is probably something of a cliché everywhere in the Tamil-speaking world, but in the Batticaloa region, where the matrilocal household provides a kind of socio-spatial continuity, where dowry is the main channel of property transmission, and where the matrilineal clan plays a role in social identity, it seems to reflect a more substantive feature of the social structure. Reasoning about conception and sharing of parental blood can, and does, diverge along matrilateral, patrilateral, and bilateral lines, depending upon which elements of the ethno-reproductive theory are stressed. Yet, although local theories of bodily substance are not uniform, and the behavioural reality can vary a great deal, the child's connections and emotional bonds are typically said to be much stronger with the mother than with the father.

In fact, the notion that members of a single kinship category, matriclan, or caste might actually think of themselves as 'sharers' or 'uniters' of unique blood or natural substance, as David (1973a) has argued for Jaffna, was untenable in the face of what informants said.[23] No one spoke of any qualities of the blood aside from the medical or diagnostic ones. Blood can be reduced, thinned, weakened, or have an imbalance of Ayurvedic humours, in which case the individual's health and vitality must suffer;[24] or blood can be copious, thick, strong, and in Ayurvedic equilibrium, in which case one's health must prosper. No one voiced a belief in the 'purity' of blood; in fact, as with the nonexistent institution of hypergamy, there is no readily recognized way to speak about such a concept in the local language. I asked whether the blood of particular matriclans and castes could be said to have distinctive 'qualities' (*kuṇam*) but the reply was consistently negative: instead, informants said 'Blood is all the same' (*irattam onṟu tān*).[25] The stereotypic behavioural traits attributed to certain castes (e.g. Goldsmiths as dishonest, or Drummers as sorcerers) are often seen as the result of seizing opportunities associated with their caste-occupational milieu (e.g. tampering with weights, or access to human corpses). The public reputation of certain families for temperament or moral character is sometimes expressed in terms of good or bad 'quality' (*kuṇam*), e.g. in discussing possible marriage partners for one's son or daughter, but the exact locus of this 'quality' is never easy to disentangle. It arises from both environment and heredity in the broadest sense of the term, but it is not discussed or explained in the language of 'blood'. In other words, neither blood, nor any other indigenous category of natural bodily substance seems to operate as the conceptual focus of caste or matriclan membership in the Batticaloa region.

4.2. States of purity and pollution

It is an assumption shared by Yalman (1963; 1967: 137–8) and Dumont (1970: Ch. 2; Dumont and Pocock 1959) that temporary states of individual pollution arising out of contact with birth, menstruation, death, and other such contaminating junctures with 'organic life' (Dumont 1970: 47) are assimilated to, and equated with, states of caste pollution, thus defining the essential purity/pollution continuum which underlies caste society. It is certainly true that high caste informants in the Batticaloa region will say that the *kuṭimai* castes (Barber, Washerman, Drummer) are immersed in the inescapable contamination associated with cutting hair, bleaching menstrual cloths, and conducting burials. But while there is a standard term (*tuṭakku*) which refers to states of individual or group 'ritual impurity', including the polluted condition of the lowest castes, there is no corresponding vocabulary for 'ordinary' and 'enhanced' states of purity, such as described for Havik Brahmans, Coorgs, and Koṇṭaikkaṭṭi Vēḷāḷars in India.[26]

The Tamil dictionary lists a number of terms for 'purity', but only one or two words are in common use here. The most general word is *cuttam*, which may connote secular cleanliness, lack of admixture, or ritual fastidiousness, depending upon context. A second word is *tuppuravu*, which often connotes secular cleanliness and is more often heard in its negative form, *tuppuravillai* (uncleanliness). Actually, the vocabulary of purity in Batticaloa seems underdeveloped and under-utilized, while the ethnosemantic domain of uncleanliness and impurity is far more open-ended than most South Asian ethnographic sources might lead one to expect. Here, the most general word is *acuttam*, the opposite of *cuttam*, which must be similarly defined by context. Specific types of physical dirtiness include *aḻukku* and *ūttai* (filth, stain, contamination), *kuppai* (rubbish), and *narakal* (revolting substance, e.g. excrement, entrails). Occasionally one hears the word *tīṭṭu* or the expression *vīṭṭukku tūram* ('away from the house'), referring specifically to states of menstrual pollution. The most universal word for 'ritual pollution', however, is *tuṭakku*, which refers to the varying degrees of metaphysical contamination resulting from sexual relations, menstruation, childbirth, and, especially, death. The removal of *tuṭakku* must invariably culminate in the bathing of the entire body, *talai muḻukiratu* ('head bathing').[27] As noted in Jaffna (Ryan 1980: Ch. 4), the vocabulary of ritual pollution also tends to overlap with that of moral and spiritual defects, so that in Batticaloa, *tuṭakku* is sometimes called *kuṟṟam* (fault, blemish) or *tōsham* (malevolent influence).

Although the processes of conception and the nature of blood had not proven to be the key to local thinking about the identity and ranking of castes and kuṭis, it still seemed possible during fieldwork that an underlying theory of purity or bodily substance might inform local attitudes and behaviour in situations of severe ritual pollution, particularly death pollution. It is known from a number of South Asian ethnographic and shastric sources that patrilineally related kinsmen typically constitute a community of pollution when a member dies (e.g. Beck 1972: 4; Banks 1957: 117; the sapinda rule of Manu V, 59), and a corresponding matrilineal observance of death pollution is known to occur in the Nayar matriclan, the *taravād* (Gough 1959; 1961: 323–4). In the Batticaloa region, death pollution (*tuṭakku*) is observed for 31 days by all Hindu castes except the Vīracaiva Kurukkaḷs, who claim a shorter period (12 to 15 days) or none at all.

It seemed reasonable to expect a substantial regional consensus as to the spread of pollution at death, since bereavement is so universal a life experience and one so governed by cultural rules. Instead, as with the interpretation of the blood connection, there was a striking divergence of opinion, and many informants were as surprised as the anthropologist to discover that outlooks varied so greatly. A detailed analysis of the surprising variety of views on death pollution would require an essay in itself, but a general classification of responses is summarized in Table 2. Almost half of the informants made explicit reference to the principle of matriliny, *tāy vaḻi* or *peṇ vaḻi*, or the pollution diagrams which they drew showed obvious matrilineal reasoning. Many of the bilateral opinions stressed the idea that the most severe pollution affected the nuclear kin group (spouse, siblings, parents, and children), and especially the residents of the 'death house', *cāvīṭu*, but approximately half of the bilateral opinions also gave secondary or partial acknowledgement of the matrilineal idea (e.g. effects upon daughters' but not sons' children, or sisters' but not brothers' children). The patrilineal principle, however, had a strong minority of defenders, a few of whom said that pollution follows the father's blood (semen), but most of whom could offer no theoretical justification commensurate with the force of their convictions. Several of the latter were forced into perplexed silence in public discussions instigated by the anthropologist, although their views remained unshaken. There was also a group of 'other' opinions which were idiosyncratic, including several statements that the principle of pollution must vary depending on the sex of the deceased.[28]

There was no standard genealogical depth to the pollution, and no one viewed the matriclan, the sublineage, or any other specific grouping as the 'unit' of pollution. The justifications offered for the matrilineal spread of death pollution sometimes mentioned matrilateral ethnoreproductive ideas (e.g., uterine blood), but most often they appealed to an image of the matrilocal household and its linked mothers and daughters as a sort of enduring socio-spatial 'establishment' cemented by ties of matrifiliation and physical propinquity. Unlike the minority patrilineal view, the matrilineal theory of pollution made constant reference to the importance of emotional bonds (*anpu*, *pācam*, etc.) in defining who was susceptible to death pollution. Sometimes the matrilateral stress in these remarks was unduly formulaic, so that it occasionally became awkward to account for

Table 2. *Opinions regarding the principle governing the spread of death pollution among kinsmen*

Matrilineal	Bilateral	Patrilineal	Other	TOTAL
13	9	7	4	33

children's pollution on the death of the father. The father is unquestionably a source of pollution for the household when he dies. All are agreed that the chief mourner should be the eldest son, but the matrilineal theory of pollution stipulates that only the daughters' children observe *tuṭakku*. Ideas of sexual/commensal intimacy and emotional attachment are cited as reasons for the pollution of the spouse, who nonetheless remains fully susceptible to pollution from all deaths in his or her natal family. Not unsurprisingly in such a matrilocal society, there is no belief that the wife's bodily substance is metaphysically assimilated to that of her husband at marriage, nor is there any element of the marriage rite which could bear such an interpretation, such as David (1973a) describes for Jaffna (see also Barnett 1970; 1976; Fruzzetti & Östör 1976; Inden and Nicholas 1977). Pollution transmitted via affinal connections with a member of the matrilocal group is always intensified when there is a close reinforcing kinship link, as when a daughter's husband is also her true MBS or FZS. It is frequently said that, failing such kinship reinforcement, such in-laws need to observe only eight days of real pollution. Pollution is tacitly recognized in such varying degrees, although there is a countervailing concern to maintain a public image of greater propriety through seemingly stricter observance.

4.3. General implications

It will be useful to consider the implications of what has been presented so far. Fieldwork has revealed two major drawbacks to reliance upon the 'purity' and 'coded-substance' approaches in the Batticaloa region. The first problem is empirical: none of the key symbolic themes such as 'blood purity', 'hypergamy', or 'sharers of natural substance and code' suggested by various writers is found to be salient in local thinking about the nature of castes and kuṭis. Although a negative idea of 'caste impurity' can be directly observed in local attitudes toward the lowest castes, whose duty it is to remove polluting states and substances from the higher castes, the positive attribute of 'caste purity' is only indirectly evident in the actions and statements of the higher castes. We shall see later that such an idea of 'caste purity', in the sense of ritual excellence or the right to perform certain special services for the deity, is only one component of the wider ideological field in which castes and kuṭis compete for rank. Complex indigenous theories about blood and reproduction are important in an ethnomedical framework, but they do not completely rationalize or clarify the nature of matrilineal descent. Instead, like local theories of the spread of ritual pollution, they are open to widely divergent interpretations. In general, local thinking about blood, descent, and pollution constitutes a more complex, more disjunct, more contextual, and more open-ended ethnosemantic field than the parsimonious theories of purity and natural substance would tend to imply.

The second type of drawback is heuristic: to assume the existence of a pervasive and coherent ideology of purity or substance underlying the behavioural reality simply leads to erroneous interpretations. Yalman's account of east coast matriclans as purity-conserving hypergamous units bears witness to the pitfalls of such assumptions. Many of the same assumptions impeded my own understanding of social organization in the Batticaloa region, and it is fair to say that a great deal of my time and effort has been consumed in examining these relatively unproductive hypotheses.

5. MUKKUVAR VANNIMAI

I now propose to formulate a more accurate and fruitful picture of caste and matriclan structure in the Batticaloa region, one which stresses the nature of political dominance within a regional frame of reference and which incorporates a historical component to explain some of the unusual features of culture and social organization which are found there. In this account, ideas of purity and natural substance will be treated, not as uniform, universal conceptions immanent in South Asian culture, but as historically contingent, socially transmitted ideas, the strength and configuration of which depends considerably upon competing interests and ideologies within a regional setting.

5.1. Mukkuvars

Let us consider first what is known of the major high caste groups. The politically dominant Tamil group throughout the Batticaloa region as a whole have been the Mukkuvars, also known by the more literary title,

Muṟkukar.[29] A similarly named caste is found in coastal areas of Puttalam, Mannar, Mullaittivu, and Jaffna (Casie Chitty 1834: 274–80; Raghavan 1971: 152–61),[30] as well as along the coasts of central and north Kerala, where they are recognized as hereditary fishermen (Anantha Krishna Iyer 1909: 266–76; Thurston 1909 vol. V: 106–17). They seem never to have considered themselves fishermen in Batticaloa, where they have settled in greater numbers than anywhere else in the island and have assumed the role of chiefs and powerful landlords (*pōṭiyār*). The Sinhalese historical chronicles mention numerous invasions of mercenary armies often including warriors from Kerala, particularly in the 12th and 13th centuries A.D. The earliest historical mention of the Mukkuvars is in the *Daṁbadeṇi-asna*, which lists them as soldiers for King Parakramabahu II between 1236 and 1270 A.D. (Indrapala 1965: 180). A collection of regional traditions from Batticaloa, the *Maṭṭakkaḷappu Māṇmiyam* (Nadarajah 1962), celebrates the arrival of the Mukkuvars under the banner of the rapacious Māgha (*Mākōn*), who claimed Kalinga ancestry.[31] Māgha is known to have seized Polonnaruwa and the northern centres of Sinhalese power with an army of 'Tamils and Keralas' in 1215 A.D. and to have held power for about 40 years (Indrapala 1965: 236ff.). After the 13th century, a number of rivalrous and recalcitrant regional chiefdoms claiming the title of *Vanniyār* arose on the margins of Sinhalese power in the North Central and Eastern Provinces, of which Batticaloa, under the Mukkuvars, was one. In the light of the available historical evidence, which is supported by folk traditions of the region, it seems likely that the Mukkuvars were granted lands and regional chiefships in Batticaloa as their reward for soldierly service in the armies of Māgha (Indrapala 1965: Ch. 5).

The oral and textual traditions of Batticaloa make constant reference to an ideal geographical model of seven constituent sub-chieftaincies (*vannipam*) within the region and to an ideal social model of seven constituent kuṭis within each caste. The origin of this pervasive model of 'seven' is clearly attributed to the ruling caste in one of its common epithets: *ēḻukkuṭi Mukkuvar*, the 'seven-kuṭi Mukkuvars'. Today the system of Mukkuvar sub-chieftaincies within the Batticaloa region has almost disappeared under the impact of 300 years of European colonial rule, yet the temple histories which are still recited and the symbols of the *Mukkuvar vannimai* (regional chiefship of the Mukkuvars) leave no doubt as to the traditions of conquest and warrior dominance which distinguish this group. We have seen earlier that the names of the Mukkuvar matriclans often celebrate kingly and martial honours, and the matrilineal succession to traditional political offices, such as the *Ūrppōṭiyār* of Akkaraipattu, is a recognized prerogative of certain Mukkuvar kuṭis. The relative status of these kuṭis varies within the region, and there is every likelihood that the Mukkuvar political system based on these clans was highly segmentary and fractious. Mukkuvars seldom make formal claim to membership of the Kshatriya *varna*, however, and it is significant that they share with all the castes of the region (except the Vīracaiva Kurukkaḷs) the 31-day period of death pollution associated with Sudras (Manu V, 83). Solid historical evidence of how the Batticaloa region was colonized and settled is still quite meagre, but legendary accounts credit the Mukkuvars with expelling the Timilar fishing caste and establishing strict dominance, which was symbolized in many aspects of domestic and public ritual and was maintained by possession and control of the largest share of the land. The distinctive term for a large landowner in Batticaloa is *pōṭiyār*, and the late records of the Dutch East India Company show that the cooperation of the Mukkuvar 'Chief Podies' was very difficult to obtain (Burnand 1794).

5.2. Vēḷāḷars

The major rivals of the Mukkuvars for social preeminence are the Vēḷāḷars, the renowned high-status cultivating caste of Jaffna and Tamilnadu. There are certain clusters of Vēḷāḷar villages which today claim never to have been subjected to traditional Mukkuvar chiefs, but this seems highly unlikely. It is true, however, that these Vēḷāḷar centres have now largely succeeded in eliminating the tangible evidence of their political inferiority during the period of Mukkuvar rule. It is now known from both historical and ethnographic evidence that the Vēḷāḷars of Tamilnadu have a strong tradition of association and alliance with the Brahman priesthood of South India (Stein 1968; 1969; Barnett 1970). This South Indian evidence of Vēḷāḷar religious connections is consistent with the traditions of Vēḷāḷar settlement in the Batticaloa region, which assert that Vēḷāḷars were brought from India and installed as Saivite temple functionaries in perpetuity by local kings. They were not given ownership or control of the temples, but they were given responsibility for overseeing the conduct of temple ritual, and they cultivated a share of the temple lands as payment for their services. The songs and legends in the *Maṭṭakkaḷappu Mānmiyam* reiterate the theme that conquering kings brought seven groups of *Kōvaiciyar* ('Herding Vaishyas', one of the three kinds of Vaishyas which Vēḷāḷars claim as their puranic ancestors: see Thurston 1909 vol. VII: 361–6; Winslow 1862: 967) to perform such essential domestic tasks for the deity as polishing the vessels, tending the lamps, storing the temple's grain, and carrying the palanquin of the god. The names of these seven groups are among the most common matriclan names of the Batticaloa Vēḷāḷars today (Nadarajah 1962: 70–1; Canagaratnam 1921: 35; Kandiah 1964: 435–6). The matrilineal clan organization of the Vēḷāḷars is similar in every respect to that of the Mukkuvars, and the Vēḷāḷars seem also to have followed the Mukkuvar law of inheritance and succession in every respect.[32]

The Vēḷāḷars are also believed to have been the first group to have brought with them an entourage of service castes. These are sometimes referred to as the '17 *ciraikaḷ* (slaves, dependents)', but this is a stereotyped formula which greatly exceeds the number of service castes present today, i.e., the three *kuṭimai* castes of Barber, Washerman, and Drummer. The Mukkuvars, however, appropriated control of the service castes to themselves, though allowing the Vēḷāḷars to share their services. We have already seen that neither Vēḷāḷars nor Mukkuvars express an ideology of blood purity, but the Vēḷāḷars do make a point of dissociating themselves from the violent warrior heritage of the Mukkuvars. As in South India, the Vēḷāḷars cherish an image of being custodians and inheritors of the soil, peaceful and honourable.[33] In fact the present aura of the Vēḷāḷar title is very strong, even in this region which has sometimes been called *Mukkuvatēcam* (country of the Mukkuvars: Denham 1912: 226). This shows through in the caste opinion-ranking (Table 1) as well as innumerable instances of 'borrowing' and 'attaching' the Vēḷāḷar title to castes and kuṭis (Thurston 1909 vol. VII: 376–7; Yalman 1967: 329; McGilvray 1974: 29–33). Both Yalman and I experienced much initial befuddlement attributable not only to the fact that every landowner would like to consider himself a 'Vēḷāḷar', on the spurious grounds that the name derives from *vēḷāṇmai* (cultivation, especially of paddy), but also to the fact that the word 'Vēḷāḷar' is a recognized component of certain kuṭi names not specifically associated with the Vēḷāḷar caste, e.g. *Vēṭa Vēḷāḷar kuṭi* ('Hunter' Vēḷāḷar, i.e., Veddah Vēḷāḷar). It is clear that 'Vēḷāḷar' prestige is gaining ground in most parts of Batticaloa today.

It will soon be apparent that, although the idea of distinct Vēḷāḷar and Mukkuvar castes is often invoked by informants (and it is useful here for the purposes of exposition to maintain this convention), there is in reality a wider universe of respectable matriclans ('good/big/high people'), some of which have explicit, textually-validated links to caste categories such as Vēḷāḷar and Mukkuvar, and some of which are more free-floating and amenable to being assimilated to different 'castes', depending upon the circumstances in different localities. However, these ambiguities never blur the line between the high caste stratum and the lower professional and service castes, so that, for example, the equivocal *Ciṅkaḷa kuṭi* ('Sinhalese *kuṭi*') of the Mukkuvars and Vēḷāḷars is never confused with separate kuṭis of the same name occurring in the Smith, Washerman, and Drummer castes.

It must also be added that the textually-specified duties of the Vēḷāḷars to perform the often menial tasks of temple service have, in the course of time, been relegated to a professional temple servant group known as *Kōvilār* (people of the temple, *kōvil*). The historical facts are very difficult to disentangle, but at the present time the Vēḷāḷars interpret their traditional mandate as amounting to supervision of the Kōvilārs, whom they prefer to treat as a separate and inferior caste. The Kōvilārs, however, maintain that they are themselves Vēḷāḷars of separate but equal origin. Significant numbers of Kōvilārs are found today only in the vicinity of the major regional temples, e.g. at Kokkaṭṭiccōlai and at Tirukkōvil. They prefer to be historically identified as Kāraikkāl Vēḷāḷars, as opposed to the others, who are given the contrasting designation of Maruṅkūr Vēḷāḷars.

5.3. Vīracaiva Kurukkaḷs

The third component of the high caste stratum are the Vīracaiva Kurukkaḷs, who are non-Brahman priests affiliated with the Vīracaiva or Lingāyat sect of South India, particularly Karnataka (Mysore). Yalman was the first to suggest such a connection (1967: 331), and although the historical steps are not yet clear, he was quite right in pointing to the symbols of Vīracaiva identity. The group is only partially endogamous today, made up of three intermarrying matriclans: Caṅkamar Kurukkaḷ, Tēcāntara Kurukkaḷ, and Canniyāci Kuṭi. There is conclusive evidence of a strong marriage exchange relationship between the first two kuṭis, which are the largest and most prestigious, although this endogamous tendency is much clearer in the genealogical record than in current practice. Today there are a great many marriages with members of the Vēḷāḷar and Mukkuvar castes. The two main Kurukkaḷ matriclans are associated with two of the five traditional Lingāyat preceptors, and both groups are said to have a vague historical connection with the Vīracaiva religious 'throne' or centre at Mallikārccunapuram in South India.[34] The full name of the first kuṭi is Vīramakēsvara Kuruliṅkacaṅkamar, a title which displays the major symbols of Vīracaiva doctrine,[35] and it is this kuṭi which traditionally conducted an annual procession through the Akkaraipattu region (*pakuti*) to purify and protect the villages from malevolent forces in the damp and ghostly month of Mārkaḻi (December–January). For this reason, the senior Kurukkaḷ in this matriline was sometimes called the *Pakuti Kurukkaḷ*. The second major kuṭi, the Tēcāntara ('foreign, wandering') Kurukkaḷs, seem to have been exclusively temple priests, and there is some evidence of rivalry in this ritual division of labour.

The Vīracaiva Kurukkaḷs of Batticaloa stoutly maintain their superiority to Brahmans and the Brahmanical 'varna doctrines' (*varuṇa vētam*), reflecting an antipathy well known from South Indian ethnography (Parvathamma 1971). Their theory is that a truly desire-less (*paṟṟillāta*) person, having received proper initiation (*tīṭcai*, *liṅkatāraṇam*), having performed the prescribed daily and preprandial worship of the personal lingam stone which is worn in a silver casket suspended on a chain from the neck, and having realized true spiritual union with Civa, is impervious to all forms of contamination, from whatever source. The title of Caṅkamar (Jangama) is recognized as referring to this ideal: the word derives from *caṅkamam*, which means both 'union', e.g. union with Civa, and 'moving', e.g. the priest as a living abode of Civa (Winslow 1862: 387; Enthoven 1922: 373; Ramanujan 1973).

Today in the Batticaloa region, the lingam is worn only by practising temple priests and a few independent Caṅkamar Kurukkaḷs, and many of the strict Vīracaiva doctrines are abridged, qualified, or attenuated. Practically the entire group, or Kurukkaḷ *vamicam*,[36] as it is called, originates from a few small villages, and today its younger members are not taking up the priestly profession. Nonetheless, the long historical association of the Vīracaiva Kurukkaḷs with villages and temples on the east coast has bequeathed an ideological legacy of great significance when compared with the usual Brahman tradition. Some of the important features to keep in mind are the Vīracaiva belief in the universal prophylactic quality of initiation and wearing the personal lingam, the emphasis upon the Vīracaiva priest's duty to protect and purify the village with his presence and his *pātōtakam* (water from washing his feet), and the injunction that the Vīracaiva priest should eat ordinary cooked food offered at such life-crises as birth, female puberty, and death.

Within the past 40 years, some members of the Kurukkaḷ *vamicam* in the Akkaraipattu area have begun to resist the principle of commensality on potentially polluting occasions such as the 31st day *amutu* domestic food offerings to the departed soul, and the response of the high caste population has been indignant and vocal. Most everyone agrees, regardless of their attitude, that until recently all Kurukkaḷs shared the food at life-crisis rituals. Even in India, of course, the Lingāyat Jangama priest observes commensality only with other Lingāyat castes, whereas in Batticaloa there are no such other groups with whom the Kurukkaḷs might form a sectarian bloc. The Vīracaiva Kurukkaḷs of the Batticaloa region found themselves in the puzzling situation of being patronized by the ruling castes in preference to Brahmans, yet being denied the underlying support of a true Vīracaiva sectarian social order. In this situation, the Kurukkaḷs were able to maintain some of their own distinctive customs, such as burial in a seated posture with the lingam placed in the mouth of the corpse, but they were inevitably led to accommodate their Vīracaiva ideology to the realities of the local Mukkuvar and Vēḷāḷar-dominated caste system. Ironically, some perceptive members of the Kurukkaḷ group, having come to a greater awareness of the theological and social implications of Vīracaivism through exposure to modern South Indian religious literature, have become quite pessimistic about the laxity of their practices and the prospects for the maintenance of a Vīracaiva priesthood in the future. The alternative is the continued growth of a heterogeneous priesthood composed in large part of local caste members who officiate at their own caste-supported temples, but there are also indications that a Jaffna-based Brahmanical style, and in some cases Jaffna Brahman priests, may gradually supersede the Vīracaiva Kurukkaḷs of Batticaloa.[37]

5.4. The Mukkuvar–Vēḷāḷar relationship

Part of the difficulty in comprehending the structure and the dynamic of caste and matriclan organization on the east coast arises out of one's initial temptation to mistake a particular constellation of local inter-caste and inter-clan relationships for a uniform regional pattern. The two high caste groups, Mukkuvar and Vēḷāḷar, are the dominant elements in the social structure of the Batticaloa region, but there may be either tension or accommodation, either a greater or lesser degree of perceived distinctiveness between them, depending upon their relative strength in different sub-regions, the evolution of joint political and ritual institutions in certain areas, and the degree to which local communities have come to recognize a wider range of respectable kuṭis in the high caste stratum, that is, beyond the typical list of seven kuṭis attributable to each caste. The Vīracaiva Kurukkaḷs, on the other hand, have provided a distinctive, and not so markedly hierarchical, priestly idiom which has been congenial to both groups.

A dynamic model of relationships within the high caste stratum, based on an analysis of sub-regional variation and reinforced by a reading of the local legendary-historical traditions contained in the *Maṭṭakkaḷappu*

Mānmiyam,[38] can now be sketched in outline. We must disregard for the moment the effects of social change during European colonial rule and the post-Independence period in order to delineate some of the important features of traditional inter-caste relations. It appears that the Mukkuvars came to exercise widespread control of the land in the Batticaloa region through some combination of conquest and colonization, probably following the invasion of Māgha (1215 A.D.), but certainly well before their political and economic dominance of the region is acknowledged in Dutch records of the 18th century (Burnand 1794). Whether there were some Vēḷāḷars already present in the region whose social organization was transformed under Mukkuvar influence, or whether, as tradition attests, they all came from India after the Mukkuvar conquest is not presently known. In any event, the role allocated to the Vēḷāḷars by the Mukkuvar rulers was, and in certain isolated areas until recent years remained, a politically subordinate one, although the grip of Mukkuvar domination was probably at times weakened by sub-regional and inter-clan rivalries and occasionally reduced to a kind of titular sovereignty over some of the more well-established Vēḷāḷar villages. Today, even Vēḷāḷar informants who are hostile to Mukkuvar status will acknowledge that the Mukkuvars were the rulers of Batticaloa by right of conquest; the disagreement is over how tangible this Mukkuvar dominance was at the level of Vēḷāḷar village life.

The Mukkuvars, and possibly other warrior contingents which local tradition indicates amalgamated with the Mukkuvars to create the regional *vannimai*, had made themselves masters of the land, guardians of the temples, and arbiters of the social order. They claimed the status of heroic Saivite crusaders who had come to expunge alleged Vaishnava sympathies and to restore the Civa temples built during the era of Rāvaṇa, before his demise as recounted in the Rāmāyana epic. We know at least that this is the sort of mythic charter which their descendants have propagated. The social system in which such a vision of pious kingly glory could be actualized, however, required the presence of ritual specialists and menial service groups, ostensibly to serve the gods, but also to serve the rulers who built and protected the sacred shrines. All the legendary accounts stress the point that contingents of Vēḷāḷars, with their own dependent service castes, were summoned by the kings to come from India and settle in the vicinity of certain famous 'regional' temples (*tēcattukkōvil*), such as Tirukkōvil, where they were enjoined, under threat of both kingly and divine sanction, to maintain the prescribed pūjas and festivals in perpetuity. In the texts they are not depicted as priests, but rather as devout, abject, hereditary servants of the temple (e.g. *aranakattoṇṭūḻiyar*). The Vēḷāḷars also cultivated the temple lands on behalf of the deity and retained a share of the crop for their own support. The priests in the textual sources are referred to as *Antaṇar* (Brahman), *Pūcurar* (performer of pūja), and *Tampaṭṭar* (apparently a reference to the Vīracaiva Kurukkaḷs, whose ancient village is named Tampaṭṭai). No specifically Brahman settlement is ever mentioned in the textual and oral traditions, nor is there any such Brahman settlement today. In fact, there is a strong tradition that the Brahmans (*Antaṇar*) were ousted from one particularly famous temple for their alleged selfishness and aloofness (Nadarajah 1962: 77, 99).

The Mukkuvar ruling group also required artisan castes, various other professional castes, and above all domestic service castes (*kuṭimai*), to staff the sort of hierarchical agrarian society they wanted. The origin of the middle range professional castes, such as Smiths and Climbers, is not emphasized in the regional traditions, and most informants today imagine these groups to have come and settled voluntarily. However, it is the Vēḷāḷars who are usually credited with bringing and installing the *kuṭimai* castes, and it is clear that at some point the Mukkuvar rulers came to appropriate control of these low castes and to regulate their domestic and temple services as part of a widespread system of caste and kuṭi 'honours' (*varicai*).

The admittedly idealized circumstances I have described can be seen to have provided the basis for an ideological split between the Mukkuvars and the Vēḷāḷars, the former strongly asserting their right to political and economic domination, and the latter circumspectly developing their claim to greater purity and spirituality as the non-violent servants of the temple deity (Nadarajah 1962: 77–80, 99–101). Although one can see in this familiar elements of the tension between temporal and spiritual power evinced in medieval European society as well as in Dumont's formulation of the Kshatriya–Brahman duality, the historical outcome in the Batticaloa region seems to have largely vindicated the martial caste, the Mukkuvars, and devalued the ideal of an aloof, non-reciprocating, and reclusive priesthood. The latter trend was in the interests of both the Vēḷāḷars and the Mukkuvars, neither of whom cared to subordinate their status to Brahmans. The Mukkuvars, as chiefly guardians and overseers of the major temples, naturally sought to confine priestly charisma to its purely service aspect, the performance of pūja in the restricted sanctum of the temple. The same Mukkuvar overseers even today insist that the priest must first confer the blessed offerings of the deity upon them before distributing it to others. The Vēḷāḷars, as the god's household staff within the temple, similarly resisted any priestly encroachments upon their sacred duties and their day-to-day management of the temple economy.

With no independently endowed Brahman lands or villages in the entire region, and two landed castes vying keenly to demonstrate high rank through an accepted idiom of temple ritual which was largely predicated on the concept of command, there was really no prospect for widespread Brahman influence.[39] Conversely, it is likely that few Brahmans would have been attracted by the idea of serving warrior patrons who had originated from a coastal fishing caste in South India, who had fought with notable ferocity in Māgha's mercenary army, and whose social status was low in other parts of the island. The historical mixture of groups comprising the seven chiefdoms of the Vanni region of north-central and eastern Sri Lanka at the time of European contact is still not fully understood, but even assuming that Mukkuvar settlements in Batticaloa may have contained elements of other warrior groups, such as south Indian Vanniyārs (Indrapala 1965: Ch. 5), the general implication is that these ruling groups would not themselves have been likely carriers or patrons of a strongly Brahmanical world-view. It is easy to see how Vīracaiva doctrines, which are also espoused in somewhat attenuated form by such lesser priestly groups as Paṇṭārams in Tamilnadu and Kerala (Thurston 1909 vol. VI: 45–52; Anantha Krishna Iyer 1912: 396–8), as well as by numerous lower caste South Indian groups, including various castes of weavers (Dēvānga, Sēṇiyan, Padma Sālē, and Kaikōḷan) and fishermen (Bestha, Sembadavan – all references in Thurston 1909), would also prove compatible with the interests of the dominant groups in Batticaloa. And if Māgha himself held Vīracaiva beliefs, this would naturally have provided further impetus to this development (Liyanagamage 1968: Ch. 4).

5.5. The matrilineal rule

A final, but crucial, element in the set of background factors which I wish to bring forward is the 'matrilineal principle' (*tāy vaḻi*) and the specific role it plays in local thought and in local institutions. It is necessary to be especially careful here, since it is quite possible inadvertently to superimpose on the situation a set of assumptions or an image of matriliny derived from the anthropological literature which is quite different from the image the people themselves have of it. It is also necessary to recognize that many matrilineal institutions have vanished during the past 150 years under the impact of radically altered political and legal systems imposed at the national level. What remain today are mere traces of the traditional Mukkuvar political and economic system, somewhat fuller vestiges of the caste and matriclan basis of domestic and temple ceremonial, and a language, a rhetoric, of matrilineal identity and honour which draws upon the distinctive but somewhat jumbled corpus of oral/textual traditions represented in the *Maṭṭakkaḷappu Mānmiyam*.

It has already been shown that there is no consistent underlying reference to matrilineal purity or coded natural substance detectable in what informants say about castes and kuṭis, but that there is a pervasive belief in an idea of matriliny arising out of a combination of more subtle factors: maternal nourishment and affection, matrilocal residence, and matrilateral transfer of property through dowry. To this must now be added the theme of matrilineal inheritance and succession which, despite its increasing irrelevance to modern life, is still seen as a firmly rooted, historically sanctioned, jural rule. There is a certain legalistic quality to the phenomenon which I immediately confronted in informants' responses to preliminary questioning about why people in Batticaloa recognized matrilineal descent and about what the 'meaning' of this custom might be. It is also this aspect which seemed so unsatisfying from the point of view of the operant purity and/or coded-substance assumptions which I was initially trying to apply. Informants eagerly volunteered that 'matrilineal kinship reckoning' (*tāy vaḻi muṟai*) was the basic rule, but when pressed for further justification of this practice they simply asserted it was the 'custom' (*vaḻakkam*) or 'law' (*caṭṭam*) of the Batticaloa region. Several more scholarly informants even referred me to a nineteenth-century codification of the Mukkuvar law written by a Colombo lawyer (Brito 1876). It was really only after the various 'symbolic' or crypto-cultural theories discussed at the beginning of this paper had been tested and been proven largely irrelevant that the explicit, formal, and 'legal' aspects of matriliny could be seen as important in their own right. I hasten to acknowledge that indigenous concepts of received usage such as 'law' or 'custom' are also fundamentally symbolic, but it appears that anthropologists can sometimes be too clever, passing up such conventional symbols in the search for hidden meaning.

The basic tenets of the traditional system of inheritance and succession for the entire Batticaloa region, in the few extant formulations which have come to light, are explicitly attributed to the Mukkuvars. Brito writes of the 'Mukkuva Law' (1876). Burnand describes the matrilineal customs enforced by the Mukkuvar 'Head Podies' (1794), and a Tamil document (Anon.: n.d.) in the Sir Alexander Johnston Papers gathered in the early 19th century summarizes the *Mukkuvarin cātivaḻamai* (Mukkuvar caste customs).[40] This set of Mukkuvar legal principles figured in some regional case law during the early British period, from which Brito extracted his codification, but the Mukkuvar law was ignored in the 1876 Matrimonial Rights and Inheritance Ordinance and thereafter ceased to have legal force (H.W. Tambiah 1954: 157; Nadaraja 1972).

The Mukkuvar law recognized the categories of *mutucom* which was ancestral property transmitted through females, *teṭiyateṭṭam*, which was acquired property of either spouse, and *cītanam*, which is dowry bestowed upon daughters. Similar terminology is found in the Jaffna legal code, the Thesawalamai, but the systems are not identical, most notably in the fact that in Jaffna the *mutucom* devolves upon sons (H.W. Tambiah 1950: Ch. 10; S.J. Tambiah 1973a: 111–27). A discussion of the detailed aspects of the Mukkuvar law and the Thesawalamai must not preoccupy us here. The essential thing to note is that the available evidence on the Mukkuvar law indicates that most property, especially land, was either classified as ancestral property (*mutucom*), which passed to one's sister's sons, or as dowry property (*cītanam*) which is passed to one's daughters. The historical significance of dowry is still a bit uncertain; the most detailed source, Brito's account, makes little reference to it, yet it is mentioned earlier (Anon. n.d.) and today it constitutes the primary mode of property transmission. A couple's acquired property (*teṭiyateṭṭam*) was disposable at the discretion of the husband, according to the sources, but it does not appear that traditional Mukkuvar society offered much practical scope for 'acquisition' apart from matrilineal inheritance and dowry. Burnand's description in particular stresses how the Mukkuvars jealously guarded their domination over a static agrarian order even, it seems, to the detriment of their own people.

> The greater half of the Batticaloa fields still belong to the Mockuva families . . . & the remainder to their temples, to the Bellales or to other Casts as Accomodessans [service tenures] & to the Maurmen.
>
> All the great & petty Headmen of the Mockawass keep it as an ancient custom not to sell any of their lands to other Casts, nor even to alienate them out of their families, however they may be burthened with debts, and it is a further custom with them . . . to hypothecate their Lands for these Debts. The other Pagan Inhabitants in the Country as well as some Maurmen follow the same custom, to the great prejudice of Agriculture.
>
> But as the headmen & inferior Mockawas podies [chiefs] possess

> almost half of the Fields, this Cast (which consists of about 500 families) is the wealthiest, that is to say 40 or 50 of them, for all the rest being greatly indebted are in a state of insolvency.
>
> (Jacob Burnand 1794: 57, 86, 138)

The extent to which Mukkuvar inheritance rules imply the former existence of a corporate land-holding matrilineal descent unit is also uncertain. Brito asserts that the eldest brother acted as chief manager of the matrilineal property, but today there is very little evidence of 'jointness' in household structure or cultivation patterns. It is possible that the estates of the wealthy ruling Mukkuvar *pōṭiyārs* were managed on collective matrilineal lines, while most Mukkuvar households were too poor to bother with such practices. There is no evidence, historical or contemporary, indicating the existence of joint matrilineal households, but there are a few examples of jointly held lands in scattered parts of the Batticaloa region today. These instances are extremely rare, and they do not conform to a single pattern. The principle of joint matrilineal management of land seems capable of being implemented in specific ways to serve particular material or civic interests.[41] In a larger sense, of course, the general pattern of matrilineal inheritance would ensure that no land left the matriclan (kuṭi), although distribution of land among members of the kuṭi might be quite unequal. Regardless of how land may have been distributed among effective management units within the kuṭi, the idea of local matriclan members as corporate 'share-holders' in the management of temples and in the sponsorship of rituals presupposes an effective internal system for collecting the necessary tithes and donations. Although such fund-raising today is sometimes transacted in money, the traditional medium was grain (paddy). It is easy to see how the liability of kuṭi members to such an agrarian tithe would have contributed to an image of the kuṭi (i.e., a local or sub-regional segment of the kuṭi) as having at least some material basis in land. Similar 'shares' in temple ritual are found among the middle and lower castes, who were allotted particular tracts of land by the Mukkuvars in return for their services (lands called *accomodessans* in the early colonial records). Some of the common features of kuṭi and caste 'shares' will soon become apparent.

5.6. Matrilineal rights, shares and honours

The language of Mukkuvar inheritance law says nothing about matrilineal blood or purity, but it says a great deal about the importance of matrilineal rights. The same word (*urimai*) means both 'right' and 'inheritance', which is to be expected in a society where virtually all traditional rights were secured by reference to some aspect of birth-status, e.g. *peṇ vaḻi urimai peṇ piḷḷai* may be translated as 'woman with matrilineal rights' or 'female heir from a female line' (Brito 1876: 12).[42] The very same word, *urimai*, is encountered whenever political and ritual privileges are being discussed, along with the word *paṅku*, which means 'share', and the word *varicai*, meaning 'mark of honour'. The principle of matrilineal succession to office is largely irrelevant in the political sphere today, since the local and regional Mukkuvar chiefships and the councils of high caste village elders have no legal sanction. The traditional matrilineal rights to hold political office are nonetheless firmly linked to specific kuṭis, who have the 'right' to supply the incumbent. The succession to such office is said to pass from mother's brother to sister's son, but genealogical evidence shows that the adult male kuṭi membership is regularly called upon to decide the succession and ratify the outcome of the numerous disputes which arise. One of the few Mukkuvar political offices still in existence is that of the area chief (*Ūrppōṭiyār*) of Akkaraipattu, who must be drawn from Paṇikkanā kuṭi. It must be emphasized that it is not just the *Ūrppōṭiyār*'s own restricted kin group, but the kuṭi as a whole, which shares the honour and prestige associated with the right to this office.

In other Mukkuvar settlements where the more distinctly political offices have vanished, and in Vēḷāḷar and lower caste settlements where such offices either never existed or played a subordinate role in the Mukkuvar authority structure, the principle of matrilineal succession and formal kuṭi representation still operates in the selection of temple and mosque trustees. The actual mixture of kuṭi representation on temple and mosque boards varies greatly from locality to locality, but in every case it reflects a balance between two opposed tendencies: on the one hand, claims to individual kuṭi rights (*urimai*) to local preeminence backed by a local historical charter and force of numbers; on the other hand, aspirations for the local integration of all kuṭis as part of a single 'system' which would both reflect the larger political realities as well as fulfil the image of society as an organic instrument of collective worship. There are a number of different ways in which these two tendencies have been expressed in temples and mosques in different areas, and there has also been no lack of special pleading to demonstrate that the first tendency is merely a more concrete embodiment of the second.

For the Tamils in Batticaloa, as for Tamils elsewhere (Baker and Washbrook 1975; Appadurai and Breckenridge 1976; Pfaffenberger 1977; Stein

1978), the temple plays an extremely important organizing role in society. In informants' statements and in textual sources from Batticaloa, the existence of the temple is depicted as conceptually prior to the founding of the settlement. By no means all of the temples which exist today are viewed in this light, but it is clearly true of the major 'regional temples' (*tēcattukkōvil*) which figure prominently in regional history and legends. Some of these temples are seen as having been founded originally by epic figures such as Rāvaṇa, who, for all his faults, was a pillar of Saivism. Other temples are believed to have been built at the command of kings, who wished to insure the perpetual veneration of sacred icons (*lingams*, *vēl* weapons, *cilampu* anklets, etc.) either accidentally 'discovered' in the forest or brought to the region by wandering devotees. The warrior kings of the Vijayanagar period (14th–17th centuries A.D.) in South India have been noted for their consuming interest in temple construction and religious patronage which legitimated their systems of 'tributary overlordship' (Stein 1969: 188–96), and the historical legends of Batticaloa seem to reflect much the same ideology. It is the king who is depicted as having first appreciated the sacredness of a particular place; it is the king and his group who appropriate all subsequent glory by proclaiming themselves protectors of the shrine; and it is the king who colonizes the surrounding lands with the requisite functional castes. In the language of these idealized accounts, it is the provision of an elaborate system of hereditary services to the temple deity which is depicted as the central achievement, the creation of society merely an incidental byproduct. The whole scheme fits very well with Hocart's image of the caste system as a sacrificial organization instituted by the king (Hocart 1950). The tradition endures today, particularly at the *tēcattukkōvils* and proportionately so at lesser temples, that the overall constitution of society should be reflected and validated in temple rituals, especially in the annual temple festival (*tiruviḻā*).

There is still today a language of 'rights' (*urimai*), 'shares' (*paṅku*), and 'honours' (*varicai*) which is expressed in the entire range of ritual display from grand temple and mosque festivals to humbler domestic life-crisis ceremonies. Among the Tamils, all participating groups, both castes and kuṭis, are said to have a 'share' in the affairs of the temple if they fulfil at least one of the minimal conditions: public sponsorship of some segment of the annual festival or provision of ritual services during the festival. It is the essence of such festivals, of course, that some shares are smaller or more servile than others, but at least the rhetoric of shares is uniform. The biggest shares include the sponsorship of specific 'nights' of the festival, and the most glorious of these are usually the last few evenings before the morning *tīrttam* or bathing of the deity which closes the festival. This is perhaps one of the most dynamic arenas of kuṭi ranking, since sponsorship of the festival requires both manpower and financial resources which may fluctuate over time. The re-allocation of 'nights' to different castes and kuṭis, as well as the arrangement of joint sponsorship by several smaller groups on a single night, is a well-attested feature of the system. The display of a preeminent position in temple ritual, particularly one dramatized at the climax of the ceremony by receiving the god's garland and first offerings, is a recognized honour called *munnīṭu* (foremost position). On most evenings of the annual festival, this honour is given to one or more people called *tiruviḻākkāran*, who are the designated leaders of the group(s) sponsoring the ritual that night. On the final night of the festival, the *munnīṭu* is typically accorded to the temple trustees (*Vaṇṇakkar*) representing the dominant local matriclans. In colonial and pre-colonial times, however, it might have been claimed by a regional political chief.

The term *varicai*, on the other hand, is applied to the set of ritual privileges accorded to different castes and kuṭis during domestic observances such as weddings, female puberty celebrations, and funerals. The traditional consistency and rigour of the *varicai* system is difficult to judge today, as the lower castes and lower-ranking kuṭis have begun to seize honours which were never before accorded to them and the higher castes and kuṭis have consequently begun to regard *varicai* as a kind of debased currency which may be disregarded.[43] The list of *varicai* honours starts with entitlement to have domestic services from the Washerman, Barber, and Drummer. High caste groups have the services of all three, but middle-ranking castes such as Smiths and Climbers were traditionally accorded only the first two. Other *varicai* honours included the right to place specific numbers of decorated pots of water (*vīṭṭu muṭi*-s, 'house crowns') on the roof and to hang certain numbers of cloths beside the doorway. Certain high caste kuṭis also claim the honour of having the Washermen spread clean cloths on the path in front of the funeral procession (*nilappāvāṭai*). Each of the castes, and many of the high caste kuṭis as well, have recognized insignia (*virutu*) which are used primarily as cattle brands, and these are also considered to be a *varicai*. The list could be expanded. Most informants laboured mightily but were unable to give a fully standardized account of the '18 *varicai*', reflecting no doubt some potential for insinuating new *varicai* honours, as well as the present decay of this entire ritual idiom.

5.7. Matrilineal caste affiliation vs. bilateral status

All of the 'rights', 'shares', and 'honours' which have been described are acquired by virtue of membership in units constituted by the common rule of matriliny (*tāy vaḻi, peṇ vaḻi*). One of the most important of these is the kuṭi, with its shallow and unsystematically segmented sublineages, which, although not a 'classic' matrilineal descent group, can be seen to share certain features of matrilineal descent as a conventional anthropological category (Schneider 1961). However, it is just as true, if more difficult to accept from a conventional anthropological standpoint, that castes (*cāti*, jāti) are also matrilineal in the Batticaloa region, and that they are associated with much the same cultural imagery as kuṭis.[44] Castes differ from kuṭis chiefly in having a much stronger functional/occupational component.[45] The survey of ethnoreproductive and ethnophysiological beliefs revealed no underlying theory of distinctive caste purity or bio-moral substance, but it did reveal a consistent view that caste membership derives from the mother. This opinion was voiced by members of all castes, and it was supported by appeal to the same principles of intimate maternal care and affection, the same mixed factors of matrilocal residence, propinquity, and property, and the same jural rule of matrilineal 'rights' as one encounters in discussions of kuṭi membership. In both kuṭi and caste contexts, though without perhaps undue reflection in either instance, informants quoted a well-known proverb: *vērōṭi vaḷartti muḷaittālum, tāy vaḻit tappātu*, 'Although the root may grow out, develop, and sprout up, the maternal connection is never lost'.

Admittedly, the matrilineal rule of caste affiliation is largely hypothetical when considering cross-caste unions involving the lower castes, since the members of the high caste stratum advocate and enforce a rule of strict caste endogamy among these groups. Apart from the effects of the common Dravidian kinship terminology which encourages marriage within a close, localized kinship universe, members of low castes said they saw no intrinsic reason to refuse an opportunity for marriage with higher caste groups. They quickly pointed out, however, that the higher caste groups would never tolerate such unions and that, formerly at least, the traditional Mukkuvar political authority would have meted out swift punishment for such a violation of the social order. The high caste people, in turn, confirmed this. It is not a concern with protecting purity or with preventing the mixture of bio-moral substances, but an adamant refusal either to permit the erosion of their 'rights' and 'honours' or to acknowledge the equality implied by marriage in this culture, that motivates these high caste restrictions. Other comments reflect the strong high caste image of society as a historically-instituted system of social differentiation, a functional division of labour laid down by kings 'in the time of the Cheras, Cholas, and Pandyans', deviation from which represents a breach of faith or the breaking of a commitment to the past. The function of low castes in such a social order is expressed as a 'duty' (*kaṭamai*) to perform 'service' (*ūḻiyam*) to the higher castes and to the deity of the temple. The high castes, ever willing to see evidence of an organic design in such arrangements, also refer to these obligatory low caste temple services as 'shares' (*paṅku*), in the formal sense that any group participation in temple ritual is a 'share', or as 'rights' (*urimai*), in the sense that these specific ritual responsibilities can never be usurped. In some cases, low caste groups which eagerly quit their demeaning and no longer legally-enforceable temple duties 40 years ago are still wistfully said to be welcome if ever they wish to resume their hallowed 'shares'. The ideology of the high castes vis-à-vis the lower castes is very strongly coloured by such traditions of historically-sanctioned political subordination, and as a consequence the theory of matrilineal caste affiliation is very seldom put to the test with members of these groups.

It is also true that overall birth status is never utterly and solely determined by the caste and kuṭi of the mother. Ethnoreproductive theories acknowledge, and genealogical research confirms, that the father plays a role with the mother in endowing the child with bodily substance, personal qualities, and social identity. While it is uniformly asserted that the child's formal affiliation is always with the caste and kuṭi of the mother, the personal standing of the child within his caste and kuṭi will be enhanced or diminished by the high or low caste origins of the father. In one documented example, the illegitimate offspring of a Barber woman by a high caste Mukkuvar landlord have gained prestige from the union and are fond of teasing the nephews and nieces of their Mukkuvar genitor as 'cross-cousins'. In another case, a respected Vēḷāḷar schoolteacher's daughter is married (matrilocally) to a Karaiyar Fisherman caste man, and although the children carry their mother's caste and kuṭi affiliation, the neighbours still talk. It is always understood that the class, occupational, and educational status of a man, as well as his appearance and character, can compensate for some shortcomings of caste and kuṭi when marriage is being considered.

The latent bilateral aspect of overall individual status poses much less of a problem, however, when both parties to a marriage are drawn from the high caste stratum of 'good people'. Status distinctions between the categories of Vēḷāḷar, Mukkuvar, and Kurukkaḷ, as well as between the constituent kuṭis of these groups and the residual 'free-floating' kuṭis of the high caste stratum, do not approach in magnitude the distinction between the high caste stratum as a whole and all of the lower castes. Marriage between the high caste people and any of the middle or lower castes, or between the middle and lower castes themselves, violates fundamental canons of ritual subordination and functional separation of low caste groups. On the other hand, marriage between kuṭis in the high caste stratum, some of which are historically 'tagged' to specific castes and others of which are more equivocal in caste identity, can be more general or more restricted depending upon local political, economic and demographic circumstances. The following discussion deals specifically with the relationships between elements in the high caste stratum.

The factor always to be kept in mind is that, here, marriage between groups implies equality between groups, even though the parties to any given match may exhibit different degrees of wealth, occupational prestige, education, and personal attractiveness.[46] The equality asserted in one marriage must sooner or later be reinforced by another marriage in the opposite direction, in accordance with the stated and behaviourally verified ideal of bilateral cross-cousin marriage. Perhaps no more vivid demonstration can be offered of the lack of asymmetrical marriage principles in this society than the acceptability of a double marriage between two brother–sister pairs, termed a *māṟṟukkaliyāṇam* ('exchange marriage'), which simplifies dowry negotiations and cements a strong bond between two families. The most visible evidence of the importance of connubial equality between groups is, however, to be seen in the recognized patterns of reciprocal marriage exchange between the leading high caste kuṭis in different localities, which have already been mentioned.

5.8. Patterns of local variation

An understanding of the regional dimension of high caste dominance, together with a recognition of how the basic assumptions of matrilineal rights and group affiliations operate in local thinking, makes it possible now to see a broad range of social structural variation within a single historical and analytic framework. The ambiguous listing of castes and kuṭis which Yalman recorded in Tambiluvil, and similarly jumbled accounts which I initially recorded in Akkaraipattu, reflect the distinctive similarities between castes and kuṭis in Batticaloa: they are both formally defined by a doctrine of matrilineal rights which is strongly sanctioned in the traditional Mukkuvar law and which also makes sense to Batticaloa people in the context of their general matrilocal domestic pattern. The potential for *selective emphasis* on either kuṭi or caste identity is implicit in the nature of these categories and is clearly evident in actual fieldwork situations.

Indigenous theories of purity or bio-moral substance are undeveloped, equivocal, and context-restricted; they seem to have played, at most, a secondary role in organizing and justifying the traditional relationships between castes and matriclans in Batticaloa. Instead, an explicit, formal political symbolism of matrilineal honours, rights, offices, and shares, along with a highly static and authoritarian control of the land, was sufficient to sustain the traditional *Mukkuvar vannimai* in close, if not always harmonious, partnership with the Vēḷāḷars. It is precisely the *formal quality* of these matrilineal connections that seems to allow for the selective emphasis in group identities noted above. At one extreme, it is possible to emphasize the historic and poetic ideal found throughout the Batticaloa region that every caste is comprised of seven specified kuṭis; and in smaller settlements where a set of such single-caste-linked matriclans forms the largest segment of the population, it is possible to maintain a claim to 'unmixed' Mukkuvar or Vēḷāḷar caste identity. Strong marriage exchange alliances are found in such situations between the largest and most prestigious kuṭis within the designated caste category, and there tends to be an ideology of caste endogamy. At the opposite extreme, in the larger and more complex 'peasant towns' for which Batticaloa is noted (Ryan 1950: 10n.), it is common to stress the strictly matrilineal rule of caste and kuṭi affiliation regardless of which caste-linked matriclans form the marriage 'pool'. In such localities, the range of high caste kuṭis tends to be more heterogeneous, intermarriage between kuṭis 'tagged' to different castes is unrestricted, and there tends to be an ideology of Mukkuvar–Vēḷāḷar alliance reinforced by an inter-caste marriage exchange relationship between the most powerful and prestigious kuṭis. The same principles apply to the third group in the high caste stratum, the Vīracaiva Kurukkaḷs, but the numbers and the resources of this group have always been tiny in comparison to those of the Mukkuvars and Vēḷāḷars. Because of this, and because of their circumscribed role as priests and spiritual servants to the Mukkuvars and Vēḷāḷars, the theme of equality through cross-caste marriage exchange with these dominant groups has never been fully developed.[47]

All three high caste groups illustrate the fact that perceptions of the degree of authenticity of caste identity vary in proportion to the degree of reinforcement available both from local demographic patterns and from the ideal, somewhat poetic, model of society enshrined in regional texts. When such reinforcements are weaker, the emphasis in most informants' comments is upon markers of kuṭi identity, rather than upon caste boundaries. In this case, it comes down to a question of how much meaning can be imputed to a matriclan name, with all the local rights and symbolic associations that name evokes.[48] In more populous and heterogeneous settlements, like the town of Akkaraipattu, the kuṭi name is frequently taken as the basis for the inference of caste membership: a man is known to belong to Paṇikkanā kuṭi, which is one of the 'seven-kuṭi Mukkuvar' clans, therefore he must be a Mukkuvar. When kuṭi identities cannot find such clear textual validation, there is always respectability to be gained from appending the portmanteau 'Vēḷāḷar' label to the names of the residual clans. In more traditional contexts, and in smaller scale settlements, on the other hand, rights to exercise a particular caste or kuṭi privilege, or to fill a matrilineal office, often carry the corollary stipulation that a man's father as well as his wife should belong to a traditionally allied matriclan. That is, the exercise of such matrilineal rights and offices is fully legitimated by observance of a complementary marriage rule which, in effect, attaches a latent bilateral condition to a putatively matrilineal right. At this end of the sociological spectrum, not merely the kuṭi name, but reciprocal alliance obligations of a more multi-stranded sort, are taken into account in assessing finer degrees of entitlement to recognized matrilineal statuses.

Against the historical and ethnographic background which has already been sketched, there are at least four major 'tactical resources' which are mobilized in varying combinations to produce different configurations of caste and matriclan relationships in different localities: (1) an assumption of high caste, especially Mukkuvar, control over the land and over the disposition of lower caste services, although this is growing weaker; (2) a fundamental implication of equality and alliance which is established and maintained by reciprocal marriage exchange; (3) a widely recognized principle of matrilineal descent and matrilineally transmitted rights defining both castes and matriclans; and (4) a set of shared assumptions about the temple as a conceptual paradigm for society and as the setting for ceremonial transactions which validate the position of castes and matriclans in the social order. The underlying continuum along which high caste, and high caste kuṭi, relationships may vary in different localities can be seen in a comparison of data from three separate settlements, one of which is in a strongly 'Mukkuvar' area, another of which is a strongly

'Vēḷāḷar' village, and the last of which is a larger and more heterogeneous semi-urban settlement where a joint ideology of Mukkuvar and Vēḷāḷar alliance and intermarriage is basic to local perceptions.

5.9. Mukkuvar dominance: the Kokkaṭṭiccōlai temple

In the isolated vicinity of Kokkaṭṭiccōlai, located on the *paṭuvān karai*, the western or 'sunset shore' of the Batticaloa lagoon, the patterns of Mukkuvar solidarity and dominance persist today in perhaps more traditional form than anywhere else in the region. The ancient Tāntōnrīsvarar Kōvil (Temple of the Self-appearing Civa) at Kokkaṭṭiccōlai is still considered to be one of the most important of Batticaloa's 'regional temples' (*tēcattukkōvil*), and despite the inevitable erosion of their traditional power, the Mukkuvars here still cling strongly to the symbols and prerogatives of temple overlordship which validated the *Mukkuvar vannimai* or regional chiefship. The temple is governed by three trustees (*Vaṇṇakku* or *Vaṇṇakkar*) representing the three most prestigious kuṭis in the region (Ulakippōṭi kuṭi, Kālinkā kuṭi, and Paṭaiyāṇṭa kuṭi), and the three temple priests claim to be Vīracaiva Kurukkaḷs. The lesser servants of the temple are members of the Kōvilār caste whose hereditary duties are differentiated among six named matrilines. Direct 'supervision of the inner-duties' (*uṭkaṭampai atikāram*) of the temple staff was, until quite recently, delegated by the Mukkuvar trustees to a hereditary Vēḷāḷar temple officer called the *Tēcattu Vannimai* (chief of the region), who acted as a sort of prestigious ritual factotum for the Mukkuvars. This Vēḷāḷar temple chief was by right always a member of one of the two high-status kuṭis (Attiyā kuṭi and Vaittinā kuṭi) which predominate in the Vēḷāḷar village of Paḷukāmam about eight miles south of the temple. This office was seen as the joint prerogative of these two matriclans, which are strongly allied in a reciprocal marriage exchange relationship. These two kuṭis also enjoyed specified prebendary rights over a large tract of temple land named after one of the clans, *Attiyā munmāri*, in return for the ritual services they rendered to the temple, particularly during the annual festival. A special committee of elders, known as the *Kaṭukkeṇṭār*, representing all the major sub-lineages within Attiyā and Vaittinā kuṭis had special responsibility for selecting each new Chief as well as for overseeing the management of the prebendary lands and the marshalling of revenue from these lands to fulfil the hereditary Vēḷāḷar duties at the temple. At the time of the annual festival, the Vēḷāḷar temple chief took up temporary residence near the temple and directed the conduct of the ritual, including the provision of extra Vēḷāḷar manpower (from Attiyā and Vaittinā kuṭis) to perform certain high-status tasks such as carrying of the deity's palanquin in procession and riding with the idol atop the temple car.

At the close of the festival, a ceremony is still performed which is called variously *kuṭukkai kūṟutal* or *kañci muṭṭi kūṟutal* ('calling out the pots' or 'calling out the rice-gruel pots') or *paṅku kūṟal* ('calling out the shares'). It was the Vēḷāḷar temple chief who, until recently, called out in strict order a list of arcane titles identifying all the castes and kuṭis recognized as having a 'share' in the celebration of the temple festival. When the list was recited in 1975 by a respected Mukkuvar schoolmaster, it contained a total of 120 titles, some of which appeared to commemorate mythological figures, but most of which represented specific castes and kuṭis holding recognized positions in specific localities throughout the Batticaloa region. Three pots for members of the Moorish community were recited, but no one took them up. When a representative of a group stepped forward to receive a pot in front of the image of the god, the onlookers sometimes challenged the recipient to explain his qualification to receive that share. If necessary, this would have to be done by reciting from memory a passage from one of the recognized textual sources of Batticaloa tradition. The list of titles began with *Vētam* (Veda, or scripture in general) and ended with *Mūppan* (chief of the Paṟaiyar Drummers). In the middle of the list the elaboration of titles and sub-titles in the list bore scant relationship to present day realities. Ten different kinds of *Ceṭṭi* shares were called but not taken up, and in the end, only 36 pots were actually distributed. The principle behind the ritual is nevertheless clear: it is intended as a traditional recapitulation of the entire social order, validating group status in terms of rank-order as the shares are called. At the same time, the uniform size, shape, and content of all the pots reflects the principle that all share-holders, however humble their contribution, play a recognized role in support of the deity.[49]

Much more could be said about inter-kuṭi and inter-caste relationships dramatized during the Kokkaṭṭiccōlai temple festival, but the important point here is to recognize the elements of a traditional, but unequal, balance between the clear kingly dominance of the Mukkuvars, expressed in overall control of the temple, and the competing claims of Vēḷāḷar ritual excellence ambiguously sanctioned by their historical 'servitude' to the temple. The Vēḷāḷars from the village of Paḻukāmam were given considerable recognition and status in the affairs of the temple, but the Mukkuvars always retained ultimate control. Tradition recalls that even when the Vēḷāḷars were given the right to assume the former priestly duty of passing out the *kañci muṭṭi* pots, they were required to cover the first pots, i.e. the Mukkuvars' pots, with a silk cloth, while their own pots and those of all other groups remained uncovered. The Mukkuvars, then and now, see the Vēḷāḷars as the hereditary servants of 'their' temple and, within the context of temple ritual, as their delegated overseers of the lower service castes. As such, the Vēḷāḷars are seen as liable to kingly Mukkuvar discipline whenever they betray their hereditary obligation to serve the deity. Temple history preserves the memory of one such misdemeanour, the complicity of the Vēḷāḷar temple store-keeper in a theft of temple valuables. A public expiation of this sin was incorporated by the Mukkuvars into the annual temple rituals: at the end of each festival, a representative of the Vēḷāḷars was symbolically tied and beaten by women of the Kōvilār caste at the order of the Mukkuvar trustees.

The Vēḷāḷars have come to chafe increasingly under this symbolic domination by the Mukkuvars in recent years, and the ensuing intensification of hostility has been reflected in electoral politics within the local legislative constituency. An old antagonism seems also to have been exacerbated between the higher-status absentee 'Maruṅkūr Vēḷāḷar' functionaries from Paḻukāmam, and the lower-status permanent Kōvilār temple servants resident in Kokkaṭṭiccōlai, who are now seeking recognition of their equal status as 'Kāraikkāl Vēḷāḷars'. Several years ago the Vēḷāḷars finally severed their service relationship to the Kokkaṭṭiccōlai temple entirely. They retained, however, *de facto* possession of the temple lands, which the Mukkuvars angrily claim had been given to the Vēḷāḷars strictly on service-tenure. This claim has failed in the courts, and now the responsibility for 'supervision of the inner-duties' of the temple has fallen quite happily on the Kōvilārs, who were formerly in chronic friction with the Vēḷāḷars over day-to-day running of the temple. Their recent promotion has also had the unforeseen effect of amplifying the Kōvilārs' claim to be considered genuine Vēḷāḷars themselves, and, ironically, the same kinds of symbolic rights and disabilities which fuelled the Mukkuvar–Vēḷāḷar dispute now figure prominently in Mukkuvar–Kōvilār tension.

The Kokkaṭṭiccōlai evidence is extremely useful in establishing a traditional base-line for judging data gathered elsewhere. The characteristic assumptions of matrilineal caste and kuṭi descent are found here, but the Mukkuvars of Kokkaṭṭiccōlai and the Vēḷāḷars of Paḻukāmam also observe mutually exclusive endogamous caste boundaries and considerable residential segregation. There is a rather clear distinction between the two castes, not to mention, nowadays at least, considerable hard feeling. Vivid evidence of the Mukkuvar cultural ideal of political domination can be seen in the temple ritual, and it is interesting to note that even where Vēḷāḷar claims to caste precedence carry an implication of intrinsic religious superiority, these claims are given concrete expression in much the same metaphor of power, honour, and authority. Thus the Vēḷāḷar temple chief, whose responsibility was ostensibly limited to the strictly religious conduct of the temple festival, nevertheless carried the full kingly title of *Pūpāla Kōttira Tēcattu Vannimai* ('regional chiefship of the earth-guarding lineage'). It is also 'supervision' (*atikāram*) of the rituals, rather than performance of historically recognized 'hereditary service' (*toṇṭūḻiyam*) to the temple deity, which is emphasized in contemporary Vēḷāḷar ideology. Although caste boundaries seem fairly strong in this region, there are still exceptions, notably in the considerable degree of intermarriage between Mukkuvars and Kōvilārs in the vicinity of the temple. Here, not only is the matrilineal rule invoked to distinguish the castes, it is still the basis for allocating specific categories of temple work among the different Kōvilār matrilines. No doubt this Mukkuvar–Kōvilār connection has been an additional factor in the temple quarrels which have taken place over the privileges and responsibilities of the Vēḷāḷars from Paḻukāmam.

5.10. Vēḷāḷar dominance: Tambiluvil and Tirukkōvil

Forty miles south of Kokkaṭṭiccōlai, it is the Vēḷāḷars who dominate the affairs of an equally famous 'regional temple' to Lord Kantacuvāmi, known here as Cittiravēlāyutacuvāmi ('Lord of the Beautiful Lance') at Tirukkōvil. The nearby village of Tambiluvil, which has been discussed by at least three anthropologists including myself (Yalman 1967: Ch. 15; Hiatt 1973; McGilvray 1974: 130ff.), is typically described by its inhabitants as a 'Vēḷāḷar village'. Two textually-attested Vēḷāḷar matriclans share undoubted preeminence within the village, which is consolidated by an explicitly preferred pattern of reciprocal marriage exchange. One of the leading pair of matriclans, Kaṇṭan kuṭi, furnishes the single trustee (*Vaṇṇakkar*) of the Tirukkōvil temple by ancient matrilineal right, while the other leading clan, Kaṭṭappattān kuṭi, enjoys a similar right to appoint the single *Vaṇṇakkar* of the Kaṇṇakiyamman temple in Tambiluvil.

Many more features of the traditional temple organization and festival ritual have undergone change at Tirukkōvil than at Kokkaṭṭiccōlai, but they are still remembered by local people. In fact, it was Yalman's informants from Tambiluvil who first mentioned the existence of the *kañci muṭṭi*, or as they expressed it, the 'kuṭi-calling', ritual which was still being conducted at Tirukkōvil in 1955 (Yalman 1967: 326–7). There is no sign of the ritual today, nor is there much left of the Mukkuvar regional chiefship which formerly 'presided' over the annual festival. There is an acknowledged, but presently rather uninvolved, Mukkuvar *Talaivar* or *Vanniyār* (regional chief) whose title and office descends matrilineally in Paṇikkanā kuṭi, but his home is 20 miles away, and he works as an engineer in Colombo. Mukkuvar traditionalists argue that the Vēḷāḷar *Vaṇṇakkar* of the temple was originally a rough equivalent of the Vēḷāḷar temple chief at Kokkaṭṭiccōlai: that is, a sort of domestic overseer of temple ritual appointed under a historic Mukkuvar mandate. The temple has been the subject of endless legal suits brought by leading Mukkuvars and others from outside the immediate vicinity, claiming mismanagement and arrogation of authority by the Vēḷāḷar (Kaṇṭan kuṭi) trustee, but the truth is that wider Mukkuvar regional dominance can no longer be enforced over Tirukkōvil in the modern legal and social setting. The annual festival is still a major regional event, and there is still widespread sponsorship of nightly 'shares' of the ritual. However, along with the lapse of the *kañci muṭṭi* ritual, there has been an evident change of emphasis from the validation of fixed hereditary ranks in society to a more pragmatic and 'devotional' pattern of voluntary sponsorship by local settlement areas.[50]

The local demographic concentration of Vēḷāḷar matriclans in Tambiluvil has enabled the local population to maintain their sense of Vēḷāḷar identity and to consolidate greater control over the 'regional temple' at Tirukkōvil as tangible Mukkuvar dominance has weakened. Inhabitants of the village are sometimes heard to say that they are 'unmixed' (*cutta, kalavillāta*) Vēḷāḷars, but the strongest adherents to this claim are members of the two large, high status kuṭis who have a tradition of marriage exchange and who manage the two main temples. In fact, nearly half of the population of Tambiluvil belongs to one of these two leading matriclans (Hiatt 1973: 248), and succession to matrilineal office, e.g. temple *Vaṇṇakkar*-ship, is predicated on the assumption that the candidate's parentage has been restricted to members of these two allied kuṭis. The existence of two separately governed temple complexes in the village provides scope for some degree of 'friendly rivalry', but there is no evidence of hypergamy (Hiatt 1973: 237–8, 248). In the view of leading Vēḷāḷars, the Vīracaiva Kurukkaḷs are merely a lesser matriclan within the Vēḷāḷar category, and the Mukkuvars are a distinctly inferior group living in other settlements, such as Akkaraipattu.

The conceptually salient pattern of shared preeminence between Kaṇṭan kuṭi and Kaṭṭappattān kuṭi in Tambiluvil shows some of the features of Yalman's Kandyan 'micro-caste' or ideally endogamous bilateral kindred (Yalman 1962; 1967: Ch. 9). From the remarks of some Vēḷāḷars here, one might initially conclude that these two allied matriclans 'are' the village of Tambiluvil and virtually 'are' the Vēḷāḷar caste. Such boastful implications are soon muddled, however, by readily available evidence that over 50% of Kaṇṭan kuṭi and Kaṭṭappattān kuṭi marriages are contracted with other, lower-prestige, matriclans (Hiatt 1973: 248). Some of these lesser kuṭis are unique to the village, but 20% of the inhabitants belong to kuṭis found also in the town of Akkaraipattu, a place which residents of Tambiluvil like to stigmatize as a 'Mukkuvar settlement'. There is little evidence of a Vēḷāḷar ideology of intrinsic kuṭi substance or blood in Tambiluvil, but there is, once again, a strong ideology of matrilineal rights and honours which are heavily monopolized by the two dominant kuṭis. Vēḷāḷar identity receives pronounced symbolic emphasis in Tambiluvil, but the actual degree of Vēḷāḷar endogamy and caste separation is less than in the Kokkaṭṭiccōlai/Paḻukāmam area.

5.11. Mukkuvar–Vēḷāḷar alliance: Akkaraipattu town

In Akkaraipattu, a mixed Tamil and Moorish town located about eight miles north of Tambiluvil on the main coastal road, the elements of a sort of sociological compromise can be seen, combining both Mukkuvar and Vēḷāḷar caste affiliations within a stable framework of shared local prestige. The Tamil sector of the town was formerly the seat of Mukkuvar political hegemony over the surrounding district (*paṟṟu*, 'pattu'), including Tambiluvil and Tirukkōvil, an authority which was symbolized and implemented through the office of the Mukkuvar *Ūrppōṭiyār*. This office descended in the female line within Paṇikkanā kuṭi, but as in Tambiluvil, there was a clear preference and obligation to sustain a reciprocal marriage exchange relationship between a leading kuṭi and its 'traditional partners', in this case the people of Maḻuvaracan kuṭi. These two allied matriclans in Akkaraipattu account for about 36% of the total high caste Tamil population of the town, while the two dominant kuṭis in Tambiluvil account for about 48% of the population there. What is noteworthy in Akkaraipattu, however, is the fact that Paṇikkanā kuṭi retains its clear identity as a Mukkuvar matriclan, while its marriage ally, Maḻuvaracan kuṭi, is given a strong acknowledgement as a Vēḷāḷar matriclan. In other words, the high caste kuṭis of Akkaraipattu stress the strictly matrilineal aspect of caste affiliation, and the high status marriage exchange alliance which unites the two leading clans is seen as symbolic of a larger cross-caste alliance between the Mukkuvar and Vēḷāḷar castes as a whole.

An interesting mythical charter, a variation on a more widespread regional legend, is perpetuated in Akkaraipattu, particularly by leading members of Paṇikkanā kuṭi. According to this story, the Mukkuvars, led by chiefs of the Paṇikkanā kuṭi, conquered and inhabited the Akkaraipattu region, but for many years they lacked any lower castes to perform domestic and ritual services for them. When a Vēḷāḷar chief of Maḻuvaracan kuṭi moved into an uninhabited tract of land nearby with his accompanying retinue, including Washerman, Barber and Drummer castes, the local Mukkuvar Paṇikkanā kuṭi chief sought to marry one of the Vēḷāḷar chief's sisters. He was refused but managed to abscond with the woman, who was later discovered and killed by the Vēḷāḷars. The Mukkuvar, however, succeeded in abducting a second sister of the Vēḷāḷar chief, and this time she became pregnant before she was located. By this time the Vēḷāḷar chief had come to recognize that it was futile to resist the political domination of the Mukkuvars, so he gave his blessing to the marriage and relinquished his exclusive rights to control the service castes (*kuṭimai*). Henceforth, as the tale is told, the Mukkuvar chiefs of Paṇikkanā kuṭi assumed supreme power in the region, particularly with respect to the disposition of the service castes and the regulation of the system of caste and kuṭi honours (*varicai*). The Vēḷāḷars, for their part, were given formal recognition of their high status, and their role in originally bringing the service castes, by the perpetuation of the marriage exchange alliance between Paṇikkanā and Maḻuvaracan kuṭis. While the latent rights of the Vēḷāḷars are thus said to be enshrined in the rule that the father and the spouse of the *Ūrppōṭiyār* must always be of Maḻuvaracan kuṭi, it is surely just as important to note that the myth explicitly recognizes the Mukkuvar tactic of forced intermarriage as a means of asserting caste equality.

In Akkaraipattu, and not merely among the two leading matriclans, the caste honours of the Mukkuvars and Vēḷāḷars are reckoned strictly matrilineally. If a person's kuṭi is historically and textually tagged to the Mukkuvar caste, he is a Mukkuvar; if to the Vēḷāḷar caste, he is a Vēḷāḷar. When the kuṭi name is more vague or anomalous (accounting for approximately 28% of the high caste population in a relatively cosmopolitan settlement like Akkaraipattu), adding the charismatic 'Vēḷāḷar' title to the matriclan name seems to be common practice, e.g. Vēṭa Vēḷāḷar ('hunting Vēḷāḷar'), Ciṅkaḷa Vēḷāḷar ('Sinhalese Vēḷāḷar'), Vīra Vēḷāḷar ('Heroic or Martial Vēḷāḷar'). The local high caste temple to Lord Piḷḷaiyār is administered by a board of 13 kuṭi trustees (*Vaṇṇakkar*) representing all the numerically significant matriclans in the vicinity, but traditionally Paṇikkanā kuṭi and Maḻuvaracan kuṭi enjoy special preeminence in ritual. The temple priests are Vīracaiva Kurukkaḷs of the Tēcantira kuṭi. The membership of all the Kurukkaḷ matrilines together constitute a group strong enough numerically in this area to have their own *Vaṇṇakkar* on the temple board and to be able also to share modestly in the sponsorship of their own festival 'share'. Both Mukkuvar and Vēḷāḷar kuṭis share similar rights to the display of *varicai* honours, and there is no evidence of any local Mukkuvar–Vēḷāḷar antagonism. The Vēḷāḷars of Tambiluvil admit that Maḻuvaracan kuṭi is a Vēḷāḷar matriclan, but they deem it of lesser rank because it is not mentioned in the standard textual sources and because of its close intermarriage with Mukkuvar clans. Conversely, the Vēḷāḷars of Tambiluvil are seen by the people of Akkaraipattu as somewhat arrogant and exclusive, although some of the more 'reasonable' people of Tambiluvil have married and settled matrilocally in Akkaraipattu with no apparent problem. The caste and matriclan system in Akkaraipattu, where much of my initial research took place, shows no dependence upon an ideology of ritual purity or coded bodily substance; rather it exhibits once again all the symbolism of political hierarchy which is characteristic of the Batticaloa region and which seems to have been codified and enforced under the reign of the Mukkuvars. In Akkaraipattu, it is not some anthropologically reified notion of ritual purity which the prominent Mukkuvar–Vēḷāḷar matriclan alliance preserves, but the vestiges of real political condominium.

5.12. The Mukkuvar cultural paradigm

There are many aspects of social organization in Batticaloa which have been omitted from this summary account, as well as others requiring further research, but the importance of the cultural paradigm which was traditionally imposed throughout the region under the *Mukkuvar vannimai*, the chiefship of the Mukkuvars, deserves a final comment. Much of what has been described here relates specifically to the high caste stratum of Mukkuvars, Vēḷāḷars, and Kurukkaḷs, but it should never be forgotten that the same complex of matrilineal caste affiliations, matriclan rights, and matrilocal kinship institutions is shared across the entire Hindu caste hierarchy. Where certain caste groups have broken away from their subordinated roles in Mukkuvar- and Vēḷāḷar-controlled temple ritual, for example, they have endowed their own matriclans with responsibilities and honours in their own caste temples which replicate many of the patterns of the high caste kuṭis. Today some high caste informants are unaware of the intricacies of low caste matriclan organization and disdain to enquire about them, but in fact the matriclans of most of the lower castes are generally as viable today as those of the higher castes. Succession to the office of lower-caste headman, where such office still exists, is in many cases matrilineal. Numerous court cases, both past and present, attest to the strength of lower-caste feeling about preserving matrilineal temple honours, particularly among the Taṭṭār Smith caste. If economic resources permitted, it is likely that additional low caste disputes would surface in the courts. Under the traditional *Mukkuvar vannimai*, of course, such disputes would have been settled by the local Mukkuvar chief and his councillors.

The pervasive Mukkuvar cultural paradigm of seven sub-chiefdoms within Batticaloa, and seven kuṭis within each caste, is both elaborated in the local texts and sung in the songs of local informants. The circumstantial evidence, at any rate, suggests that the society of the Batticaloa coast was profoundly influenced by the ideas and the institutions of the Mukkuvars, who (it would appear) encouraged, perhaps even enforced, the structural replication of their matrilineal clan system in all of the lower castes.[51] Whether any of the Vēḷāḷars or Vīracaiva Kurukkaḷs, or any of the lower castes, brought matrilineal institutions with them when they arrived in Batticaloa is presently unknown. Despite the likelihood of Mukkuvar origins in Kerala, the names of the remaining castes of the region nearly all correspond to well-known castes of Jaffna and Tamilnadu.[52] Some names of matriclans and some regional place-names show resemblances to those of Kerala, but the language spoken in Batticaloa has been identified simply as an archaic and rather literary dialect of Tamil (Zvelebil 1966).

Whatever the origins of the various castes, and whatever their mode and sequence of arrival in Batticaloa, it is clear that the dominant Mukkuvar political system sought to uphold a distinctive pattern of matrilineal rights and institutions throughout the entire population. Even the Moors, a major segment of the population who have presumably been present throughout the period of Mukkuvar rule, follow clearly derivative social institutions based upon matrilineal organization. In fact, it seems quite likely that the size of the Moorish population of Batticaloa (44% in the 1971 Census) is attributable in some measure to the voluntary conversion of both ordinary Mukkuvars and members of other castes under circumstances of harsh domination by Mukkuvar chiefs.

6. CONCLUSION

6.1. A critique of purity and bio-moral substance theories

It would scarcely be feasible to 'disprove' the highly encompassing purity theory of Dumont or the immanent transactional/bio-moral substance approaches advocated by Marriott and Inden and others, nor has this been my aim in this paper. I have sought instead to suggest in a more practical way, by considering some original ethnographic data, that these approaches are typically too condensed and reductionist, or too vague and universalizing, to be of heuristic value in field research.

One might, for example, wish to discount the absence of Brahmans from the Batticaloa region and see the local Vēḷāḷars as structurally filling the 'Brahman role'. In such a Dumontian recension, the Vīracaiva Kurukkaḷs could be seen as a doctrinally weak embodiment of the hierarchical principle, posing no bar to the assertion of ritual purity by the Vēḷāḷars (surrogate Brahmans) in the context of Mukkuvar (surrogate Kshatriya) power in regional temple organization. What this paper has attempted to demonstrate, however, is that invoking a single, abstract, and highly condensed attribute such as 'ritual purity' in this context suggests a misleading identification of Batticaloa Vēḷāḷar thinking with some idealized form of Brahmanical theology presumed to exist in India. In fact, it has been found that Vēḷāḷars here do *not* tend to articulate their claim to high status in terms of an indigenous theory of blood purity or in a systematic vocabulary of purity/pollution; instead, they share the Mukkuvar ideology of authority and matrilineal rights and honours. So understated is the idea of caste purity in Batticaloa, and so pronounced is the kingly 'liturgy' of honour and authority (Hocart 1950; Dumont 1970: 216), that it is doubtful whether the concept of ritual purity would have occurred as a major focus of analysis if there were not already such a voluminous literature on the subject. With the decline of effective Mukkuvar political hegemony in modern times, the Vēḷāḷars have utilized this historically sanctioned politico-legal idiom to amplify and strengthen their latent claims to *both* religious *and* political eminence within localities having a strong Vēḷāḷar identity. This aggrandizing tendency seems to be a common feature of modern Vēḷāḷar ideology in Jaffna and in Tamilnadu (Banks 1957: 197–200; 1960: 66–9; David 1974: 51–63; Barnett 1970; 1973a: 183–5), and it is also in accord with recent research which indicates that in South Asia 'purity' and 'power' are, in certain contexts at least, aspects of the same thing (O'Flaherty 1969; Wadley 1975; Marriott 1976a: 113).

It must be obvious, also, that Dumont's whole analytic strategy of restricting the meaning of the term 'caste' to situations in which the shastric ideal of the Brahman/Kshatriya relationship constitutes the fundamental model of inter-caste structure not only rules out facile Western comparisons in the sociological jargon of 'social stratification' (one of his explicit aims), it also hinders more culturally sympathetic comparisons within the larger Indic world itself. While, for example, data from some parts of Sri Lanka or Nepal which conforms to the Brahman/Kshatriya ideal can be taken as further confirmation of Dumont's viewpoint (as such doctrines are assumed to have their origins in Indian law and scripture), any discrepant finding can be dismissed either as the artifact of an insufficiently holistic pan-Indian point of view or as a sign of mere 'quasi-caste rather than caste proper' (Dumont 1970: 216). In either event, some of the more interesting questions about how regional social systems in South Asia actually operate are neglected. What, for example, should we make of the existence of Vīracaiva Kurukkaḷs instead of Brahmans in Batticaloa? It might be taken as evidence of an 'incomplete' caste system, intelligible only as a segment of the larger Indian society; but that offers scant insight into the distinctive beliefs and attitudes of the local inhabitants, especially those of the Vīracaiva Kurukkaḷs themselves. On the other hand, if we try to settle the question by designating Sri Lankan society as having 'quasi-caste', we immediately confront a whole series of bootless classificatory quibbles. Are Saivite Tamils with 'quasi-caste' really then only 'quasi-Hindus'?

The recent 'ethnosociological' approach to South Asian caste systems, which has been developed by Marriott and Inden to supersede such rigidities in Dumont's framework, seeks to account for an even greater degree of ethnographic diversity by arguing for a widely shared set of South Asian transactional strategies by means of which social genera (including castes and kinship groups) mix, preserve, and improve their intrinsic bio-moral substances and attributes. There are no prior restrictions in this approach which would rule out data from Sri Lanka; in fact, the authors are hopeful that it will clarify Buddhist, Islamic, and various sectarian social systems as well as orthodox Hindu caste systems. This ethnosociological theory is said to be a 'generative model' based upon shastric legal, medical, and philosophical theories as well as upon 'what we know of South Asian actors' pervasively monistic cognitions of reality'

(Marriott 1976a: 113). If such a thing were possible, it seeks to 'encompass' Dumont's theory, to show it to be unduly rigid and ethnocentric.

There are two fundamental components to the Marriott and Inden formulation: the first is the concept of monistic 'substance-code', said to correspond to commonsense indigenous perceptions of an intrinsic link between the composition of living bodily tissue ('substance') and the morally-regulated actions of the individual ('code'). The second component, recently elaborated by Marriott (1976a), is a transactional grammar or logic by which actors, in their capacity as individuals as well as members of kin-groups and castes, seek to protect and improve their substance-code by following one of four logical interaction strategies in competition with other individuals and groups. The theory has a strong impetus toward universality: every genera is defined by a substance-code, every action (even non-action) is some form of transaction, every conceivable mode of human accomplishment is a medium conveying substance-code between actors. The authors illustrate the applicability of the theory to an extremely wide range of South Asian textual and ethnographic material, and in fact there are some respects in which the theory fits the data from Batticaloa quite well.

It was found, for example, that there was no one single 'symbolic vector', such as blood, which represented to Batticaloa informants the essence of matriliny. The multiple sources of matrilineal ties, such as nourishment, affection, propinquity, matrilocal household and dowry property, can all be interpreted as mutually reinforcing transactional links to the women of the matriline. Although theories of the spread of death pollution showed sharp differences of opinion, those favouring a matrilineal interpretation reflected many of the same transactional concerns. In the realms of domestic ritual symbolism and public temple 'shares' and honours, the transactional nature of caste and matriclan competition is quite explicit and formalized. Group participation in the major regional temple festivals is perhaps traditionally the most definitive transaction of all. The formal properties of the 'transactional logic' elucidated by Marriott would appear to have great analytic usefulness in Batticaloa and throughout South Asia.

What fails to match the Marriott and Inden projection in Batticaloa is the indigenous belief system which explains or justifies these transactions. It has now become a canon of the 'ethnosociological' approach of Marriott and Inden, and at least a commonly accepted working hypothesis among other writers such as Barnett, David, Östör, and Fruzzetti, that there is a Protean concept of bodily 'substance-code' underlying and informing

South Asian kinship and caste transactions. The most clearly formulated versions of this concept are adduced from Ayurvedic medical texts and shastric law books, where a highly developed Sanskritic vocabulary of flowing atom-like particles (*piṇḍa*) and in-born generic duties (*dharma*) serves to enunciate a unified theory of the world. These scholarly textual theories are said to be reflected today in 'the cognitive assumptions actually prevalent in South Asia' (Marriott and Inden 1974: 983), in the 'world of constituted things as conceived by most South Asians', and in what 'recent ethnography tells of the same sorts of cognitions among Hindus in rural areas' (Marriott 1976a: 110, 113). In the words of its authors, the ethnosociological theory 'borrows what now seems to be a repeated empirical finding – the cognitive nonduality of action and actor, code and substance – and uses it as a universal axiom for restating, through deduction, what we think we know about caste systems' (Marriott and Inden 1977: 229).

Research in Batticaloa does not support this universal axiom. Local thinking about the nature of the body is well developed, but it is seen as the domain of medicine and health (*vaittiyam*, *cukam*), not as an extension of moral philosophy and sociology. It is only within this context that informants feel at ease to discuss such impolite topics as blood, breast milk, and semen. The 'qualities' (*kuṇam*) which are attributed to the gestating foetus are usually morally neutral qualities such as appearance, stature, strength and intelligence, while propensity toward moral or immoral conduct is typically felt to develop in childhood and later life. The idea of the untainted innocence of the young child is, in fact, a very strong cultural theme, and for this reason young children often play an important role in Hindu rituals. It is evident that caste and kuṭi differences are not conceptualized in terms of bodily substance. In fact, I have already noted that questions about the possible intrinsic caste or matriclan-linked qualities of the body or of the blood met with the common reply that 'Blood is all the same'.

This finding is consistent with the lack of widespread inter-caste food exchange patterns at weddings and other domestic observances. It is also reflected in the absence of any belief in the transubstantiation of a bride's bodily substance or transfer of her descent group affiliation to that of her husband at the time of marriage (or vice versa). As for an indigenous theory of atomic particles, there is no formulation which local people cite aside from the theory of Ayurvedic humours, which is invoked in a specifically medical context. The word *piṇḍa* (T. *piṇṭam*), cited in shastric sources as the word for particles of matter, is known only in the context of funerary ritual, and there only haphazardly, as the balls of rice flour which are sometimes offered to the souls of the departed. This is recognized to be a relatively new and by no means widespread feature of funeral and death commemoration rituals in the Batticaloa region: it is presently being introduced through the influence of Jaffna Brahman-trained officiants, and there is virtually no common appreciation of its etymology or symbolism. In the area of marriage alliance, which is a pronounced feature of matriclan relationships at the local level, there is likewise no ideology of conserving bodily substance, only the idea of sharing local rights to matrilineal offices and exercising the symbols of political dominance connected with matriclan titles.

Just as Batticaloa concepts of bodily substance are confined to the ethnosemantic domain of medicine, so the local concepts of 'code for conduct' are expressed in the domain of political authority and historical honour. Everyday extensions of the shastric notion of dharma as in-born, bio-moral family and caste duty are very rarely invoked by the people of Batticaloa. During the course of fieldwork, the word dharma (*tarumam*) was most often heard in the context of alms-giving (*tarumatānam*); it was never applied to the behaviour of castes (cf. '*jātidharma*', Marriott and Inden 1973: 7). The term dharma in Batticaloa has the primary connotation of individual, particularly charitable, duty. In fact, it was striking to discover in fieldwork that such ideas as dharma (*tarumam*) and karma (*karumam*) and reincarnation were seldom mentioned even in discussions of religion. The popular religious aspiration, and apparently expectation, is that the soul should attain the heaven of Civa (*Civanaṭi*, 'the foot of Civa') after death. Souls of the dead linger about this world until the final food offerings are made on the 31st day, when the messenger of Yaman (god of death) conducts the soul to its judgement at the hands of Cittirai Puttiran, whose scales weigh its accumulated sin and merit (*pāvappuṇṇiyam*). Theoretically, punishments include consignment to various hells and/or rebirth at an appropriate level in the natural/social order. In practice, however, great hope is placed on the likelihood of at least a saintly (*tēvar*) incarnation, if not something better. Although one may elicit the orthodox theory of karmic rebirth, it is not typically invoked to explain the nature or ranking of castes. Many of these same tendencies have been noted in the popular beliefs of non-Brahman villagers in Tamilnadu (Maloney 1975; Moffatt 1979: 268, 296–7). Basic Vīracaiva doctrines rejecting rebirth (Dubois 1906: 116) may also have influenced popular attitudes in Batticaloa.

The vocabulary of caste and matriclan behaviour, as we have seen already, is one, not of transcendental dharma, but of historically instituted relationships of service, enforced obligation, respect, honour, chiefly sovereignty and the like. These 'codes for conduct', to borrow for a moment the Marriott and Inden terminology, are not conceived as immanent moral qualities of bodily substance but as rules in a geographically delimited political and legal system, sanctioned by historical precedent, and regulated by Mukkuvar and Vēḷāḷar caste authorities in subregions of the district. Patterns of inter-caste transactions between high caste people and members of the middle and lower castes are *behaviourally similar* to those reported from other parts of South India: intermarriage is forbidden, cooked food is never passed upward, and a wide range of distancing behaviours are required of the lower castes. The *indigenous explanation* of this, however, stresses not the mixing of coded substances but the need to enforce and maintain the deference (*mariyātai*) and the respect (*matippu*) of the lower castes. The ultimate justification for caste differentiation is a religious goal, i.e., the maintenance and support of temple rituals instituted by kingly vows, and the more off-hand justifications elicited from informants were also couched in the metaphor of civic duty and functional division of labour. The lower castes, particularly the *kuṭimai* castes, are indeed polluted and polluting by virtue of their intimate contact with the *tuṭakku* which accompanies birth, death, menstruation, and their (assumed) exposure to various exuviae and putrefactions. The explanation of low caste status in terms of karmic retribution is not unknown, but it seems to be mainly a 'back-up' theory not well integrated with the more readily voiced ideology of an ancient kingly division of labour (see also Sharma 1973: 362). These castes might equally well be portrayed as polluted because they are low, as low because they are polluted or sinful.

It may be objected that all of the specifically mentioned interests, such as political authority, enforced servitude, caste respect, ritual preeminence, maternal affection, matrilocal attachments, even the legendary associations of matriclan names, while divorced from concepts of blood or bodily matter, can nevertheless be subsumed under much more liberal South Asian categories of gross versus subtle 'substances'. This is the clear implication in Marriott's discussion of transactions in 'coded influences that are thought of as subtler, but still substantial and powerful forms, such as perceived words, ideas, appearances, and so forth' (1976a: 111), as well as in his treatment of honour and violence as transactional media (1976a: 132–3). The data on 'worship' substances, 'territorial' substances, and 'occupational' substances in middle period Bengal (Inden 1976: 16ff.) and the concept of 'love' as a bodily substance in Bengali kinship (Inden and Nicholas 1977: 21), exemplify some ethnographic applications of this omnibus concept. To the extent that such an exhaustively monistic concept of 'substance' is ethnographically documented and described among specific groups of people in a particular place and time, the finding is noteworthy and significant. As an *a priori* conceptual framework, however, or as a 'universal axiom', it seems likely to lead to a distorted re-definition of fieldwork experience. There is also the problem that where a popular culture of radical monism could be empirically shown to assimilate *everything* to relativized 'substance-code', the result would be a viewpoint analytically trivial and solipsistic. As a limiting case, radical monism begs the fundamental question of why individuals and groups choose particular transactional media or pursue particular transactional ends, since it is axiomatic that all substance-codes are mutually transformable. In order to anchor their substance-code theory and give it some firm reference points, the authors make their strongest appeal not to distinct, locally-situated, and ethnographically-attested models of social virtue and social status, but to 'Hindu macrosociology' (Marriott 1976a: 112), also known as 'The Theory of the Varna' (Dumont 1970: Ch. 3). Judging from the results of fieldwork in Batticaloa, the formal 'tactical' possibilities inherent in the two-dimensional matrix of transactional logic (Marriott 1976a: 114–23) may prove to have greater ethnographic usefulness in South Asia than a universal belief in miscible substance-codes.

It should be noted that Marriott and Inden have assessed the range of regional, historical, and sectarian variation in South Asian caste systems succinctly and informatively in several publications, devoting considerable attention to features of South Indian and Sri Lankan caste systems which are also found in Batticaloa (Marriott 1960; Marriott and Inden 1974). In the summary formulations of their 'ethnosociological' theory, however, they argue that regional variation and change in caste systems can be made intelligible 'as replications and deletions, as permutations and combinations, as negative and reciprocal transformations of coded substance according with the preceding cognitive repertory of kinds of nondual units, relationships, and processes'. They further state that 'deletions and replications are perhaps the commonest devices' (Marriott and Inden 1977: 236). The ideology of caste and matriclan organization in Batticaloa might seem a classic case of 'deletion', were this whole mode of interpretation not so unsatisfactory; not only does it assume what is yet unproven, i.e., the existence of a popular monistic theory of substance-codes, but it also enables the authors to bolster their case by appeal to what is circumstantially disconfirming evidence ('deletions'). One fears that 'deletions' could be made to do for Marriott and Inden what the 'encompassing' relationship does for Dumont: that is, to explain away the awkward empirical anomalies (Lynch 1977: 262).

The more ethnographically-specific works of writers like Yalman, Barnett, David, Östör, and Fruzzetti, who wish to retain something of the holistic Dumontian purity versus power distinction but who have also detected various ideas of coded bodily substance in the indigenous cultural rationales offered to explain caste and kinship patterns, are also, in these particular respects, of little help in sorting out the Batticaloa caste and matriclan data. It is in fact the *non*-substance-linked aspects of these research studies, particularly Yalman's analyses of Sinhalese kinship categories and domestic organization, which have proven most useful to the understanding of society in Batticaloa. Although Yalman was, I believe, quite misled to suppose that ritual purity and hypergamy were basic features of matriclan structure on the eastern littoral, his consistent attention to the implications of marital residence and domestic patterns in other parts of the island has provided extremely useful insights which apply equally well to the matrilocal households of Batticaloa. His attention to the 'contradictions' of bilateral caste affiliation implied in aristocratic Kandyan patrilineal *wamsa* titles and his general emphasis upon the capacity of unilineal descent rules to produce dramatic regional variation in the degree of 'bilaterality' expressed in caste and kinship also suggest important parallels with Batticaloa. His concern with empirical flexibility and variation in both social organization and social ideology within the relatively small geographical compass of Sri Lanka and adjacent parts of South India suggests a more pragmatic and constructive orientation to the data of South Asian anthropology than the single-minded pursuit of pan-Indic varna dichotomies, or pan-Indic bodily substances, or pan-Indic monistic cognitions.

6.2. The social and historical context of caste ideologies

I have argued that the ideology of Mukkuvar dominance, emphasizing martial values and matrilineal rights, is not a thin kingly veneer but rather a pervasive cultural influence at all levels. However, it would not merely be sufficient to demonstrate that this ideology of Mukkuvar dominance deviates from the caste ideologies of Brahmanical purity or coded bio-moral substance which are reported in other parts of Sri Lanka and India. In this highly compressed account, I have also tried to suggest some plausible historical, cultural, and social structural *reasons why* this particular ideology occurs in this region and among these particular groups. It is this type of intellectual concern which seems lacking in much recent South Asian research into the cultural symbolism of caste.

The transactional substance-code approach of Marriott and Inden, although put forward as a more generally applicable and more culturally valid theory than that of Dumont, actually shares with the latter the same kind of theoretical goal: a single formula to explain all South Asian caste systems. Both of these approaches, if not ahistoric as a matter of principle, are predicated upon an assumption of the underlying uniformity of 'Indian thought' since Vedic times. Both of these approaches recognize the existence of regional and sectarian variation, but their true goal seems nevertheless to capture the essence of South Asian social thought as if by heroic application of Benedict's theory of 'cultural wholes' to the entire Subcontinent. Both of these approaches argue for the existence of a culturally-immanent and, at some level, uniform set of assumptions governing caste behaviour, but ambiguities about just *where* these postulated ideas reside and *how* they are empirically manifested in South Asian culture make it difficult to know exactly what should count as evidence. My approach in this essay has been to remain as empirical and as close to overt culture and behaviour as possible; if 'purity' or 'substance-codes' are meant instead to represent unconscious models, allegorical themes, or otherwise indirect formulations of reality, it is not apparent from what these authors have written.

The extent to which highly developed caste ideologies of purity or of bio-moral substance predominate in South Asia is an empirical question which we will no doubt know a great deal more about as ethnographic research proceeds, but it seems just as important to consider the origin and disposition of these cultural beliefs within historical and social structural settings. The need for this may seem more obvious with anomalous or recalcitrant data such as I have presented from Batticaloa, but it is really a basic concern of any anthropological study. A strictly 'cultural account' of symbol systems and indigenous classifications may have its uses (Schneider 1968), but it also prompts a whole range of behavioural and social structural questions. It is also relevant to consider, for example, (a) who generated, codified and transmitted the ideas and why; (b) who had exposure to the ideas and who did not; (c) what degree of selective emphasis, scepticism, apathy, or ignorance may have been entailed in this process; and (d) why these ideas may have been congenial to certain groups and not to others. The existence of an ancient literate tradition in

South Asia, and the historical role of Brahmans and other castes as professional scholars and scribes, suggests not only the wide distribution of indigenous South Asian theories of caste; it also points to the likelihood of some formal arbitrariness, discontinuity, and lack of fit between the elements of the received pan-Indian textual tradition and local socio-cultural systems (Goody and Watt 1963; Goody 1968). While literate religious traditions commonly feature the jealous preservation of orthodoxy and the adoption of an esoteric vocabulary among the professional literati, it is by no means certain that theoretical concepts and lexical fragments found in the everyday thinking and parlance of ordinary villagers will always reflect the textual definitions (*vide* the word 'dharma' in Batticaloa).

Even the most well-founded 'emic' approach to South Asian cultural materials cannot consist solely in the anthropological admiration of indigenous categories and their 'monistic' or 'dualistic' logic; it must also seek to understand the limits of cognition, the experience and social manipulation of symbolic forms (Geertz 1964; 1973), and the effects of both 'ideal and material interests' upon the content of indigenous reasoning (Weber in Gerth and Mills 1958: 280). Although it would add an element of plausibility to their interpretive schemes, both Dumont and the 'substance and code' writers seem indifferent to the need for a sociology of knowledge. Numerous precedents for such an approach to the study of South Asian civilization can be found in Max Weber's analysis of Hinduism (1958), in Robert Redfield's concept of the 'social organization of tradition' (1956), and in Milton Singer's work on the propagation of Sanskritic Hinduism in South India (1972). Indeed, these issues are central to Marriott's own earlier work on the interconnections between the Indian village and its civilizational matrix (1955) and on 'multiple reference' in Indian caste systems (1968b). Even the rare epigram I have chosen from Dumont's *Homo Hierarchicus* acknowledges the need for greater attention to variation and discontinuity in ideologies of caste. This essay has presented some data on Tamil caste and matriclan ideology in eastern Sri Lanka in the hope they will stimulate, if necessary resuscitate, these concerns in South Asian anthropology.

Caste rank and verbal interaction in western Tamilnadu

Stephen C. Levinson

1. INTRODUCTION

Recent approaches to caste have been largely of two major and opposing kinds. On the one hand there are those approaches that treat the ideology of caste, and native ideas about caste, as central to an understanding of it; on the other hand there are those that are Marxist, or at least Marxistic (by which I mean inclined to economic determinism), which view the ideology and native ideas about caste as 'mystifications' of a dramatically exploitative economic order (see e.g. Meillassoux 1973; Mencher 1974).

I shall have little to say to or about the latter kind of approach for a number of reasons. First, if an ideology fits and reflects an economic order it is claimed that this proves the dominance of the latter, while if it fails to fit, the notion of mystification can be invoked to prove the same thing. There are thus no possible counter-examples to such a theory, and consequently it can have no empirical content. Secondly, while specialized ideologies may indeed be Malinowskian charters or Marxist mystifications and thus largely peripheral to an understanding of how a social system actually works, I cannot see how one can possibly relegate the entire structure of native concepts to the same peripheral status (cf. Harris 1968). While there undoubtedly are material forces that tend to shape human intents and beliefs, it would be impossible for a social theory to proceed profitably without according those conceptual structures their central importance as the templates of social action. It is the very basic facts about the subjective nature of the system in which South Indian villagers live that are the focus of this essay; and these subjective perceptions, far from being 'mystifications' of underlying realities, closely reflect the complex web of economic exploitation, power relations, patronage and alliance that can be objectively observed.

The other major approach to caste, now in the ascendant, takes indigenous ideology, or ethnosociology, as central to an understanding of Indian society. There are many sub-schools of thought that can be distinguished here, but Dumont's writings are undoubtedly central (see especially Dumont 1970). By judicious selection from a wealth of indigenous and largely ancient textual materials Dumont has constructed a framework that can be successfully applied to a wide range of Indian materials, including, notably, empirical studies of village organization. Crucial to his scheme are two specifically Indian cultural principles: the opposition between purity and impurity, and the ancient Varna scheme. The first provides a source for the ranking and proliferation of castes, while the second allows (as its principal virtue) the accommodation of the importance of material power. The scheme makes some empirical predictions that seem to hold: for example, and most importantly, it predicts that there should be no local ranking system, in the great diversity of such systems, in which Brahmans rank lower than the often distinct and more powerful dominant caste.

The problem with this ingenious application of text to context (a strategy now followed by Tambiah 1973 and others, and most vociferously by Marriott and Inden 1974; 1977; and other members of the Chicago school) is that while some degree of 'fit' between the (highly selective) textual model and the observable facts is demonstrated, it is quite unclear what this proves. For a start the 'fit' is engineered: from the vast repository of Hindu texts a few themes are selected from which to construct a sometimes very abstract and synthetic metaphysic (see e.g. Marriott 1976a), while from the indefinite numbers of observable facts a few are selected as crucial (e.g. the supremacy of the Brahman). There are already rival metaphysics (cf. Dumont 1970; Marriott and Inden 1977), and there is no reason to believe that there is any limit to the number of alternative frameworks that would also fit the facts. I would hold that the 'fit' is only sociologically significant if the framework in question can be reasonably held to *govern* the facts and *because* of this to match them. Social life is so richly textured that any number of recurrent patterns can be found; we need to have some theory that will pick some of these out as determinative and show others to be epiphenomenal.

What we need, I believe, are ways of getting at the normal, everyday subjective perceptions of caste – the unconscious, unpremeditated maps of their social environment that members of caste society use to guide their actions. We can expect such maps to contrast with the prestige-motivated charters and models that the articulate informant can provide. The problem of course is how to tap this level of everyday belief and perception, and my argument will be that the study of language usage provides privileged access to it. There are other sociological payoffs from such a mode of study too, but consideration of these may be postponed to the concluding section.

1.1. Ethnographic background

The linguistic work to be described here was done in precisely the same research locus as one of the most detailed ethnographic accounts of any Indian village, *Peasant Society in Koṅku*, by B.E.F. Beck (1972). In addition the linguistic situation is described in Levinson 1977. Here then I shall provide just the minimal background required for an understanding of this paper, and refer the reader to these sources for a full account.

The facts to be reported here hold for a unit of local administration called Kaṉṉapuram Kirāmam, a 'revenue village' in Coimbatore District in Tamilnadu, South India. The unit, which I shall henceforth refer to simply as 'the village', is really a collection of no less than 50 hamlets (agglomerations of contiguous dwellings) dispersed through the agricultural land, comprising an official recorded total of over 5,000 souls. There are two main kinds of hamlet: untouchable hamlets (*cēri*) where members of the Harijan castes live (usually one caste per hamlet), and touchable hamlets where one usually finds an incomplete set of the touchable castes living together (but concentrated in caste-wards, or distinct portions of each hamlet reserved for members of each caste). Touchables do not go, if they can avoid it, to untouchable hamlets, although untouchables frequent the streets and compounds of the touchable hamlets where they provide necessary services.

It is not a simple matter to determine the caste inventory of such a revenue village. Neither ordinary villagers nor local officials have a clear idea of how many castes there are, principally because of three factors: firstly, caste titles obscure subdivisions into a number of smaller endogamous kinship units; secondly, quite a few castes are represented by only a few or single families, which may come and go; finally, there are real transients, gypsy-like castes, selling wild honey, salt, charms, stone mortars, or telling fortunes. A full list of minimal endogamous caste units resident in the village at any one time would run to somewhere about 35 in number.

In this study I shall be concerned with just seventeen of these smallest endogamous units, usually termed 'subcastes' in the literature, but which I will simply refer to as castes. The selection came about partly for practical reasons: I was based in a particular touchable hamlet, Ōlappāḷaiyam, wherein members of all these castes were in frequent daily interaction which could be observed, tape-recorded and analysed without difficulty. But there is also reason to think that these castes form the back-bone of village society; together they account for the great proportion of the local population, and historically form a stable and largely ancient core, with the consequence that they have clear rights and duties in the local ritual framework and the local analogue of the *jajmāni* system. This selection of castes corresponds closely to Beck's eighteen; sixteen are the same, while I have recognized a subdivision among the Mutaliyārs that she chose to ignore. I have therefore been able to retain her caste identification numbers, based on putative rank at a Brahman feast, with the minor modification that her caste 7 is my 7a, and its related subcaste of Mutaliyārs is labelled 7b. Cross-reference to her account of each caste is thereby facilitated.

Table 3, largely based on Beck (1972: 5, 58–9, 113), introduces these seventeen castes, and gives an indication of the traditional occupation of each (at which at least one family of each caste continues to work), together with approximate percentages of the village population contributed by each caste (it may help to know that 0.1% is very roughly equivalent to one family). From the population figures it is immediately clear that the population is very unevenly distributed across the castes. Over half of the total village population belongs to the dominant landowning caste 5, which is one reason for its continued hegemony. Another fifth of the total are Harijan leather-workers of caste 18, who provide the bulk of the permanent hired labour force. The remaining quarter of the population are distributed between fifteen main, and several other minor, castes.

Before passing to a brief summary of Beck's findings, a sketch of the politico-economic relations between the castes is in order, as this is one of the few areas not covered in detail in Beck 1972. Some idea of the distribution of economic interdependencies can be conveyed quickly if crudely by means of the diagram in Figure 4. Here each circle represents one of the seventeen castes, identified by the code numbers assigned in Table 3, the area of each circle very roughly in proportion to the population of each caste. Solid arrows indicate the major economic dependencies of each caste, that is, the source of the bulk of its members' income; the arrow head pointing to the left indicates those castes that derive the major portion of their incomes from extra-village connections or occupations. One can immediately grasp from this diagram that ten of the castes depend primarily on service to the dominant caste 5, the landowning caste, and that together with caste 5 they account for the great bulk of the rural

Table 3. *Inventory of castes by division membership, percentage of local population, traditional occupation, and native language*

Left division	Neutral bloc	Right division
	1. Aiyar Pirāmaṇam, 0.3% Brahman priest, Tamil[a]	
	2. Karuṇīkar Piḷḷai, 0.1% Accountant and scribe, Tamil	
3. Cōli Ācāri, 0.5% Artisan, Tamil		5. Koṅku Kavuṇṭar, 54% Farmer and landlord, Tamil
4. Kōmuṭṭi Ceṭṭiyār, 0.2% Merchant, Telugu		
6. Koṅku Ācāri, 0.5% Artisan, Tamil		
7a. Kaikkōḷar Mutaliyār, 1.5% Weaver and merchant, Tamil		7b. Ceṅkuntam Mutaliyār, 0.5% Temple musician and merchant, Tamil
		8. Okaccāṇṭi Paṇṭāram, 1% Cook and local priest
		9. Koṅku Uṭaiyār, 1% Potter and builder, Tamil
		10. Marameṟi Nāṭār, 7% Palmyra-palm climber, Tamil
11. Vaṭuka Nāyakkar, 2% Well-digger and builder, Telugu		
13. Vaṭuka Vaṇṇār, 2% Washerman, Telugu		14. Koṅku Nāvitar, 2% Barber, Tamil
17. Kūṭai Kuṟavar, 0.5% Harijan basket-maker, Tamil[b]		16. Koṅku Paṟaiyar, 5% Harijan drummer, Tamil
18. Muracu Mātāri, 21% Harijan leather-worker and labourer, Telugu[c]		

Notes:

a. Another Brahman caste, the Aiyaṅkār, speak Telugu.

b. Related Kuṟavar subcastes speak Kannada. Two subcastes, Nari Kuṟavar and Uppu Kuṟavar, have native languages other than Tamil, the former an Indo-European language.

c. A related Mātāri subcaste speaks Kannada.

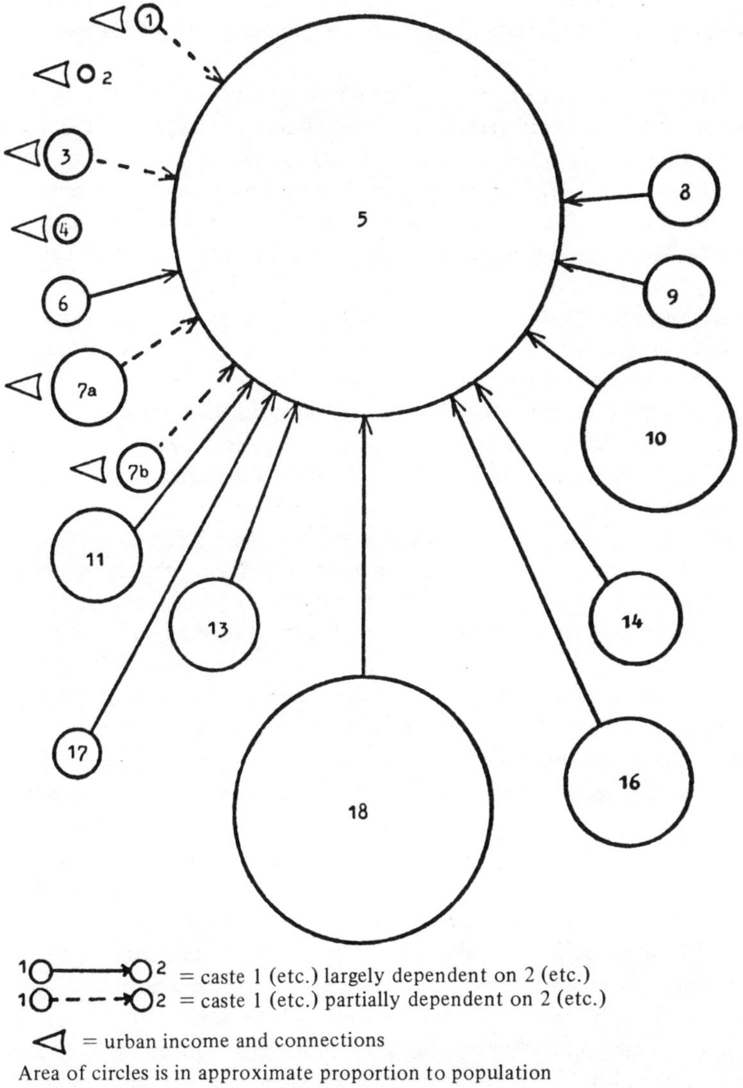

Figure 4. Economic dependencies among castes

population. In contrast to these castes tied closely to the local agricultural production system, six castes represented by relatively few households each have some independence from this rural economy. These independent castes belong to the 'left-hand division', the significance of which will be made clear below.

Caste 5, the dominant caste, has an almost absolute monopoly over landownership (the only exceptions are landholders of castes 1 and 2, each represented by only a few families), as it has had for the last millennium or so. This absolute kind of caste-based monopoly is of course no longer a common feature of modern rural India, having been broken up in many areas by legislation and economic forces, and it accounts for the fact that the local caste structure preserves some of the well-defined interdependencies of earlier times. However it is important to realize that the great majority of households of this caste are impoverished or at a subsistence level: in one hamlet, for example, only 44% of such households actually made a living from their own land and two thirds of these were at a subsistence level unable to employ additional labour (Beck 1972: 192). The remaining 56% of households of this caste derived their livings from agricultural labour or transport or other small business.

The great proportion of rural capital or land is thus concentrated in the hands of just a few families of the dominant caste, and of these just a few of the most wealthy occupy a status of considerable prestige and power not unlike the gentry of Tudor England. While not themselves actually titled aristocrats, they are proud of connections to the *Paṭṭakkārar* or traditional feudal lords who reside in distant villages and are themselves members of caste 5. They run manorial establishments with household servants, and have traditional rights over the labour of Harijans residing within their estates. They have managed to retain political control despite democratic processes in local government. Their traditional status is recognized and inherited by members of their families, while *nouveau-riche* members of the same caste are not (at least immediately) admitted to this status. All castes treat them with due respect, and most reserve the highly honorific title *ecamāṅka* for them, for their power is very considerable indeed. For these reasons, I have called them 'squires' or 'aristocrats', and they play an important role in the facts presented below.

Besides land and traditional authority, other important sources of power are wealth, and more surprisingly, simple numbers or manpower. The fact is that Koṅku is an area of violent crimes with one of the highest rates of homicide in South India. And the more able-bodied men of one's own family, lineage and subcaste in one's village, the safer one is, and the more able to impose one's wishes on members of other groups. From this one may correctly surmise that the caste with the lowest ritual status in the area, namely caste 18, as second largest caste in the village, is by no means the least powerful caste, while a high caste like 4 with only two families is extremely vulnerable.

Let us turn now to the main substance of Beck's findings. After a great deal of study of the internal organization of each of eighteen castes, Beck found that every group has predictable internal customs and structure in relation to its place in the overall inter-caste system. In particular, she found that internal organization varied in relation to two dimensions of the overall system: the rank of the caste in the local caste hierarchy, and the membership of the caste in the left-hand, right-hand or neutral divisions. The caste hierarchy is what it sounds, namely a unidimensional ranking of local castes in a manner which will much concern us later on. But 'division-membership' is not a familiar concept in Indian studies. We might say that it was a sociological construct invented by Beck to deal with an added dimension of variation. But there is more to it than that. In the first place, historical documents make it clear that an explicit division of the castes into two political blocs named with the Tamil terms for 'left' and 'right' was an all-important feature of earlier South Indian politics (see Stein 1980). In the second place, Beck found a few elderly informants who could actually produce lists of such division membership. Thirdly, the distinction runs so deeply into the cultural life of castes, with ramifications from kinship structure to ritual to interactional style (Beck 1972: 8–15), that it must have at least unconscious significance for villagers, a conclusion that this study vindicates.

Some of the main differences that Beck found between right-hand and left-hand castes are these. In social organization, right-hand castes exhibit an internal structure that is closely tied to territorial units via caste temples and caste functionaries. Left-hand organization, on the other hand, is un-territorialized. There are different emphases in kinship too: right-hand castes favour matrilateral cross-cousin marriage with the consequent potential for great alliance chains, while left-hand castes favour the patrilineal alternative facilitating the formation of closed small marriage circles. Right-hand castes have extensive and functionally important patriclans and lineages, while left-hand descent-group organization is minimal. The left-hand castes maintain the shastric ideals of joint families to a greater extent than the right. They stress education and urban advancement and the worship of gods of the 'great tradition', in contrast to the tendencies of right-hand castes. Finally, in life-style and style of interaction, right-hand castes tend to value instrumentality and power, meat and liquor, force and swagger, while left-hand castes favour Brahmanical detachment, non-involvement, vegetarianism, and interactional circumspection.

The differences as here related hold only for the high castes of each division; as one descends the hierarchy, the distinctions become less marked. Beck suggests convincingly that these apparently heterogeneous traits typical of left- and right-hand castes become coherent and rival systems when one considers the two divisions as constituting alternative paths to social prestige. On the one hand we have the right-hand castes with their landed interests preoccupied with expressions of material power; on the other hand we have the left-hand castes with their wider-flung, often urban, connections concentrating on the prestige derivable from a Brahmanical way of life. The leader and model for the right-hand division is the dominant caste 5, while the model for the left-hand division is provided by the unaligned castes of Brahmans (and Piḷḷais to a lesser extent). In short, although in the south of India the classical Varna scheme is not a conscious frame of reference as it is in the north, we find here an expression of the Hindu theory of the balance and hierarchy of different powers: the Brahman at the top, the king at his right hand, balanced by the merchant at his left, with the peasants and service castes below.

This analysis of Beck's fits well with the historian Burton Stein's analysis of the once overt bifurcation of South Indian society into 'right' and 'left'. Stein suggests that the opposition was essentially between those groups whose interests and powers were tied to the land, and those groups whose influence and strength were based in the towns, and who historically probably arrived later than the original land-settlers, remaining to some extent 'outsiders' (Stein 1980). There is more, then, to the local caste system than merely a linear ranking of caste groups. Nevertheless, as we shall show, villagers do operate with the notion of an overall hierarchy.

1.2. The language situation in the village

An important initial observation is that Tamil is by no means the only language spoken in the village and in those around. A very few educated persons can speak English, but apart from that there are a number of castes whose native language is Telugu or Kannada; that is, members of these castes speak these languages at home and to other members of their castes. And one quite obvious but interesting thing is that those castes that have a native language other than Tamil *invariably* belong to the left-hand division. Table 3 shows how native languages are distributed among the seventeen castes selected for this study. We may mention in addition that two other castes with just a few resident families have native languages other than Tamil: one is the Naidu caste, who speak Telugu, and the other is a variety of Mātāri, closely affiliated to caste 18, who speak Kannada, and who provide the bulk of the Mātāri population in neighbouring villages. They may both be assigned to the left-hand division. There are some resident Brahmans (Aiyaṅkārs) who speak Telugu, and some Kuṟavars (possibly local) who speak Kannada.

The four castes included in this study who do not have Tamil as a native tongue, namely 4, 11, 13 and 18, all speak Telugu. But in two cases this is dying out: it is in fact no longer spoken in the homes of caste 13 members except amongst some elderly people, although members of the same subcaste speak Telugu in the local towns. And the children in at least one home of caste 11 are no longer brought up speaking Telugu at all. So Telugu remains the basic domestic medium for only castes 4 and 18. The Telugu spoken by these castes is mutually intelligible although clearly different, but they strongly avoid speaking Telugu to each other, for as the domestic language it presumably carries (as always in cases of code-switching) the connotations of solidarity. Members of 18 do, however, speak Telugu to each other in front of Tamil speakers, in a way that members of 4 avoid.

The correlation of non-Tamil native language with the left-hand castes fits perfectly with the view of Stein's, mentioned above, that the left-hand castes were late-comers to the area and continue to be viewed as outsiders. Notice that in the case of caste 3, Cōḻi Ācāri, even though they speak Tamil they continue to bear the designation that indicates they came from *Cōḻa* country to the east. In fact, they speak a dialect of Tamil that seems to contain less Western Region dialectal features. But this also is a general feature of the left-hand caste speech.

Concerning caste-differentiation by dialect, this is a feature that seems to have been exaggerated in the literature. In the region of this study only Brahmans could be held to exhibit a clear caste dialect, and even they avoided this when not talking amongst themselves. However, various clues, like traces of non-Tamil native tongue, strength of regional dialect features, avoidance of Brahmanical or English lexical terms, confidence of verbal expression and so on, can be used to guess with some success at a speaker's division membership and even approximate caste rank. Table 4 summarizes verbal clues to division membership, which are only strongly in evidence among the higher castes of each division.

Table 4. *Linguistic features associated with caste division membership*

	Left division	Right division
Native language:	sometimes Telugu	always Tamil
Regional dialect:	negligibly or weakly Western Regional; towards standard colloquial	strongly regional: Western Region features including lexicon
'Purity'	many English loans	avoidance of English loans
Brahmanical lexicon:	a few ritual elements, kin terms, and a few items of general vocabulary adopted by non-Brahman castes	non-Brahman alternates used instead

1.3. Caste categories and verbal interaction

What immediately strikes the visitor to the village are not the details of dialect differences or even different mother tongues (those being reserved for intra-caste affairs), but the general way in which social relations are dramatically expressed in social interaction. Rank differences and feelings of solidarity between persons drawn from different castes are immediately observable. An interaction between a Harijan and a member of the squire class of the dominant caste 5, for example, is often marked by an elaborate display of deference on the part of the Harijan: he stoops, puts his hands under his armpits, puts on a show of bumbling ineffectuality, speaks in a high-pitched voice, and generally is concerned to display his own insignificance; meanwhile the landlord expresses his power and position in brusque authority, swear-words, dishonorifics and sometimes benign paternalistic concern. Gestures, voice-quality, choice of expression, honorific and dishonorific terms in Tamil, and general demeanour all play a part in this. Similarly, relations of cordial alliance between members of two high ranking castes in the left division, say, will be marked by mutual intimacy, gossip, sharing of benches on the verandahs of houses, frank discussions of intimate topics and the like.

These features of the modality of interaction are sensitive enough to map out many different degrees of rank, respect, friendship and alliance. A full-scale study of these would indeed provide a map of the social relations of the entire village, and thus a model of the social structure. But the features involved are often subtle, concerned with the way that messages are expressed, and a cataloguing of them is in itself a full-scale enterprise (Brown and Levinson 1978).

In the study reported here recourse was therefore made to some few features of interactional style that lend themselves to rigorous collection and analysis. The features in question are *forms of address* used in face-to-face interaction, that is, terms used to refer to or otherwise indicate the addressee. The local variety of Tamil offers a nice range of alternative forms of address to choose from: there are six alternatives for you-singular, a dozen or so common titles in addition to caste titles, there are hierarchies of summons terms (ranging approximately from *hey!* to *excuse me, sir*) and a range of ranked honorific and dishonorific particles that can be thrown in to indicate degree of respect for the addressee. There are also incidentally ranked series of terms, pronouns and titles, for referring to third parties not present in the speech event, but these show much variation in use and will not concern us here.

Linguistic items of this sort can be considered elements of *social deixis*, that is, ways in which social aspects or dimensions of the speech event are encoded directly in linguistic structure (see Brown and Levinson 1978: 183ff. and Levinson 1979 for a review of this field). I shall therefore sometimes refer to them as socially deictic items. They carry as part or whole of their meaning a social significance, typically a valuation on just two social dimensions, vertical social distance or 'power' and horizontal social distance or 'solidarity'. Brown and Gilman (1960) were the first to point out the general importance of these two social dimensions in connection with the European pronouns of address typified by the French *tu/vous* (T/V) distinction. We shall identify below two pronouns that function just like the European T/V systems used in medieval times.

Unfortunately space prohibits a full treatment of all the socially deictic items used in the village in daily interaction, including titles of address and honorific/dishonorific particles. The main focus of this paper is the usage of *pronouns* referring to a singular addressee. Table 5 provides a list of forms used in the village. It is immediately clear that in a sense there is only one 'real' second person singular pronoun, *nī*, the others being drawn from elsewhere in the pronominal paradigm. On a smaller scale this is a familiar fact: the *vous* of polite address in French is, of course, drawn from the plural second person pronoun. Here, although we have a confusing array of person-number switches to convey respect, the principles at work are quite systematic and universal (see Levinson 1978; Brown and

Table 5. *Alternates for second person singular pronoun in Tamil*

Form	Literal meaning
nī	you-singular
atu	it (distal)
nīr	archaic you-plural, now you-singular with connotations of respectful equality
nīṅka	you-plural (in written Tamil, *nīṅkaḷ*)
nām	we (inclusive of addressee)
tāṅkaḷ	themselves (third person plural reflexive)

Levinson 1978: 203ff.). In the table these pronouns are ranked from least honorific (top) to most honorific (bottom). In fact, this paper will concentrate almost exclusively on just two of these forms, *nī* and *nīṅka*, the T and V forms respectively.

In order to pick out the underlying regularities in pronominal usage, it is necessary to identify a number of factors responsible for special or 'marked' usage. Some of these special features are transitory or ephemeral and reflect specific facts about the situation of speech: for example, when people request things they tend to be more polite and thus may shift their pronominal usage, or there may be some overhearer present on whom a good impression should be made. Other factors are more stable, and the most important of these is any personal office or prestige that an addressee may have acquired above and beyond the status of place in the caste system he or she may have by virtue of membership in a caste. This effect is actually rarely relevant, and it rapidly becomes clear that caste is the major determinant of pronominal choice, so that personal office or prestige can be thought of as an extra factor redirecting normal pronoun choice.

There is isolable, then, something that we may call a *basic classification* of alters, on the basis of which standard unmarked pronominal usage is produced, and a set of secondary *reclassifications* that take into account any transient situational factors together with the particular secondary characteristics of the addressee. There is some very indirect evidence that these are distinct cognitive processes utilized by villagers in assigning pronouns appropriate to particular addressees (see Levinson 1977: Ch. 2). On this analysis, therefore, only *nī* and *nīṅka* emerge as pronouns assigned to addressees on the basis of the primary basic classification of alters. The other second person alternates are 'marked' forms, occurring in special circumstances or to special addressees. Since in this paper we shall be primarily concerned only with the basic unmarked usage, the restriction to *nī* and *nīṅka* is in fact principled.

The existence of systematic but secondary determinants of pronoun choice hints at the difficulties attending data collection. It would not do simply to ask people how they address others; villagers are aware that much in the way of status and prestige hangs on such usage and they report accordingly. Nor would a few casual observations of actual usage simply serve to disconfirm their reports; the observations might be of the special 'marked' usage already described. What in fact was done here was to build up a composite picture based on self-reports, third-party reports, casual observation by the ethnographer, and a large body of tape recordings of casual interaction. Factuality in self-reports was increased by interviewing publicly in the presence of others with a vested interest in the correctness of the report, and especially by asking for usage between named specific alters ('How do you address Ramucāmi Kavuṇṭar' rather than 'How do you address anyone of caste X'). In these ways a picture was built up that is probably about as accurate as could be obtained by a single fieldworker in a relatively small amount of time.

From this mass of detail of actual usage it was then necessary to extract the basic underlying norms or expectations of usage. Once situational and other reclassifications had been allowed for, a relatively simple picture emerged: usage was primarily determined, between actors of different castes, by caste membership, and secondarily by the age of the addressee relative to the speaker. It was possible then to be quite precise in stating that, other things being equal (that is situational and personal factors not intervening), members of caste X would address members of caste Y in such and such a way, due allowance being made where necessary for relative age. It is on this possibility that the rest of this paper crucially depends.

2. LINGUISTIC INFERENCE OF INTER-CASTE RANK RELATIONS

2.1. Advantages of this method

There is a persistent problem for Indologists, namely that although there is general agreement that caste society is a holistic hierarchical system with specific properties, it is not at all clear how the system is to be objectively determined on the ground. If we ask people about the ranking of castes, we will find that they will disagree or be uncertain in many crucial cases. If we measure the wealth, or the life-style, or any other attribute of castes, we will obtain no clear overall ranking. How then are we to determine what the local hierarchy is? And how do the inhabitants themselves, who claim that there is such a ranking, know what it is? (See Marriott 1959; 1968a, for a discussion of these problems.) What we want is a method for finding out how members of the society perceive it, given that they are unable to verbalize a consistent or complete model of it. The problem can be put in a quite general way: how is the sociologist to build overall models of a social system that retain the perspective of its members?

In the answer we offer here, we shall attempt to determine the ranking of local castes as subjectively agreed upon by members, and to discover further principles that organize inter-caste relations, by studying systematically the use of certain value-laden exchanges between castes. The method is not original, and is owed in most part to the work of Marriott. However, the application to linguistic materials is novel, and this extension we shall argue is important.[1] For linguistic interaction has a number of special properties: it is universal (occurs between all castes), it is public, it is indefinitely replicated, its social valuation is precise and independently testable, and it is the most frequent form of exchange. Consequently we can derive from it attitudes and opinions that reflect the unpremeditated viewpoints of actors, with a confidence we can gain from no other source.

As a preliminary to this method, what we wish to do here is to extract the pronominal usage to be found between each and every caste. Given that we have studied 17 castes, for each caste we must ask how it addresses the sixteen others: there are therefore $17 \times 16 = 272$ distinct pairs of different castes to be examined. The obvious format to represent them is the two-dimensional matrix, which with labelled columns and rows of 17 cells each will give us 289 cells including self-reciprocal ones.

However there is a further benefit of matrix representation. For we can manipulate it to produce a scaled matrix, or *scalogram* (Guttman scale) which will allow us to infer any inherent ranking in the data. Scaled matrices, introduced originally into caste studies by Marriott (1959) and Mahar (1959), are now standardly used to represent caste ranking in South Asian studies (see Dumont 1970; Mathur 1964; Orenstein 1965; Hiebert 1971; McGilvray 1974 and many others). The only element of novelty here is the treatment of linguistic data as just another medium of transaction wherein ranks are expressed.

2.2. Initial matrix: informal observations

We may start by taking an *unscaled* matrix that simply represents the kind of T/V usage that holds between each and every caste dyad. It should be remembered that this represents an 'idealized' usage, or rather a conditional usage where the conditions are fulfilled; and further that it is claimed that this represents a distinct level of information for users.

Now we could simply produce a matrix with randomly ordered axes. However, since we have the benefit of the ranking of these castes on quite independent ethnographic criteria as analysed by Beck 1972, we may as well use one such ranking scale along both vertical and horizontal axes rather than simply jumble up the castes. Since Beck uses rank at a Brahman feast (as ascertained by the order in which castes are seated and fed) as a basic rank order on the basis of which to assign numbers as labels for each caste (number labels that we have retained), this will provide a useful if arbitrary starting point for our discussion also.

Sociolinguistic analysis (Levinson 1977: Ch. 3) suggests the partition into three major kinds of mutually exclusive T/V usage: categorical T- and V-usage, and *either* T- *or* V-usage depending on the relative age of speaker to addressee, henceforth relative age T/V. We define these as follows:

(1) *Categorical T-usage* (or simply T in the diagrams):
If caste A gives categorical T to caste B, then every member of A uses *nī* to each and every member of B irrespective of age, sex, or any other attributes of speaker or hearer except their caste memberships – unless specific reclassification operations take place.

(2) *Categorical V-usage* (or simply V in the diagrams):
If caste A gives categorical V to caste B, then every member of A uses *nīṅka* to every member of B irrespective of age, sex, or any other attributes of speaker or hearer except their caste memberships (or membership in the squire class) – unless specific reclassification operations take place.

(3) *Relative age T/V* (or simply REL in the diagram):
If caste A gives relative age T/V to caste B, then every member of A uses *nī* to every member of B who is younger in years than the speaker, and *nīṅka* to every member of B who is older than the speaker. If the speaker and hearer (addressee) are equal in age to the nearest year or so, then usage is very sensitive to other factors (social closeness or solidarity being the most important). But the unmarked usage would generally be V to coevals as to elders. Note that many individuals do not know their own, let alone others', *exact* age, and the greater the age the less likelihood of precise knowledge.

Nevertheless it is an estimation of actual age in years and not social age-grade that is conceptually relevant, even if that estimation may in part be based on behaviour indicative of social age-grade.

The initial matrix (Matrix I) simply represents the facts about inter-caste T/V usage mapped onto an independent rank order, which derives from the ranking of guests at a Brahman feast (see Beck 1972: 159–60, 173, 178). Note that we have omitted Beck's castes 12 and 15, and added caste 7b. Before we begin an analytical dissection, let us informally note that a few dominant patterns are especially striking:

(1) Starting at the top left of the matrix we see that a large bloc of castes (with a core of 2 through 7b) symmetrically exchange relative age T/V. These represent over a third of the castes in the village who are, if we accept our single independent criterion of rank, at the top end of the local hierarchy.

(2) Beneath them is a large bloc of castes (in the bottom left-hand corner) who receive categorical T from the bloc of relative age T/V exchangers in (1) above.

(3) To the right of the REL-exchangers is a large bloc of castes, very roughly the same castes as those in (2), who give categorical V to a large group of upper castes – mostly those in (1).

Although the patterns on the giving and receiving dimensions are not quite the same, we have an immediate impression of a basic caesura between what we may call *the upper castes* (1 through 7b) and *the lower castes* (8 through 18). Note, however, a somewhat intermediate status seems claimed by 8, 9, 10 on the giving dimension. Turning to an ego-centred analysis momentarily, if we take, say, column 3, which represents caste 3's usage to castes 1 through 18, we see that an Ego in the upper caste category lives in a social world which is divided (as far as inter-caste relations are concerned) into just two important areas: those (inferior) groups one gives categorical T to, and those (superior or equal) groups one gives either T or V to, according to their relative age to oneself (seniors getting V, juniors T). On the other hand taking a column, say 16, from the lower category, we see that for Egos of this category the social world divides into two rather different important areas: those (rather few) equals or inferiors one gives either T or V to according to relative age, and those groups (the great majority) whose superiority warrants V irrespective of age (or any other non-caste) considerations.

If we look more systematically at the giving dimension in this way, we can see that columns 3 and 16 are just two extreme patterns out of five major types. The three that lie between the two extremes are the patterns

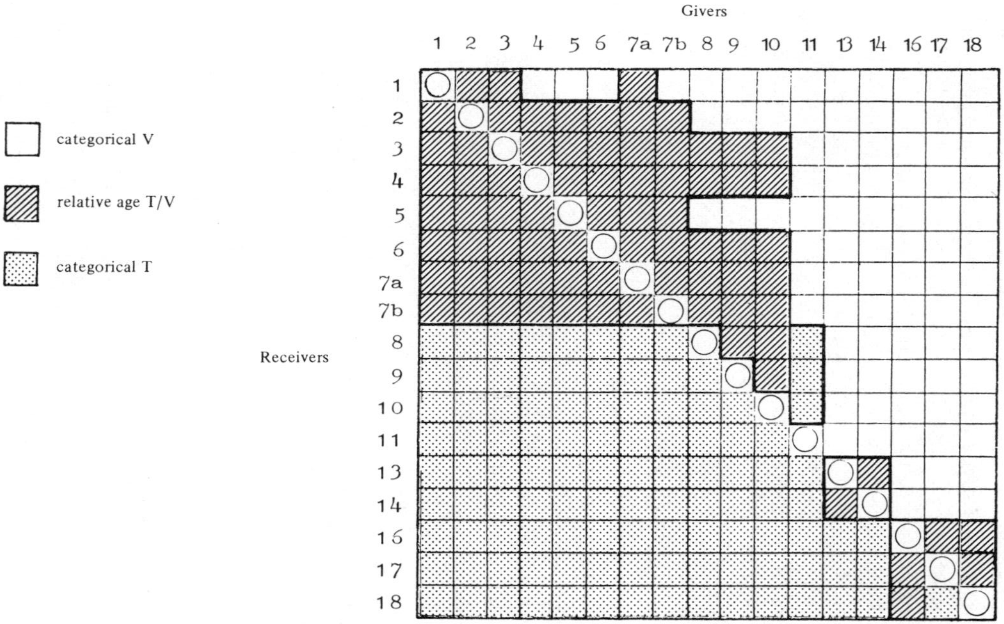

Matrix I. The initial matrix

of T/V giving by castes 5, 6, 4 and 7b, by castes 8, 9, 10, and by castes 13 and 14. The rest of the castes follow our upper caste pattern (1, 2, 7a are like 3), or our lower caste pattern (17, 18 are like 16) – except that 11 is closely similar to the pattern shared by 13 and 14 but is slightly anomalous.

We can then identify five major 'universes', or patterns of T/V giving from an egocentric point of view. We extract in Figure 5 typical columns for each universe from Matrix I which illustrate these five basic patterns. In the figure the sequence of caste identification numbers on the left is a rank order based on implications of T- and V-receiving, derived in a way to be explained below. Each column represents the spectrum of the T- and V-giving that each caste of a particular group indulges in. One caste in the group is taken as Ego for illustrative purposes, and heads the column, while the others are in brackets. In this manner an approximate indication is given of the way in which members of each focal caste treat members of castes above and below it in the caste hierarchy (as measured in one dimension).

However, we have so far begged the most interesting questions: we have been relying on an 'imported' ranking dimension which may not tally with any hierarchical order that inheres in the T/V data. Further, we have been drawing on an intuitive valuation of T- versus V-giving, the principles of which must be made explicit. We wish now to restrict ourselves to a purely internal analysis of the patterns emergent from T/V usage. In this way we shall get some idea of just how far linguistic data will take us in the understanding of an alien society.

2.3. The valuation of media and moves within them

Marriott in a series of important papers (Marriott 1959; 1968a; 1976a) has drawn attention to the extremely systematic patterning of Hindu transactions in food and services, and to the cultural presuppositions that lie beneath that patterning. Marriott (1968a: 141–6) has formulated the underlying rules of Hindu food and services transactions as follows:

For cooked food transfers

(1) If A gives to B, and B does not give to A, then A is *higher than* B. Diagrammatically:

$$\begin{array}{c} \mathrm{A} \\ \downarrow \\ \mathrm{B} \end{array}$$

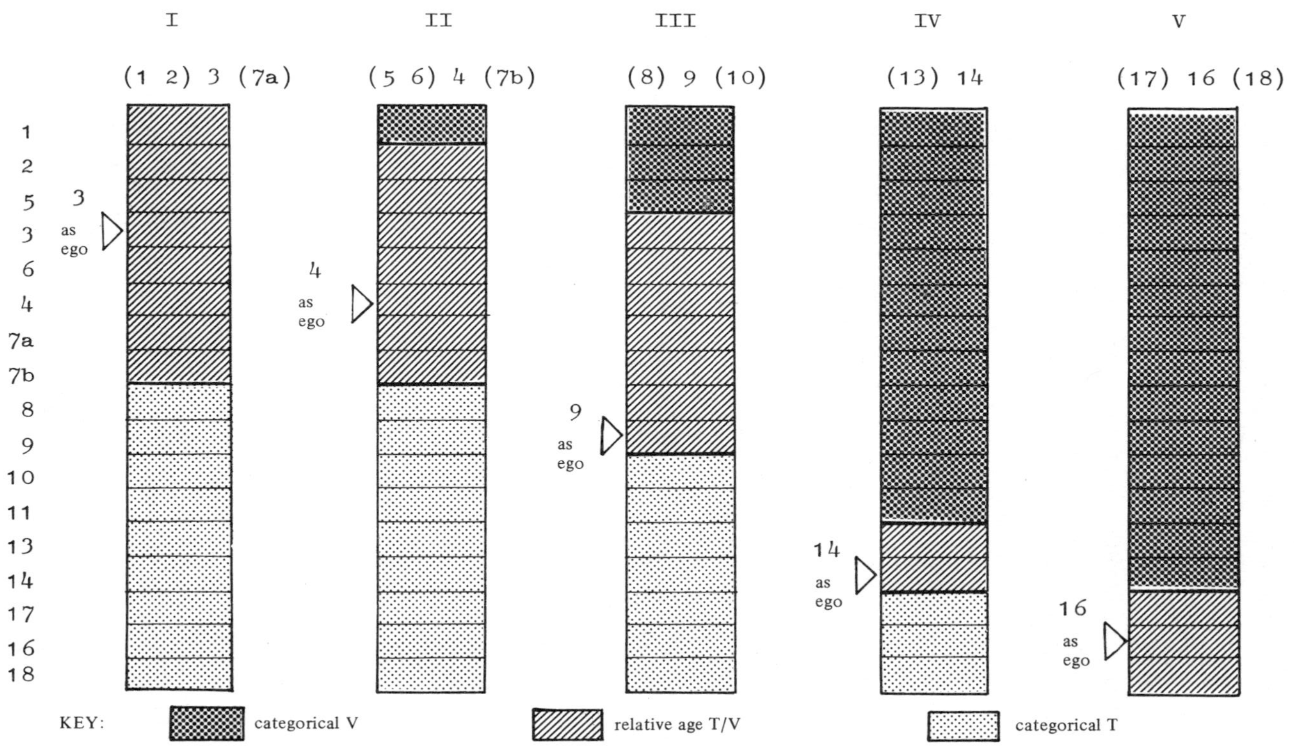

Figure 5. T/V universes, the five major types

(2) If A gives to B, and B gives back to A, then A is *equal* to B. Diagrammatically:

(3) If A gives to B (and B does not give to A), and B gives to C (again without reciprocation), then A is *higher than* C. In short the relation 'higher than' is *transitive.* Diagrammatically:

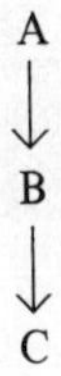

(4) If A gives one way to C, and B does not, then A is *higher than* B. Or, if A gives to C (without reciprocation), and A gives to D (again without return), and B gives only to D and not to C, then A is *higher than* B. The relation 'higher than' is thus *arithmetically scored*, or diagrammatically:

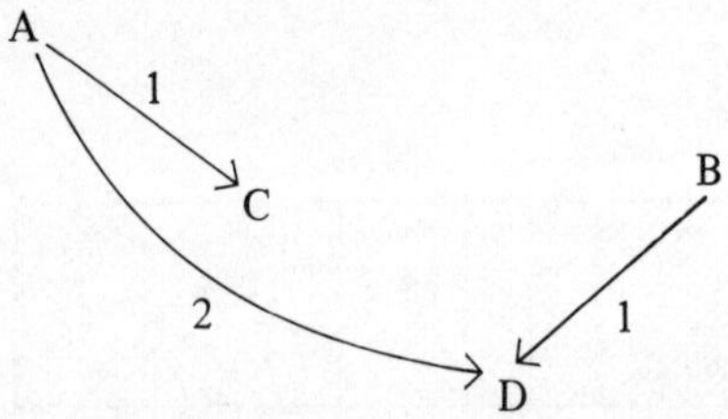

A scores twice
B scores once
So A is higher than B

Marriott does not indicate how he derived this rule of arithmetic scoring, although it is crucial to his (and our) methods. Evidence that this is a rule of valuation used by villagers themselves is presented below (2.4) and in Levinson 1977: 246–50.

To these rules of Marriott's we may add another:

(5) The relation *higher than* (as intuition tells us) is asymmetric as well as transitive: thus there will be no situation where the relation is maintained and where A gives (asymmetrically) to B, B to C, and C to A.

The reader will probably want to know exactly what plane of measurement the relation *higher than* refers to: power, prestige, ritual or sacred rank? But there is no straightforward answer – indeed the matter is contentious. For while the intake of food is avowedly related to the Hindu metaphysics of purity as Dumont 1970 insists, the provision of food is also an expression of the largesse of the powerful, and being fed a sign of subordination, as Marriott's villagers insist (Marriott 1968a: 143). Similarly, defiling services (the collection of soiled eating leaves, the removal of faeces), while clearly polluting by the same metaphysics, are also part of a broader spectrum of services that 'contribute to the refinement, aristocracy, good fortune and commanding appearance of the employer' (Marriott 1968a: 144). Further, Beck argues that different particular media of interaction may establish rankings on quite different scales: some to do with 'master–servant relations', some to do with 'dietary and ritual ideals' (Beck 1972: 162).

As Marriott notes (1968a: 142), 'the logic for deriving rank from service is the exact inverse of the logic for deriving rank from food transfers'. The rules are these:

For the provision of services

(1′) If A provides services to B, and B does not reciprocate, then A is *lower than* B. Diagrammatically:

B
↑
A

(2′) If A provides for B, and B provides for A, then A is equal to B. Diagrammatically:

A ⟷ B

(3′) If A provides for B, and B provides for C, and neither B nor C reciprocates, then A is lower than C. Diagrammatically:

C
↑
B
↑
A

In short, the relation *lower than* is transitive.

(4′) If A provides asymmetrically for C, but B does not provide services for C, then A is lower than B; if A provides asymmetrically for C, and A and C for D, but B only provides for D, then A is lower than B. Schematically:

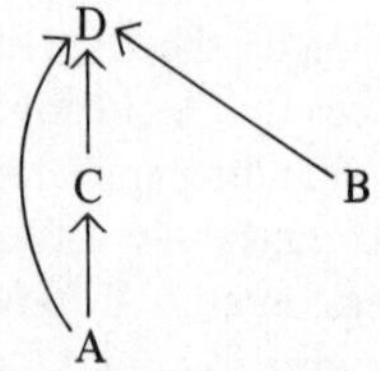

The relation *lower than* is thus arithmetically scored: A serves 2, B only serves 1, therefore A is lower than B. Further justifications for this will be given below.

(5′) The relation 'lower than' is asymmetric.

Now let us turn to linguistic media, and in particular the giving and receiving of honorifics. Brown and Gilman (1960) suggested that the 'semantics', that is the social valuation, of the European T/V system should be interpreted in relation to two dimensions: 'power' and 'solidarity' or as we prefer, vertical and horizontal social distance. A symmetrical exchange of T marked solidary relations, a symmetrical exchange of V marked relations of social distance. An asymmetrical use of T indicated that the speaker was higher than the addressee, while an asymmetrical use of V indicated that the speaker was lower than the addressee. Or schematically:

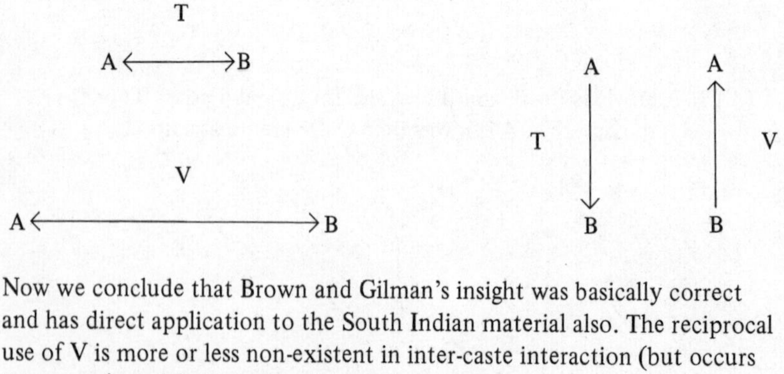

Now we conclude that Brown and Gilman's insight was basically correct and has direct application to the South Indian material also. The reciprocal use of V is more or less non-existent in inter-caste interaction (but occurs intra-caste), and further complications are introduced by the fact that there are more pronominal options in village Tamil than the European systems, at least as standardly described (but see Laberge 1976). Nevertheless the valuation seems essentially correct. A special note is required for relative age T/V. This is the pattern where the senior in years give T and receives V, a pattern that conforms to shastric familial ideals. Where this usage occurs *symmetrically* across castes, this then implies that caste is neutralized, is of less importance than relative age in determining the norms of interaction. It thereby implies a status equality, or near equality, in caste rank. It also connotes a sort of pseudo-familial inclusion, and it is worth noting that many of the castes who symmetrically use this pattern of pronominal usage also exchange kin terms ('fictitious' of course). Another way of looking at the symmetrical exchange of REL is that it is really a symmetrical exchange over a time dimension or from a group point of view, as Figure 6 illustrates. Nevertheless REL also occurs *asymmetrically*, from one group to another without reciprocation. The observable patterns in our data are reciprocations with categorical T or V. In these cases it still seems that the valuation of REL, with its inherent implications of the neutralization of caste in favour of age distinctions, must be *claims* (apparently not reciprocally felt) to some measure of equal caste status.

Now the remarkable but obvious fact is that the valuation of T-giving exactly parallels the valuation of food transfers, while the valuation of V-giving exactly parallels the valuation of service provision. Reciprocal exchange in both the material and linguistic media implies equality. In the media of food and T-usage, asymmetrical exchange implies that the giver is higher than the receiver. In the media of service provision and V-usage the reverse valuation holds. The parallelism between T and food, and V and services is thus precise (Levinson 1977: 240–1).

But this raises some fundamentally interesting equations. Let us begin by asking what there is that is similar in food transfer and the giving of T. One possible line of explanation may go like this. Food – especially in an Indian context – is intimate stuff: the most intimate, closed unit in village society is the *kuṭumpam*, the household as defined by the sharing of a common hearth. More than one *kuṭumpam* may live under the same roof and share the same sources of production – but unless they share the same food cooked at the same hearth, co-residents belong to different *kuṭumpams* (Beck 1972: Ch. 5). If food sharing is intimate behaviour, so is reciprocal T-exchange: this is the universal (pan-caste) language of mother–child relations, indeed of familial relations in general in non-hierarchized families. Mutual T-exchange is also the language of intimate

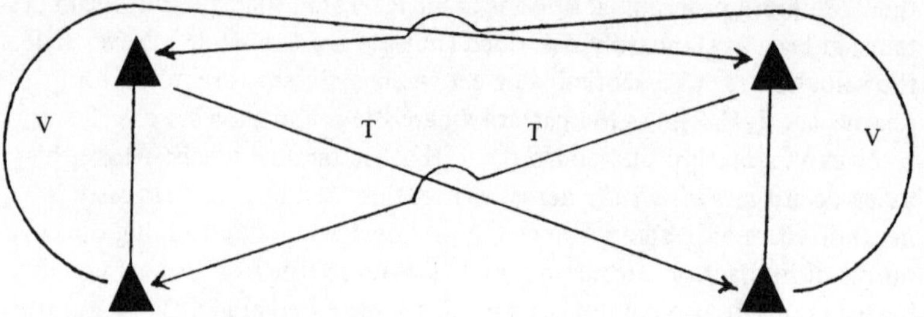

Figure 6. Symmetrical REL-exchange

friends (but not the language of spouses). In short, wherever we find islands of intimacy, where rank does not intrude from the highly hierarchized orders that structure most transactions in this society, we find mutual T-exchange.

Now if we take the valuation on the horizontal social dimension as basic, we can put our question this way: why should giving asymmetrical intimacy be an expression of superiority? And why should the giving of asymmetric distance (V – and possibly services too) be an expression of inferiority? The answer lies, I believe, in certain very general principles of social interaction: persons who are deemed to have high social rank have the right of access to the personal lives of social inferiors who relate to them, but the inferiors do not have the reciprocal right of access to the lives of their superiors. This seems to be a universal principle (see Brown and Levinson 1978, where an account is given in terms of the notion of 'face').

We have stressed the parallels between food transfer and T-giving, service provision and V-giving, because they hold out encouragement for some general theory of transactions that would encompass material and communicative transfers. However there are inherent differences between linguistic and material media that cannot be ignored. Perhaps the most important of these are the following:

(i) Material exchanges (e.g. food transfers) require two independent acts by different parties in order for a transfer to take place: an act of giving and an act of receiving; linguistic exchanges on the other hand can be delivered without the acquiescence of the other party. Thus a transfer of cooked rice at a feast requires that one party presents the rice, and the other takes and consumes it, while if one party addresses another with a T pronoun, the other party – unless it feigns hard-of-hearing – can hardly avoid having received it. Of course these differences inhere not so much in the media themselves as in the rules that guide their usage. Thus there are cases reported from Melanesia where food transfers occur against the will of the recipient, and the food is simply dumped on his threshold (as reported for example by Malinowski); and on the other hand hearing what is spoken to you is not so much automatic as the product of powerful norms of attention (see Sacks, Schegloff and Jefferson 1974; and Reisman 1974, for a case where such norms are claimed to be partially non-operative). Nevertheless given these cultural ground rules, if that is what they are, we can see that food transfers involve a larger measure of consensus by both parties to the transaction than a particular pattern of T- or V-giving.

(ii) One area of difference between the particular linguistic and food and service media here considered is that, whereas asymmetric food and service transfers, like T- and V-giving, empirically never flow in the same direction because of their inconsistent valuations, symmetric food transfers can co-occur with symmetric service provision. Thus every household of a caste will theoretically be willing to dine with every other household of the caste, and also to remove the eating leaves of every other member-household (as indicated by the self-reciprocal cells in Figures 4.8 and 4.10 in Beck 1972). Note, however, that symmetric food and service transfer obtains not between individuals but between households (*kuṭumpams*) within a caste. For no man will eat with a woman, nor will a man clean away the eating leaves of women: men rank higher than women and the asymmetric rules for such transactions operate within the household also. Similarly it is the most junior competent woman who will clear away the eating leaves, and eat last. But in that case, taking the same unit, symmetric T- *and* V-giving can be seen to co-occur. If we sum the overall transfers of T and V between particular members of each household, equal numbers of each kind of T- and V-transfer will be seen to flow between households (or at least households of the same demographic make-up). We can probably conclude, therefore, that this difference between the media is more apparent than real.

We now have in hand a *valuation* for T- and V-givings. It is important for the argument that follows that this valuation is seen to be at least potentially arrived at by a method independent from the observation of inter-caste behaviour, otherwise the inferences made below would be circular. But we can in fact produce independent empirical or theoretical sources for these rules and valuations:

(i) It is possible to give an account, on the basis of a theory of strategic language use oriented around face-preservation (as in Brown and Levinson 1978), of why plural pronouns will be used to express deference to singular addressees. The same theory predicts that reciprocal use of such plural second person pronouns would indicate social distance on a horizontal dimension; and that asymmetrical and symmetrical usages of T would have the values they do.

(ii) Similarly on the basis of Brown and Gilman's theory one would expect the same valuation, and that theory intuitively extends to the Tamil data.

(iii) The valuation may be independently checked against data from another domain: intra-caste behaviour. Here we find that the same rules apply, although the rank thereby established has to do with hierarchical relations between kin (seniors, affines, cross-kin) rather than between castes.

(iv) The rules have an independent existence in informants' minds, and can be elicited from them. Similarly, on the basis of participant-observation the ethnographer intuitively built up the same rules, which were accessible to introspection.

The arguments that follow then can, I believe, be made on solidly independent grounds. One point that should be borne in mind is that these valuations are *inherently* interactional. If A says T to B, then the valuation of T depends crucially on what B says back to A.

2.4. Scaling as a members' activity

Many of those who have used scaled matrices in the study of caste seem to have been interested in the question 'is there any *objective* method for determining caste ranks?' (Hiebert 1969: 434, see also Freed 1963). But for us the question is 'is there any *subjective* method, used by members to determine their rank vis-à-vis others?' Scaling may not seem a likely subjective method, but in fact it only represents a determination of ranking on the basis of a simple set of numerical scores. In order to maintain a potentially subjective viewpoint, we must be careful to observe the following principles. First, the behaviour to be scaled must be accessible to public observation and knowledge. Indeed if it is to be assumed that subjective rank assessments are inter-subjectively available (as appears from behaviour we shall later call 'retaliative'), then all the relevant behavioural outcomes must be mutually known (in the sense of Schiffer 1972: 30–5). Second, the valuation of the atomic behaviour types must be shown to be subscribed to by members on independent grounds, i.e., the valuation must be subjective. Moreover the subjective valuation must be consonant with the preconditions for meaningful scaling: in short it must be phrased – intuitively for members – in terms of some asymmetric transitive relation (in the sense employed in finite mathematics). We must now establish that each of these conditions is met. We will take them in order.

(i) *Public knowledge of the behavioural outcomes.* One problem with the 'attributional' theory of caste ranking (Marriott 1959; Stevenson 1954), which stresses caste attributes such as vegetarianism, is that members of society (in this case the village) do not have a detailed knowledge of these attributes and their distribution. For instance the Village Accountant, a reasonably intelligent man with administrative responsibilities, did not know that the two distinct castes of Ācāri (craftsmen: castes 3 and 6) were distinguished by the following culturally important attributes: members of 3 are *caiva*, that is vegetarian, while members of 6 are *acaiva*, non-vegetarian. And this despite the fact that the Accountant belonged to caste 2, a left-hand vegetarian caste like 3. Castes 3, 2, 4 and 1 were the only vegetarian castes in the village. Admittedly most persons of these castes did know this, but such knowledge of attributes does not seem to be a *sine qua non* for understanding and operating in village society. Only a full survey of the extent of such knowledge of attributes throughout the village would fully establish this point, but I believe that it would put paid to any attributional theory of ranking once and for all, assuming the aim of such theories is more than simply to obtain some 'objective', etic, culture-independent assignment of ranks by social scientists.

Compared with the public availability of attributional criteria (which are often private prescriptions of ritual), interactional facts are necessarily public, and matters of daily experience. Potentially, and I believe empirically, every adult member of the village will witness the interaction, at least occasionally, between members drawn from each and every caste. This is especially true for linguistic and kinesic interaction: for even those castes that would by preference avoid each other (e.g. Brahmans and Christian Paraiyars) are drawn together by mutual duties of a ritual, official or commercial kind. For instance, Brahman children are taught by a Paraiyar teacher, and at temple festivals Paraiyars still do their traditional service as musicians – and of course all such arrangements involve talk of one kind or another.

(ii) *Members' knowledge of the valuation of patterns of T/V giving and receiving.* One of the independent bases for this valuation is that it may be directly elicited from members, and another is that it operates in another arena, namely intra-caste behaviour. Of behaviour in that arena members say:

> 'We give *māmā* (MB category) *matippu* (respect): we say "*vāṅka māmā*" (come-V MB). But he says "*vāppā, pōppā*" (come-T + dishonorific, go-T + dishonorific) because we are just young people.'

For them V-giving maps the direction of respect, T-giving maps the direction of disrespect. Similarly:

> 'One thing is important: to *māmiyār* and *māmanār* (parents-in-law) respect must be given. It is better for the groom to say nothing: but if he must speak then he must say "*vāṅka māmanār*" (come-V father-in-law). But *māmanār* must also say "*vāṅka, vāṅka*" to the groom. They must give each other respect.'

Thus, for members, reciprocal V-exchange establishes mutual respect. In the same way mutual T-giving establishes or expresses intimacy, or close friendship:

> 'They are good friends, nothing will part them. When they see each other they say "*vāṭā, pōṭā*" (come-T + dishonorific, go-T + dishonorific). A pair of rascals mind you!'

As for the asymmetric transitivity in rules (3) and (3′), what evidence is there that members make inferences based on the assumption that such a relation obtains? First and foremost is the fact that informants found it hilarious that the ethnographer did not find it obvious that T/V usage was based on such a relation, as instanced by an episode in which the ethnographer's question (whether, if caste 9 gives T to 11, and 11 gives T to 16, then does caste 9 give T to caste 16) was greeted with laughter. Everyone knows that 11 gives T to 16, so there is a chain of T-givings from 9 to 11 and 11 to 16, and *on the assumption of transitivity*, 9 must therefore give T to 16. What if 9 gave V to 16? The grave answer was cosmological chaos: it simply couldn't happen.

It is clear that the asymmetric transitive relation that underlies T/V usage is 'socially higher (more respected) than', and/or 'socially lower (less respected) than'. Further evidence for the strict asymmetry and transitivity of the underlying relation is provided by the fact that honorifics and dishonorifics can themselves be scaled by members. For instance the implicational scales shown in Figure 7 were elicited, and correspond to all the facts that were collected. That is, forms to the left imply the possibility of the usage of all forms to the right, to the same addressee. Thus if A uses *cāmi* to B, then A may on occasion use *nām*, *ṅka*, V and will never use B's name to B. (Further details about some of these forms will be presented

Scale of honorifics

$$\left\{\begin{matrix}\text{cāmi}\\ \text{ecamāṅka}\end{matrix}\right\} > \text{nām} > \left\{\begin{matrix}\text{ṅka}\\ \text{ayyā}\end{matrix}\right\} > \text{categorical V} > \text{name-taboo}$$

Scale of dishonorifics

$$\left\{\begin{matrix}\text{li**}\\ \text{ṭi**}\end{matrix}\right\} > \left\{\begin{matrix}\text{ṭā*}\\ \text{ṭē}\end{matrix}\right\} > \text{use of name} > \left\{\begin{matrix}\text{-ppā}\\ \text{-mmā}\end{matrix}\right\} > \text{categorical T}$$

**used only to women, but ruder than forms restricted to men
*form used only to men

Figure 7. Scaled usage implications of verbal status markers

later.) But one cannot infer from the fact that A uses V to B that A may on occasion use *cāmi* to B; i.e., one cannot make inferences from right to left. This shows that whatever underlies the usage of honorifics is a strictly asymmetric and transitive relation. Similarly for dishonorifics: one can infer from the rudest that the least rude may be used to the same addressee, but not vice-versa.

Let us now turn to rules (4) and (4′) of the valuation, which assert that there is an arithmetic computation of rank: the more numbers of positively valued receipts (V's) and the less numbers of negatively valued receipts (T's) the higher the rank of the receiver (again treating castes as the units of giving and receiving). Informants spoke this way too: 'We Washermen, Barbers and all say "*vāṅka*" to the Brahmans: everybody does. They are the highest caste compared to all.' They also spoke in terms of rank estimates by least giving of valued outgoings (V): 'We Cōḻi Ācāri do not have to say *nīṅka* (V) to Brahmans: I for instance say "*vāyyār*" (come-T Brahman) to the *Kurukkaḷ* (Brahman priest). But the Koṅku Ācāri they have to say "*vāṅkayyār*" (come-V Brahman). Cōḻi Ācāri are a high caste.'

In a way the point of arithmetic scoring is that it takes into account not only the rank relations established by asymmetric exchanges, and thus the inferring of the asymmetric transitive relation of rank, but also the notable absence of such exchanges between particular parties. Rules (1) through (3) simply attach no valuation to the non-occurrence of some particular exchange: no rank is thus established, nothing is said. But for villagers this is patently not the case: if caste 7b does not give V to caste 2, and neither does 3, 4, 5, 6, and 7a, then clearly castes 3 through 7b do not think 2 worthy of categorical V. (That this is confirmed by the alternative employed does not diminish the validity of this mode of thinking in terms of negative occurrences of V.) So members keep tabs on such non-occurrences: for instance a member of 9 pointed out that there is a big difference between members of 10 and 11, for 11 gives V to all the 'upper castes', while 10 gives V to only the top three. So 11 admits to more relations of social asymmetry, and this directly implies that it is lower in rank. Since this judgement can only be made on the basis of counting occurrences versus non-occurrences of the behaviour in question it does imply that arithmetic computation is involved. It may not take the fully specified form that our computations here will take, but it seems that it must follow at least some approximate analogue of these.

2.5. Two media and four scales

Having now established a cultural valuation of particular patterns of pronominal exchange, we wish to know what social inferences (to do with rank) members can make from the overall patterns of pronominal usage accessible to them. We here consider two media: (categorical) T-usage and (categorical) V-usage. These are independent media, for there is a third major option, REL (considered below in 3.1), that precludes the possibility of inferring T-usage from the non-usage of V. Nor, as the results will show, are the inherent patterns established in one medium totally consistent with those established in the other.

Within each medium the rules of valuation establish two potentially independent scales of rank: rank as givers, and rank as receivers. As was explained in 2.2, these scales are also not inter-inferrable. Consequently we shall take each dimension of evaluation one at a time, in the following order:

1. Rank as (most) T-givers
2. Rank as (least) V-givers
3. Rank as (most) V-receivers
4. Rank as (least) T-receivers

In each case we shall construct a *scaled matrix* or scalogram, and from this infer the rank order of castes in that dimension. One point of method does need to be explained. We here effectively ignore reciprocals in our computation of ranks inherent in the data. Our justification for this is twofold:

(a) In the first place, reciprocal usage of a form never *reverses* the valuation that would be established by an asymmetrical usage, rather it can only neutralize the rank implications.

(b) In the second place, considering only the two media T and V, there are almost no cases of symmetrical usage of a medium in inter-caste usage (the single exception is caste 11's exchange of T with 8, 9 and 10), as the reader may check by scanning the basic matrix (VIII).

This treatment is, it is true, an idealization in the following respect. Asymmetrical use of V implies the use of T or REL in return, while asymmetrical use of T implies the use of V or REL in return. In our valuation of asymmetrical T and V we shall ignore the difference between a T or V and a REL return. This is an idealization which we make amends for in section 3. It is not a serious idealization for the following reason: if A gives V to B, and B gives back to A *either* T *or* REL, A is still unambiguously inferior to B; and similarly if A gives T to B, and B gives back to A *either* V *or* REL, then A is either way unambiguously superior to B. Given that virtually no cases of symmetrical exchange in one medium are attested, this ignoring of the exact nature of the reciprocal form used in each dyad will not lead to serious misrepresentations.

So passing straight away to our first dimensions of evaluation, rank as (most) T-givers, we have Matrix II. Here the castes that give most T are those with the longest *columns* in the space labelled T, namely castes 1 through 7b along the top of the matrix. These castes each give T to nine other castes, while castes 11 and 8 both give to eight others, caste 9 to seven others, caste 10 to six others, and so on, till castes 16 and 18 give categorical T to nil others. Let us call the count of T-recipients for each T-giver that T-giver's *positive score.*

All castes with identical positive scores form one undifferentiated bloc as far as each medium is concerned. Thus there are seven blocs, ranked from one to seven by the highest score. Without tabulating scores, exactly the same results emerge visually from the scaled matrix, with the highest ranking (longest) columns shuffled to the left, the horizontal edge of each step indicating rank equals, and vertical edges indicating distinctions of rank receding downwards. The heavy line delineating rank-steps has been compensated for self-reciprocal cells in the T-space (see Levinson 1977: 220–5 for detailed explanation).

For a shorthand, we can represent the rank that emerges from Matrix II as a vertical linear array of castes (labelled by numbers) from top rank at the top, to bottom rank at the bottom, where bars divide the ranked blocs and ordering within bars is arbitrary (as used by Marriott 1968a: 157; Beck 1972): we do this in Figure 8.

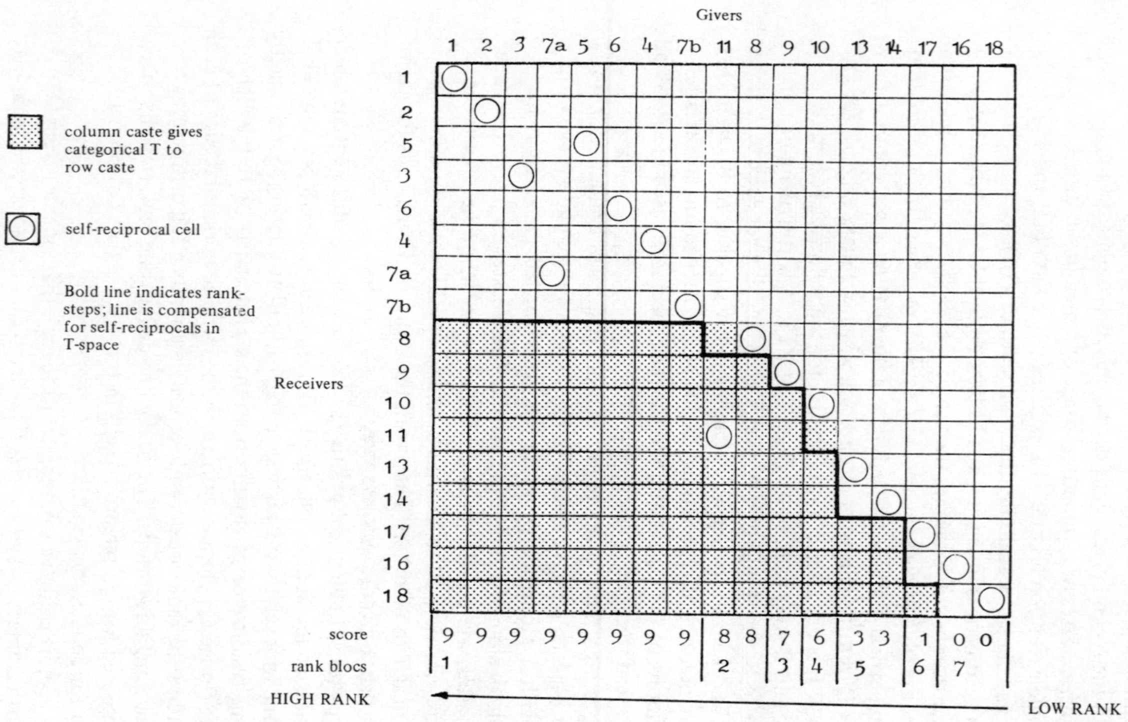

Matrix II. Rank as (most) T-givers

Highest rank		1
		2
		3
	Bloc 1	7a
		5
		6
		4
		7b
	Bloc 2	11
		8
	Bloc 3	9
	Bloc 4	10
		13
	Bloc 5	14
	Bloc 6	17
	Bloc 7	16
		18
Lowest rank		

Figure 8. Rank by T-giving

It is clear from Figure 8 that maximal T-giving does not distinguish among what we have called the upper castes (1 through 7b) at all, while it distinguishes six levels of rank among the lower castes (8 through 18). We may judge from this that success in maximal T-giving is of much more importance to individual castes of the lower category. We shall need some explanation of this.

Let us now turn to the second dimension of evaluation: rank as (least) V-givers. The scores for V-giving are negative: the more recipients of V a caste has the less its rank on this dimension.

The facts are as in Matrix III. Here all self-reciprocal cells lie outside the V area, so there are no compensations required to preserve geometrical perspicuity. Castes 1, 2, 3, 7a form the top rank-bloc with no (categorical) V-givings at all. Their score is zero (maximum on this dimension). There follows Bloc 2 composed of 5, 6, 4 and 7b, who give categorical V to Brahmans (caste 1) and thereby lower their rank by a score of 1 (hence they score –1). Then comes Bloc 3 (castes 8, 9, 10) who give categorical V to 1, 2 and 5 (hence they score –3). And so on till Bloc 6 (17, 16, 18), members of which give V to no less than fourteen castes (hence a score of

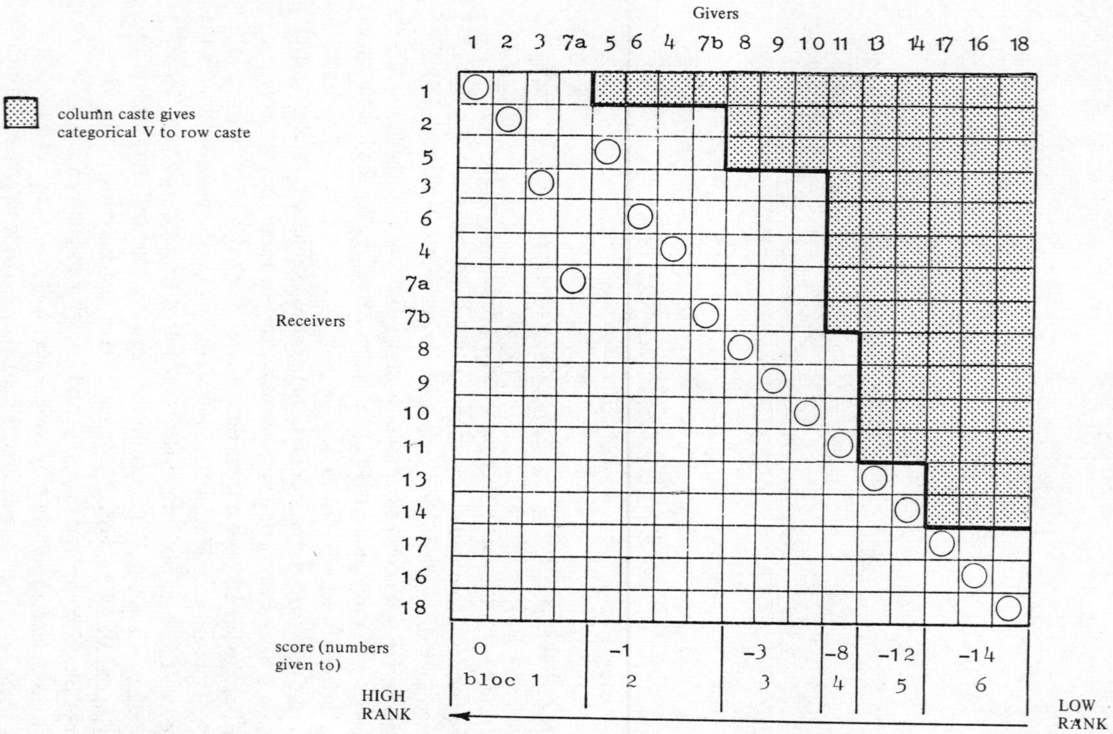

Matrix III. Rank as (least) V-givers

Highest rank		1
		2
	Bloc 1	3
		7a
		5
	Bloc 2	6
		4
		7b
		8
	Bloc 3	9
		10
	Bloc 4	11
	Bloc 5	13
		14
		17
	Bloc 6	16
		18
Lowest rank		

Figure 9. Rank by V-giving

–14). Once again we can easily extract a linear representation of rank, as in Figure 9.

Here we see that minimal V-giving makes one important cut in the array of upper castes, distinguishing Bloc 1 from 2. We may merely note here that its significance depends crucially on the usage that castes 2, 3 and 7a substitute for the V that Bloc 2 members give to Brahmans. Since that usage did not appear on Matrix II, nor on III, by exclusion we know that it must be REL, and we shall answer this question when we come to deal with REL (section 3.1). Note that again the lower castes (8 through 18) are finely distinguished into four grades of V-givers.

Now let us turn to the *receiving* dimensions. Here we have two, V-receiving, positively valued, and T-receiving, negatively valued. The facts are as in the scaled matrices, Matrix IV and V. Now, however, we are interested only in the receiving dimension, and thus in the *rows*, and their top-to-bottom scaling.

Turning to Matrix IV we see that Bloc 1, the topmost rank, has only one member caste, the Brahmans, and that Brahmans rank highest as receivers with a score of 13 categorical V-receipts from thirteen other

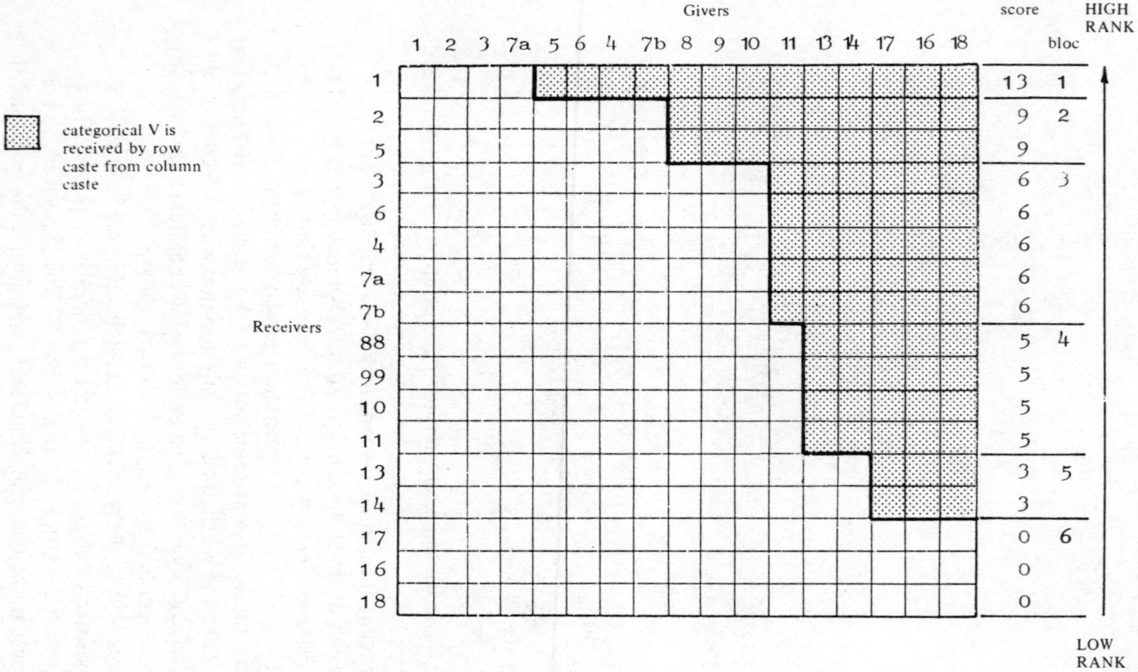

Matrix IV. Rank as (most) V-receivers

Highest rank	Bloc 1	1
	Bloc 2	2
		5
		3
		6
	Bloc 3	4
		7a
		7b
		8
	Bloc 4	9
		10
		11
	Bloc 5	13
		14
		17
	Bloc 6	16
		18
Lowest rank		

Figure 10. Rank by V-receiving

castes. Next comes Bloc 2, composed of castes 2 and 5, each with nine V-receipts; then Bloc 3, composed of castes 3 through 7b except 5, with equal scores of six receipts – and so on. The linear rank order thus established is then as in Figure 10.

Note that V-receiving cuts the upper castes into as many blocs as the lower castes. This is important: upper castes do not seem to attempt to distinguish between themselves very finely on giving dimensions, but somewhat finer distinctions emerge in their treatment by others. Also noteworthy is the position of caste 5, the dominant caste, on this dimension: it here ranks second only to the Brahman caste, sharing this rank with caste 2.

We come finally to T-receiving, a disvalued medium where scores will be negative. Matrix V repeats the facts in Matrix II, but now we are interested in the rows, scaled from top to bottom. We see that, when compensation is made for the internal self-reciprocal cell 11/11 as done in Matrix II, there are seven ranks. Bloc 1, composed of row-castes 1 through 7b, has a score of zero. But Bloc 2 (caste 8 alone) acquires immediately, and dramatically, a score of –9, while Bloc 3 has –10, Bloc 4 has –11, Bloc 5 has –12, Bloc

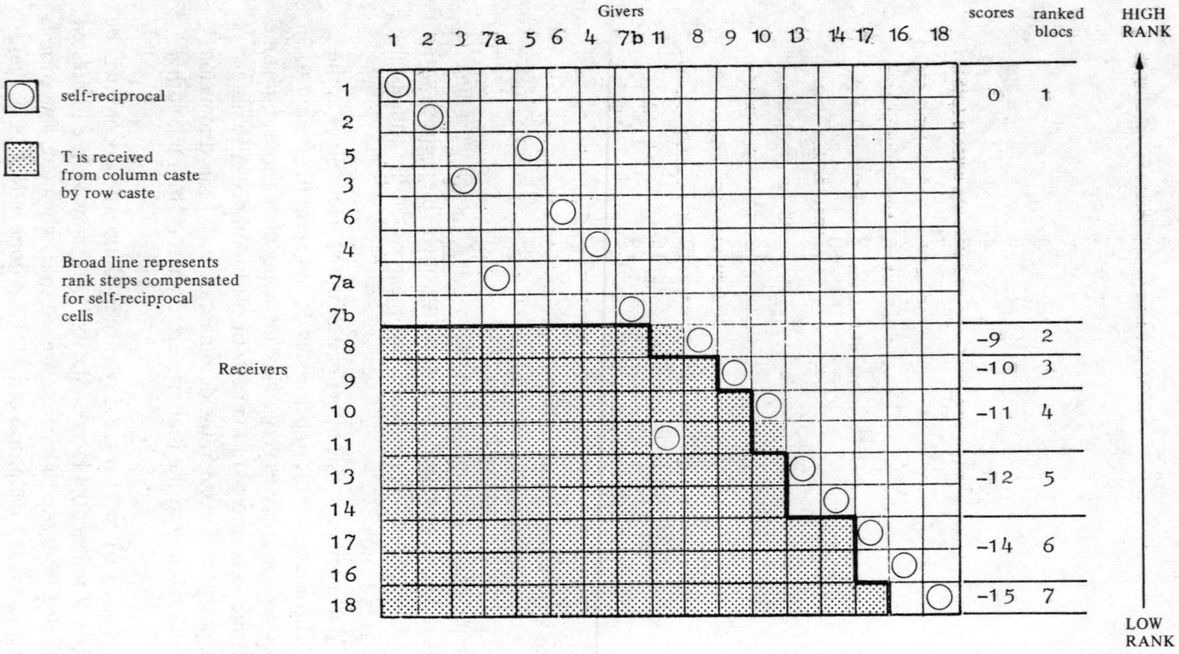

Matrix V. Rank as (least) T-receivers

Highest rank		1
		2
		5
		3
	Bloc 1	6
		4
		7a
		7b
	Bloc 2	8
	Bloc 3	9
	Bloc 4	10
		11
	Bloc 5	13
		14
	Bloc 6	17
		16
	Bloc 7	18
Lowest rank		

Figure 11. Rank by T-receiving

6 has –14, and Bloc 7 has –15. In terms of our linear representation, we have the situation in Figure 11.

The pattern here is very similar to that derived from Matrix II: in both, the upper castes are given a single rank, and the lower castes divided into six ranks. However, as we shall see, the rank order of castes on these two dimensions, giving and receiving, is not exactly the same. The dimensions make slightly different cuts in the linear ordering of castes, and one caste (11) has very different ranks in the two media. This will call for explanation.

Let us now compare the rank orders that we have obtained so far. We can do this easily by comparing the linear representations of rank, which are brought together in Figure 12. Here we compare the ranks established within the two dimensions of giving and receiving. Diagonal linking lines point to rank reversals. We can see immediately that there is only one such reversal, the relatively high rank that caste 11 has as a T-giver, is lost in the V-giving sweepstakes; that is to say that, whereas 11 manages to give a lot of T, it is not able to minimize its V-outlays. But apart from caste 11's reversals, we can see that *within* the dimensions of giving and receiving,

Rank as givers		*Rank as receivers*	
T-giving	V-giving	V-receiving	T-receiving
1	1	1	1
2	2	2	2
3	3	5	5
7a	7a	3	3
5	5	6	6
6	6	4	4
4	4	7a	7a
7b	7b	7b	7b
11	8	8	8
8	9	9	9
9	10	10	10
10	11	11	11
13	13	13	13
14	14	14	14
17	17	17	17
16	16	16	16
18	18	18	18

Figure 12. Rank on two dimensions compared

ranks established are absolutely compatible and consistent. That does not mean that ranks on V- and T-giving and receiving redundantly express the same hierarchical distinctions: for the ranks established in the two media (T or V) cut the hierarchy of castes at different locations. Thus V-giving makes five cuts establishing six rank-blocs, to which T-giving adds two differently located cuts, establishing eight rank-blocs *in toto*. Similarly V-receiving cuts the hierarchy five times, distinguishing six blocs, to which T-receiving adds three different distinctions, establishing *in toto* nine rank-blocs on the receiving dimensions. For a set of local castes only seventeen in number these are very fine distinctions of rank.

If we now turn to compare ranks *across* the dimensions of giving and receiving, far more intransitivities and inconsistencies appear. Figure 13 reassembles the linear representations of rank to make this visually apparent. Comparing first T-giving and T-receiving, we find that caste 11 slips from a position at the top of the lower castes by T-giving, to a position in the third rank down from the upper caste/lower caste boundary as judged by T-receiving. Comparing V-giving and V-receiving, a further case of rank reversal emerges, with 3 and 7a above 5 in V-giving, but 5 above 3 and 7a in V-receiving. We must seek explanations for these reversals: why is there this disjunction between ranks established as givers and those estab-

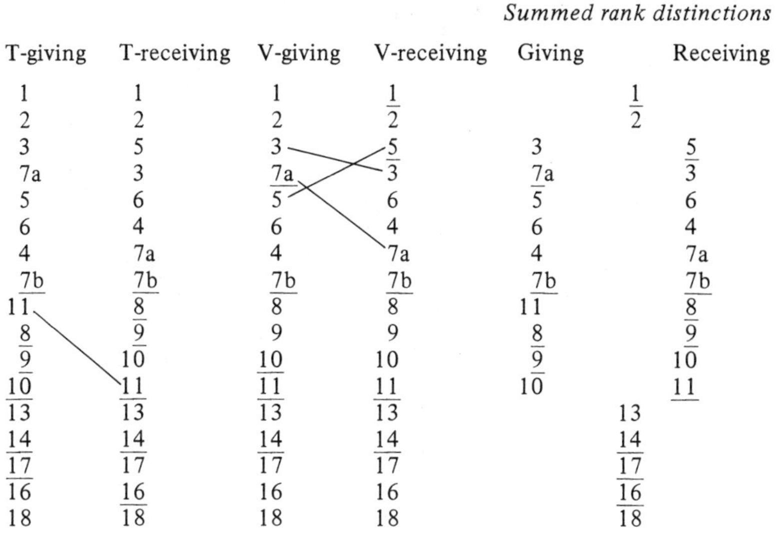
Summed rank distinctions
T-giving
1 2 3 7a 5 6 4 7b 11 8 9 10 13 14 17 16 18
T-receiving
1 2 5 3 6 4 7a 7b 8 9 10 11 13 14 17 16 18
V-giving
1 2 3 7a 5 6 4 7b 8 9 10 11 13 14 17 16 18
V-receiving
1 2 5 3 6 4 7a 7b 8 9 10 11 13 14 17 16 18
Giving
Receiving
1 2
3 7a 5 6 4 7b 11 8 9 10
5 3 6 4 7a 7b 8 9 10 11
13 14 17 16 18

Figure 13. Giving and receiving compared

lished as receivers? This is a question that will occupy us for a number of pages below. But before we turn to the analysis of these materials let us complete the harvest, and look at one of the media in more detail, and some others in addition.

If we take V-giving and examine it in detail, we soon find that we have been oversimplifying. Categorical V-giving as we have treated it so far, is not in fact V-giving *absolutely* irrespective of the age of the addressee. Some high caste children are in fact addressed as T by some categories of lower caste adults. Note that this is not a matter of *relative* age between speaker and addressee: it is strictly a question of the addressee's absolute age in years. When a certain age threshold is reached, T-address ceases, and V begins; the speaker may still be 50 years or more older than the addressee. What then is interesting is at what age addressees of certain castes pass the threshold into V-giving for speakers of different castes. And this turns out to be a systematic variable dependent on the caste of speaker and addressee.

After a good deal of eliciting, six basic thresholds were isolated. These were:

(i) 0-V: A gives V to B if B is 0 age (i.e., from birth)
(ii) 5-V: A gives V to B if B is 5 years old and over

(iii) 15-V: A gives V to B if B is 15 and over
(iv) 25-V: A gives V to B if B is 25 or over
(v) P-V: A gives V to B (where B is a Brahman), only if B has been initiated into the priesthood (anywhere from age 12 to 25)
(vi) M-V: A gives V to B if B is married

Now P-V and M-V are clearly social age-grades while the other thresholds are phrased in terms of absolute age, regardless of social grade. This distinction may well be artificial, that is, it could be that in all cases what is really involved is some measure of social maturity of which age is a cardinal determinant. This is further suggested by the fact that there was some variation from informant to informant, so that while one member of a caste, in response to the question 'when do you begin to call a boy of caste X *nīṅka*?' would respond with 'at the age of five', another might reply 'at the age of seven'. In all cases, though, the relationship between the different categories of addressees remained constant, and so did the number of distinctions. It may well be (I think it likely) that 5-V really corresponds to the social age-grade of *viḷaiyāṭappiḷḷai* (literally 'playing child', that is a dependent child), 15-V with puberty, 25-V with manhood (the period after which a male can no longer be called a *paiyan*, boy). This last social threshold is associated with marriage (although the threshold would be passed by a bachelor after about 30 in any case), and would clearly be different for girls who marry many years earlier than boys: unfortunately all my questions about these thresholds were phrased only in terms of male addressees, and I do not know how they extend to female addressees. However, it should be stressed that my informants did not speak in terms of social grades, except in the cases of P-V and M-V, but rather spoke consistently in terms of actual age, and it should also be remembered that actual age is definitely utilized in our third T/V medium REL and cannot be ruled out here. Consequently we shall continue to use the idiom that informants do.

How are we to treat these six thresholds? As defining six distinct media? Or as a single medium with a sliding valuation? This second must be the correct treatment, for to treat each threshold-V separately would be to ignore the transitive patterning between them. If we turn to Matrix VI we see that these different thresholds are extremely systematically distributed. The basic pattern is that the lower the caste of the giver, not only the more V is used in general, but also the lower age thresholds for V-use become. And this corresponds with the intuition that derives from the valuation of V: since to give V is to admit inferiority of caste rank by giving V to all members of another caste, to withhold V till the addressee

M — column caste gives V to row if latter is married

P — column caste gives V to row if latter is a priest

O — column caste gives V to row from latter's birth (zero years)

5 — column caste gives V to row from 5 years old

15 — column caste gives V to row from 15 years old

25 — column caste gives V to row from 25 years old

Givers (columns) / Receivers (rows)

Receivers \ Givers	1	2	3	7a	5	6	4	7b	8	9	10	11	13	14	17	16	18
1					M	M	M	P	5	5	5	O	O	O	O	O	O
2									5	5	5	5	O	O	O	O	O
5									5	5	5	5	O	O	O	O	O
3												25	15	O	O	O	O
6												25	15	O	O	O	O
4												25	15	O	O	O	O
7a												25	15	O	O	O	O
7b												25	15	O	O	O	O
8													15	15	O	O	O
9													15	15	O	O	O
10													15	15	O	O	O
11													15	15	O	O	O
13															O	O	O
14															O	O	O
17																	
16																	
18																	

Matrix VI. Thresholds for V-giving

is 5, 15 or 25 is to progressively diminish the respect in which the other caste is held. Conversely, the more unconditional the use of V (culminating in 0-V), the more respect is given.

On these grounds, then, it seems plausible that, in the eyes of members, the lower the age threshold at which caste A begins to V members of B, the higher the rank of B. We can then rank the values of the six kinds of V-giving, in the order already presented from (i) to (vi). We place P-V after 25-V because this social threshold can be achieved as late as 25, but in addition need never be achieved at all (although in the great majority of cases it is). Similarly M-V is a social threshold that can occur well after the age of 25: indeed males often seem to marry in the years immediately after that (cf. Beck 1972: 230). We place M-V after P-V because in general for Brahmans, marriage would occur after the passage into priesthood: it thus seems to represent a lower threshold. Let us assign decreasing unit-scores as values for each of these ranked types of V:

0-V	6 units
5-V	5 units
15-V	4 units
25-V	3 units
P-V	2 units
M-V	1 unit

In this way we can reflect the fact that receiving 0-V is more highly valued than receiving 5-V, 5-V than 15-V, and so on. What we have done, in fact, is discover that there are *degrees* of categorical V from absolute (0-V) to adults-only (25-V), and beyond to social maturity (M-V). It might be that a yet finer-grained analysis would break down our six types of V still further, suggesting an ordered continuum of V-types matching an underlying continuum of rank. However, if these six types are all anchored in fact to social age-grades, as I suspect, then there will in fact be a small set of distinct types.

It is worth mentioning here that my attempts to break down T-giving in a similar way were unsuccessful: informants were on the whole insistent that if one gave seniors of another caste T then one gave even very much older persons of that caste T too. There were just some exceptions to this on the upper caste/lower caste borderline. Thus, not all members of caste 7b received strict REL from members of 5; those members of 7b who were poor and uninfluential might receive T from junior members of 5 until these members of 7b reached the dignified age of 60 or so. Here, then, is a cell that is claimed to be in general REL in the initial matrix, but on closer examination seems to be REL for the upper *class* member of 7b only, and under-sixty-T for lower class members of 7b. We shall treat this phenomenon as a reclassification of REL in relation to the personal achieved attributes of members of 7b (here negative attributes: dependence, sloth, etc.) but we admit that this obscures some similarity between varying thresholds for T-usage and varying thresholds for V-usage.

To return to the analysis, Matrix VII assigns scores to each cell in the area of each distinct type of V-usage, on the basis of the ranked unit-scores above. A caste's score as a receiver is here a sum of the unit-scores for each cell in its row, while a caste's score as a giver is the sum of the unit-scores for each cell in its column. So, for instance, caste 1 (Brahman) has a receiving score of

$$(1 \times 3) + (2 \times 1) + (5 \times 3) + (6 \times 6) = +56$$

and a giving score of zero.

From the summed scores we may extract the linear representations of rank for giving and receiving as in Figure 14, below.

Note that the rank orders established in Figure 14 on the two dimensions of giving and receiving are not consistent with each other. On the other hand each is completely consistent with the rank order already established on its own dimension (giving or receiving), as we shall see in a moment. Note too that visually from the matrices one may observe that the diminishing thresholds are entirely consistent with the rank established on the basis of the first gross (unbroken-down) analysis of V.

Let us now gather together all the evidence on caste ranking that has been collected here. Figure 15 provides a simple visual array of the data. We can see that threshold-V distinctions add two differently located cuts on the giving dimension, but none on the receiving. Since within each dimension ranks established are overwhelmingly consistent, we may add the distinctions together to achieve an overall ranking that slices the caste hierarchy finely into eleven blocs of rank-status on the summed giving dimensions, and nine blocs on the summed receiving dimensions.

We may note in passing that such a fine discrimination of ranks within the caste hierarchy in Ōlappāḷaiyam is not achieved by the analysis of food transactions. For instance, curd giving chops the hierarchy into nine blocs, summing the distinctions in curd and rice giving achieves no further discriminations, while ranks as receivers of curd and rice together only sum to eight distinctions (Beck 1972: Figures 4.8 and 4.9). It may be noted that the maximum number of discriminations in any one transactional medium (excluding therefore ranks by opinion poll) reported from Indian materials seems to be nine, a figure reached by Marriott's *pakka* food transactions (Marriott 1968a), and Beck's curd transactions (Beck 1972).

1 — M-V, assigned unit score 1 per cell

2 — P-V, assigned unit score 2 per cell

3 — 25-V, assigned unit score 3 per cell

4 — 15-V, assigned unit score 4 per cell

5 — 5-V, assigned unit score 5 per cell

6 — 0-V, assigned unit score 6 per cell

Receivers \ Givers	1	2	3	7a	5	6	4	7b	8	9	10	11	13	14	17	16	18	positive receiving scores
1					1	1	1	2	5	5	5	6	6	6	6	6	6	56
2									5	5	5	5	6	6	6	6	6	50
5									5	5	5	5	6	6	6	6	6	50
3												3	4	6	6	6	6	31
6												3	4	6	6	6	6	31
4												3	4	6	6	6	6	31
7a												3	4	6	6	6	6	31
7b												3	4	6	6	6	6	31
8													4	4	6	6	6	26
9													4	4	6	6	6	26
10													4	4	6	6	6	26
11													4	4	6	6	6	26
13															6	6	6	18
14															6	6	6	18
17																		0
16																		0
18																		0
negative giving scores	0	0	0	0	-1	-1	-1	-2	-15	-15	-15	-31	-54	-64	-84	-84	-84	

Matrix VII. Scored thresholds for V-giving

Rank as receivers			*Rank as givers*	
caste	score	highest rank	caste	score
1	+56		1	0
			2	0
—				
			3	0
2	+50		7a	0
5	+50		—	
—			5	−1
3	+31		6	−1
6	+31		4	−1
4	+31			
			—	
7a	+31			
7b	+31		7b	−2
—			—	
8	+26		8	−15
9	+26		9	−15
10	+26		10	−15
11	+26		—	
—			11	−31
13	+18			
			—	
14	+18			
—			13	−54
17	0		—	
16	0		14	−64
18	0	lowest rank	—	
			17	−84
			16	−84
			18	−86

Figure 14. Ranks by thresholds for V-usage

(Marriott, though, sums his food transaction discriminations to reach twelve distinctions among 24 castes.) It appears from this that linguistic media are finer discriminators than any other media. Nevertheless there does seem to be some limit to the number of rank-blocs that are discriminated in any one medium, and it may be that this represents some basic cognitive limit on routine perceptual discriminations along the lines of Miller's 'magical number 7 ± 2' (Miller 1956).

We are now in a position to reassemble all our data on inter-caste T/V usage into a single, largely scaled, matrix. From Figure 15 we know that all the derived rank scales as receivers are consistent and establish an overall hierarchy in the receiving dimension. We also know that all the scales as givers are in agreement, except for the ambiguous position of 11 in the giving dimension. So we can take these two overall ranks as our axes for a

Rank as givers T	V	Threshold-V	*Rank as receivers* T	V	Threshold-V
1	1	1	1	1	1
2	2	2	2	2	2
3	3	3	5	5	5
7a	7a	7a	3	3	3
5	5	5	6	6	6
6	6	6	4	4	4
4	4	4	7a	7a	7a
7b	7b	7b	7b	7b	7b
11	8	8	8	8	8
8	9	9	9	9	9
9	10	10	10	10	10
10	11	11	11	11	11
13	13	13	13	13	13
14	14	14	14	14	14
17	17	17	17	17	17
16	16	16	16	16	16
18	18	18	18	18	18

Summed rank distinctions (*Overall rank as givers*)	Summed rank distinctions (*Overall rank as receivers*)
1	1
2	2
3	5
7a	3
5	6
6	4
4	7a
7b	7b
8(11)	8
9	9
10	10
11	11
13	13
14	14
17	17
16	16
18	18

Figure 15. Summary of derived ranks

combined matrix that will scale perfectly on the two distinct dimensions except for caste 11's transactions. The combined matrix is presented as Matrix VIII, and it encapsulates all our information on inter-caste T/V usage. Note that we know that REL (relative age T/V) must scale appropri-

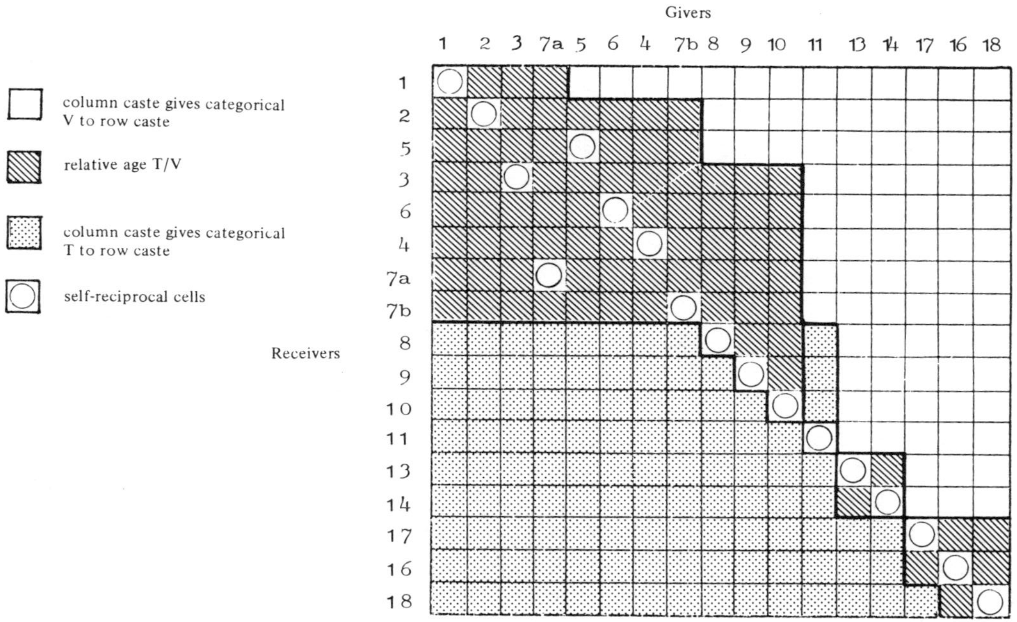

Matrix VIII. The basic matrix

ately because being the residual option it has to fill the geometrical space between T- and V-usage. Simply for readability we will omit the facts about V-threshold variability from this matrix, which we will now designate *the basic matrix*.

We are able to combine all these facts into a single almost-scaled matrix in part because of the two-dimensional matrix format introduced by Marriott (1976a), which utilizes both axes (here giving and receiving dimensions) to establish independent scales. We cannot use Beck's 1972 double-matrix format here, designed to retain geometrical representations of rank, as this requires that allowances be made for self-reciprocal cells in each medium (which would then impinge into the other media represented on the same matrix). In using Marriott's 1976a format we therefore fall back implicitly on a scoring rather than a geometrical method, but in any case the two are inherently linked. Note that now the self-reciprocal cells are somewhat displaced from the diagonal – and following Marriott we shall make some capital of this very displacement.

But the major reason that we are able to combine all these facts into a single almost-scaled matrix is that there is an overwhelming consistency and agreement between the different ranking scales. This need not have been the case: T-giving and V-giving, though mutually exclusive, could have established grossly inconsistent ranking scales, because the existence of the third basic option (REL) ensures that the scales are not inter-inferrable. Not only are the bulk of transactions in all media consistent and/or redundant, but where intransitivities of rank in different scales do occur, they occur together consistently on the giving versus the receiving dimension. And this can be accommodated in our two-dimensional matrix. There is only one set of anomalous facts, namely caste 11's column which will not scale with the rest, to remind us that we are really dealing with potentially independent media. It is caste 11's behaviour that requires that the qualification 'almost-scaled' be used to describe the basic matrix. In an effort to compare the patterning of T-, V-, and REL-exchange with other linguistic media, five commonly encountered Tamil honorifics and dis-honorifics (*ppā*, *ṭā*, *nām*, *cāmi*, and *ecamāṅka*) have also been analysed in similar fashion. Some of these additional media seem to reflect a clear social power dimension, rather than a dimension of ritual status, but the data are too lengthy to summarize here (see Levinson 1977: 293–321).

Let us now summarize our results. We find that no media are totally redundant, but are rather additive of rank discriminations. Taking all media and the scales extracted from them together, we find that there is a very high level of agreement between these independent measures of rank: the details – which constitute our major results – are these:

(i) All rank orders established on the basis of *receiving* are absolutely consistent.

(ii) All rank orders established on the basis of *giving* are consistent – with the exception of the ambiguous position of caste 11.

(iii) *Giving scales are NOT consistent with receiving scales.*

The source of the disagreement between the receiving and giving dimensions is essentially an ambiguity about the relative ranking of castes 3 and 7a vis-à-vis caste 5. For on the giving dimension 3 and 7a rank higher than 5, whereas on the receiving dimension 5 ranks higher than 3 and 7a. In addition in the T-medium, but only there, caste 11's rank as a giver places it in the third rank-bloc above 13, while 11's rank as a receiver places it only one rank-bloc immediately above 13.

2.6. T/V behaviour: passive scoreboard or competitive game?

The patterns that we have collected could reflect one of two things: either they are determined essentially outside this linguistic arena altogether and then simply reflect the ranks obtained in those other areas of social life (the 'score-board' interpretation), or they could represent the outcomes of a rank-maximizing competition that is actually played with T and V tokens to establish a rank order of winners and losers *within* this linguistic arena (the 'competitive game' interpretation).

The leading proponent, and perhaps the originator, of the 'competitive game' interpretation is Marriott (1959, 1968a, 1976a). He talks about 'inter-caste transactions in any kind of food in Kishan Garhi as a kind of tournament among the 24 teams which make up this village's society' (Marriott 1968a: 154) and of 'game-like scorings', 'victories and defeats' (ibid: 155); and although he now adopts an 'ethnosociological' interpretation of the Hindu metaphysics of transactions, he still maintains that 'the tournament-like "total-prestational" models of exchange suggested by Mauss . . . and systematized by Homans . . . and Blau . . . can all be shown to depict part of such Indian talk and action about rank fairly well' (Marriott 1976a: 112).

But this is not the only interpretation of inter-caste relations. Leach (1960: 5–7), for instance, puts forward the thesis that one major distinction between *class* and *caste* systems is that whereas in class systems competition is endemic, in caste systems it is – by definition – rigorously excluded; for the caste society is a system of interdependent units *each* of which is guaranteed exclusive monopolies. Much of what Dumont says may also be read as claiming that hierarchy is ascribed by the Hindu cultural tradition, not competitively derived, and that in so far as competition exists it occurs in a specially isolated arena of power relations – the Kshatriya varna, the domain of *artha* (Dumont 1970). And his discussion of Marriott (1959) indicates that at least in part he favours the 'scoreboard' interpretation (Dumont 1970: 89–91). The issue then is live.

How can we decide between these two interpretations? Let us ask ourselves what consequences one would expect if indeed T/V or other transactional media like food exchanges were truly competitive games. What game-like properties are there in the patterns that we have collected?

Informally, we may observe that there are some patterns of T/V behaviour that do seem indicative of the competitive orientation of caste-groups and of individuals. In the first case we have what we may call *countermoves*, including *retaliations* and *boycotts*. A clear case of retaliative behaviour is provided by the T-exchanging patterns between caste 11 and the caste bloc formed of 8, 9 and 10. If we refer back to Matrix II, we can see that 8, 9 and 10 give T to 11, and 11 also gives T back to 8, 9 and 10. The anomalous character of this bold usage by 11 shows up clearly in the basic matrix (Matrix VIII), where it is the only set of facts that obstructs a fully scaled two-dimensional composite matrix of all the types of T/V usage together. We have also noted that it is the only source of nonconsistency in the giving dimensions (Figure 15). Not yet remarked upon is that it is also the only set of facts in the data that represents reciprocal T-exchange. By the valuation in section 2.3, reciprocal T-exchange establishes (more or less) equal rank. It might then indicate an island of intercaste solidarity. However it is *only* in this T-giving that equality is asserted: on the other measures 8 and 9 at least are distinctly higher in rank than 11. Now, given that the valuation of T/V outcomes depends on a dyadic interaction, if caste A gives T to B, expecting to secure a V in exchange and thereby to assert A's superiority over B, it is in fact open to B to frustrate this assertion simply by returning T instead of the hoped-for V. And given that 8 and 9, and to a lesser extent 10, are recognized to be higher than 11 (see their respective *receiving* scores in Figure 15), it seems that 8, 9 and 10 would have little or no motive for claiming solidarity, and thus a measure of equality from 11. In that case in giving T, they must have hoped for V, and our interpretation in terms of a plan by 11 to frustrate this assertion of relative rank seems justified. If we allow a momentary departure from our restriction to internal analysis we can readily show that 8, 9 and 10 do indeed consider 11 uppish, and 11 does indeed think it is as good or better than 8, 9 and 10: both parties openly express their indignation. In short, 11 is here acting competitively towards the other three castes: if they give T then 11 will give T back; if they extend the courtesy of REL, then 11 would probably reciprocate.

Absolute boycotts are not to be found in the T/V data. But boycotts in food-exchange media are widely reported, and are found in Ōlappāḷaiyam where Beck reports that the Cōḻi Ācāri (caste 3) and the Kōmuṭṭi Ceṭṭiyār (caste 4) are blacklisted so that as givers they rank almost as low as untouchables: this in return for minimal (rank-maximizing) receiving (Beck 1972: 164–7). Thus those who claim too high a rank can be effectively boycotted. In the T/V media, as one can readily imagine, this is more impractical: it would amount to avoiding any second person pronouns in the verbal interaction that for one practical reason or another would be impossible to escape. Nevertheless, although no group systematically maintains such pronominal boycotts, I know of at least three individual inter-caste dyads where precisely such non-usage is maintained. These have arisen in response to perceived violations of REL-usage, or V-usage or T-usage. One case, for instance, concerns a 55-year old man of caste 9 (call him K.U.), and a 45-year old man of caste 7a (call him O.S.). Referring to the basic matrix (Matrix VIII), one sees that the general expectation is that members of 7a give members of 9 T irrespective of their age, while members of 9 give 7a REL, that is T or V in relation to the relative age of speaker or addressee. By these norms K.U. can expect T from O.S.S., and O.S. can expect the same back, for he is younger than K.U. But as informants commented, O.S. doesn't want T back. O.S. is a successful merchant: he has the best cloth stall in the line of shops along the trunk road outside the hamlet, and in addition lends money at interest to many local farmers. He has also been the banker for some commercial ventures of various local squires (*periya Kavuṇṭar* families). In one way or another, without being especially popular, he has considerable influence in village affairs. Clearly O.S. has visions of social advancement, and since all other members of his caste in the hamlet are closely related to him, his visions extend to them as a body. In advancing himself he hopes to advance them. He remains obsequious to the dominant caste 5 – their patronage is the source of his influence – but he would like to detach himself (or so his behaviour seems to indicate) from those castes that straddle the upper caste/lower caste borderline, namely 8, 9 and 10. If he could get these castes to give him V he would have gained their acknowledgement of his superiority.

In contrast K.U. is simply an industrious respected member of caste 9 who carries on the traditional trades of his caste with a small margin of profit, and maintains a tough self-respect. Although O.S. has let it be known that he expects more respect from K.U., K.U. will not bow to the pressures. He refuses to give V. But rather than give T (which might in any case risk measures from O.S.), K.U. as a measure of protest *boycotts* O.S. in pronominal usage: he uses *neither* T *nor* V nor any other second person form.

Faced with this protest by avoidance, O.S. has two rational strategies open to him: he may continue to give T to K.U., or he may likewise protest by avoidance. The only problem with continuing to give T is that it would seem to be an acceptance of a situation that O.S. does not in fact accept: the usage might stabilize with K.U. giving zero pronouns, and O.S. giving T. The only problem with boycotting K.U. reciprocally is that it would establish a symmetrical usage of zero pronouns with the accompanying presupposition of rank equality. Faced with the decision between these two equally unsatisfactory solutions, O.S. oscillates from one to the other. The whole affair is a matter of common knowledge and amusement to villagers (but I have the facts about the protagonists' attitudes from closer sources: K.U.'s son and O.S.'s nephew).

Despite pronominal boycott, there can be no boycott on verbal interaction: village affairs bring the two men together, and then the mechanics of second person pronoun avoidance are of interest. Instead of saying:

(1) *Eṅkēyō pōyiṭṭu vāriṅka?*
Where have you-V returned from?

one says:

(2) *Eṅkēyō pōyiṭṭu vārappale irukkutā?*
Is there as if there has been a going and coming?

or instead of

(3) *Cantaikki pōyiṭṭu vantiṭṭiṅkaḷā?*
Have you-V returned from market?

one says

(4) *Cantaikki pōyiṭṭu vantāccā?*
Has there been a returning from the market?

and so on. The point is that impersonal phrasing makes T/V avoidance possible.

We have strayed from our self-imposed restrictions to internal analysis, but hope to have established the point that there are patterns visible both in the basic matrix and in the finer analysis of individual usage that are best interpreted as rational *counter-moves*, either retaliations or boycotts, to rank-maximizing moves by others in what is potentially a competitive game. When we turn to external evidence these interpretations can be shown to be substantiated.

Let us mention one other piece of evidence, external to the data in the matrices, that indicates a measure of competitive rank-maximization. This is the fact that there are situational variabilities, particularly in relation to the composition of the audience. Where such variations occur they most often occur in the direction of speaker-rank-maximization. For instance, take a case where a male adult member of caste 8 is addressing a ten-year old boy of caste 5: the expectation here (as recorded in Matrix VII) is that the man will address the boy as V. And that expectation will be fulfilled wherever the audience includes persons who have a vested interest in the rank of caste 5 as a whole (e.g. the boy's parents, members of castes closely allied to 5, members of the other two highest castes, traditional servants of the boy's family, etc.). But outside those contexts, in the absence of any audience at all, or in the presence of members of caste 8 only, the man may feel free to use T to the boy. The interesting question then is why the man bothers to make his usage inconsistent, and one is inclined to the view that he would say T wherever he could and get away with it. Many other observations support such a view. No one seems to be inclined to give more respect than they can get away with: they attempt to maximize their rank vis-à-vis others.

Returning now to the facts internal to the matrices, two general facts about them lend some support to the competitive view of caste relations. One of these is the basic asymmetry between ranks derived from success on giving dimensions and ranks derived from success on receiving dimensions. For one possible source of this asymmetry might turn out to be that the rank that any one caste *claims* (by a certain pattern of giving) is not necessarily *accepted* by the set of all the other castes with which it must transact (this acceptance being reflected in a certain pattern of receipts). Since we examine possible sources for this dissensus below (2.8) in detail, we may simply say here that if such a system of competitive claims is one possible source it cannot be the only one. For instance it might explain that whereas castes 3 and 7a do better than 5 as givers in T/V media, when it comes to receipts there is a high level of consensus that 5 is higher than 3 and 7a (see Figure 15). However the assumption of competitive behaviour then makes 5's actions difficult to understand: why does it not challenge 3 and 7a on the giving dimension too? Other solutions are explored below.

The other general fact about the matrices that may lend credence to the 'competitive game' interpretation of inter-caste behaviour is the fact that the ranks, and especially the distinctions between rank-blocs, are established with an apparent degree of independence in each medium. If all these behaviours were simply symbolic ratifications of a rank order established in some other medium, ritual, political or economic, then there seems no reason why they should be such erratic representations. In short, if these media are 'score-boards', why are they such poor ones? Not only are there discrepancies within T/V media (Figure 15), and within the other honorifics reviewed, but also between the facts in both arrays. Moreover, if we allow ourselves another glance outside our domain, such discrepancies occur in the local food transactions too: Figure 16 (derived from Beck 1972: Ch. 4) lines up linear representations of rank orders derived from scaled matrices of food and service transactions.[2] Lines connect castes with the most erratic fortunes across different media.

It is clear that if these media are score-boards of rank attained elsewhere, then they are not score-boards of the *same* external game. They must either be games within themselves, or be representations of rank in quite different social dimensions. It is this last interpretation that seems to be accepted by Beck; she argues that whereas the ranks that are derivable from transactions in food 'are heavily influenced by dietary and ritual ideals', the rank derivable from the offering of seats on informal occasions 'comes as close as is possible to a scale of the relative power and dependence of the various subcastes . . . on the Kavuṇṭar community' (Beck 1972: 162). Two external dimensions then underlie the symbolic expressions in transactions: purity and power. Since there are more than two rank-scales symbolically expressed, one must then assume that these others are derived from some partial fusion, or algebraic combination, of positions established in the two basic external social dimensions. This at least allows for the fact that there might be competitive claims about *which* basic social dimension (purity or power) was most relevant to some particular symbolic display.

This interpretation of the transactional patterns is not easy to substantiate nor easy to falsify. One would like to be able to derive independently two ranking scales corresponding directly to the social dimensions of power and purity, and then see whether all observed transactional rankings can reasonably be viewed as lying somewhere in between these two ideal types, as partial compromises in various degrees to both. But in fact there is only one clear way that Indians measure purity, namely by transactional discrimination, Hindu actors having (as has been argued by Marriott 1976a)

Informal seating	Givers of rice and curd	Receivers of curd	Receivers of rice	Takers of eating leafs	Rank at a Brahman feast
1	1	1	$\underline{1}$	1	$\underline{1}$
2	$\underline{2}$	2	$\overline{2}$	2	$\overline{2}$
$\overline{5}$	$\overline{5}$	5	4	4	3
7	7	7	$\overline{3}$	3	4
$\overline{3}$	8	8	5	6	5
6	$\overline{9}$	$\overline{9}$	7	$\overline{5}$	6
$\overline{4}$	6	6	8	$\overline{7}$	7
8	$\overline{10}$	4	$\overline{9}$	$\overline{8}$	8
9	$\overline{12}$	$\overline{3}$	6	$\overline{9}$	9
10	14	$\overline{10}$	$\overline{10}$	10	$\overline{10}$
11	11	$\overline{12}$	12	12	11
$\overline{12}$	13	14	14	14	$\overline{12}$
13	$\underline{15}$	11	$\overline{11}$	$\overline{11}$	13
14	$\overline{4}$	13	13	13	14
15	$\overline{3}$	15	15	15	15
$\overline{16}$	$\overline{16}$	$\overline{16}$	$\overline{16}$	$\overline{16}$	$\overline{16}$
17	17	$\overline{17}$	17	17	17
18	18	18	18	18	18

———— connects castes with great rank variation

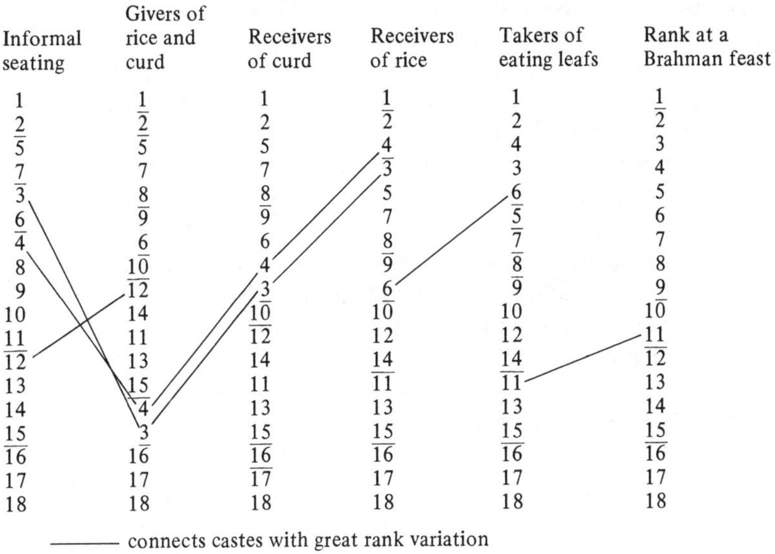

Figure 16. Ranks on a variety of non-linguistic media

as moral substance the sum of their dealings with the world. Even objective power, on a detailed search and survey, tends to evaporate into a large number of diffuse and different sources: political allegiances, connections to urban power structures, numbers of mobilizable kinsmen and retainers, economic clout, land control, etc. When we then ask which of these criteria of power assessment are actually important to members, and which castes are actually generally *judged* to have power (thus actually acquiring it of course), we find ourselves inevitably turning back to look at behaviour in transactional media. And there is every indication that members also turn back: 'he's powerful (I know because) everyone bows low before him' is the sort of reasoning presented. It seems that social dimensions like purity and power are not independent of the actions that ratify them. There are real stakes in these transactional games themselves.

So far we have argued informally that there are at least some elements in transactional inter-caste behaviour that favour the 'competitive game' interpretation. But in fact there is a formal theory of competitive behaviour, namely the mathematical theory of games. Let us ask whether T/V usage falls within the compass of that theory, and if so what predictions the theory would make. If we can find some of those predictions verified in the behaviour then the competitive game interpretation would receive very strong support indeed.

It is sometimes thought that the theory of games has only normative applications, that is, that it seeks to prescribe rational optimal behaviour in competitive contexts. But it is also, of course, descriptive and does not assume optimal behaviour but rather attempts to determine this empirically (Morgenstern 1968: 62). The theory does make certain assumptions about the nature of the game and the participants: amongst these are that the game has a definite form that defines a set of alternative moves for each player, that each player has a consistent pattern of preferences among the possible outcomes of the game, knows the other player's pattern of preferences, and seeks to maximize his own (Luce and Raiffa 1957). Games can be classified usefully in various ways: they may include elements of chance (mixed strategies) or exclude them (pure strategies); they may have 'saddle points' in which case they are called 'specially strictly determined'; they may be strictly competitive so that players' utility functions sum to zero, in which case they are called 'zero-sum games'; they may have two or more players, and may be described in that way; they may be so arranged that coalitions will benefit players ('essential games') or provide no benefit ('inessential games') – and so on.

Now one thing worth trying is to take Marriott at his word, and interpret inter-caste relations as a particular kind of competitive game. The most straightforward model would be that T/V usage and food transactions constitute *zero-sum n-person strictly-determined games with pure strategies*, that may or may not be *essential*. The rules of the game together with the nature of the outcomes is stated by the valuation of atomic dyads in section 2.3, and the utility functions of all players are a simple maximization of rank. Examination will show that utilities are zero-sum, and there are saddle points in such a game. Now let us ask how players would behave. To make the simple point that we wish to make here, no formal development is necessary. Indeed we can operate with highly scaled down mini-games with just four players.

Taking food transactions first, let us ask what each player's best strategy is, given that (a) giving food raises a player's rank while receiving it lowers it, and (b) each player prefers the outcome that maximizes his own rank. The answer clearly is that the best strategy is to give as much as possible and receive as little as possible. Now let us suppose that all players chose best strategy. Then we have a total game outcome in which none of the four players receives, but as a consequence none manages to give! All acts are abstentions: nothing takes place. However if we allow pre-game bargaining, there is another best strategy: one player can agree to receive from another, just so long as the other promises to receive from him. Then each partner in the coalition will succeed in giving, but only at the cost of some receiving. If all four players join in this coalition, agreeing to receive each other's food just so long as the others agree to receive theirs, then we have a total game outcome in which each player has three successful gifts but these are weighed against three costly receipts: the net gain is again zero. Thus although a player can do just as well by successful coalition, he can do no better than he would have done with the other strategy and no coalition. Therefore these games are *inessential*: there are no benefits to be derived from coalition. But nevertheless there are two *minimax* strategies (strategies that will guarantee the minimal loss): the one is total abstention – which we may call the *minimal* strategy – which is best in the absence of a coalition; the other is the *maximal* strategy of securing maximum gifts – but at the cost of maximum receipts, and this is only a minimax strategy in a coalition context.

If we now turn to the linguistic medium of T-giving we find a very similar pattern. This is not surprising because T-transactions have the same valuation as food transactions. However, as we noted in section 2.3, there are some differences between material and linguistic media; in particular it takes two separate acts for a food transfer to occur – an act of giving and an act of receiving – whereas for a linguistic transfer receiving is largely beyond actors' control. From this it follows that, whereas for food the best strategy in the absence of a coalition was abstention (no one being willing to receive), for T-exchange best strategy is on the contrary *maximal*: all players have no choice but to receive, so each player can maximize his giving. The outcome, if all players follow best strategy, has the unfortunate consequence that for each player his three gains (successful gifts) are neutralized by three losses (his receipts). Once again in a context without coalitions, best strategy can only yield zero-gains and zero-losses net. If coalitions are allowed, then each player can bargain to reduce his losses (T-receipts), but only at the cost of giving up a corresponding number of gains (T-gifts). If all players joined in such a coalition then once again net gains for each player are zero. So apart from the fact that maximal strategies and minimal strategies are best in different coalition contexts, food and T-transfers offer the same basic game to players: a game in which, if all players play best strategy, all players must come out with equal scores, and in which there is no advantage in coalitions.

Turning to the media with the inverse valuation, service provision and

V-exchange, it can be shown that they also constitute the same kind of game with the same basic formal properties. Even in a game allowing a mixture of coalitions and non-coalitions, those players who make coalitions will do no better than those who do not (see Levinson 1977: 339–41).

What can we show by all this? First and foremost we can show that the patterns that emerge in the empirical T/V data (as encapsulated in the basic matrix) do not even approximate to the game-outcomes that we have generated on the assumption that players are free to pursue minimax strategies. For if they were free to do so, then, with or without coalitions, they would all do equally well. *In short, hierarchy would never be generated.* And the remarkable thing about the empirical data is that it scales so very well to reveal clear blocs of ranked castes. We can conclude that T/V exchange and food and service transfers *cannot constitute strictly competitive games*. The hierarchy must come from somewhere: there must be strong constraints on players outside the game, so that game outcomes are at least partially a passive score-board of ranks achieved in other arenas. Marriott's 'tournament' then is one where fates are at least partially already decided before the tournament begins.

How can we reconcile this conclusion with the evidence of competitive behaviour that we adduced earlier, namely the existence of retaliatory counter-moves (retaliations and boycotts), the asymmetry between claims to rank and general recognition of it, and the fact that ranks established in diverse media do not match? The obvious, and I think necessary, solution is to admit the possibility that each medium constitutes *in part* a truly competitive game and *in part* a reaffirmation of ranks derived elsewhere. Each medium would then be in part a passive score-board and in part an arena of actual competition.

If we now look more carefully at the empirical outcomes in the actual media, we can readily discover *areas* of the matrices which do indeed approximate to the models generated on the assumption of minimax strategies operating freely. Matrix IX is drawn directly from Beck's Figure 4.8 which represents the pattern of cooked rice exchanges on informal occasions between each and every caste in the local arena (Beck 1972: 163). Looking carefully at this figure one can detect an area of maximal strategy: 5, 7a and 8 give and receive cooked rice from each other. No other castes exchange this food reciprocally. This must in fact represent an area of coalition: each agrees to accept if the other takes. We can also detect an area of minimal strategy: castes 4 and 3 receive from only one and two others respectively (thus minimizing their gains). There is admittedly another factor here in that caste 4 and caste 3's failure to give even

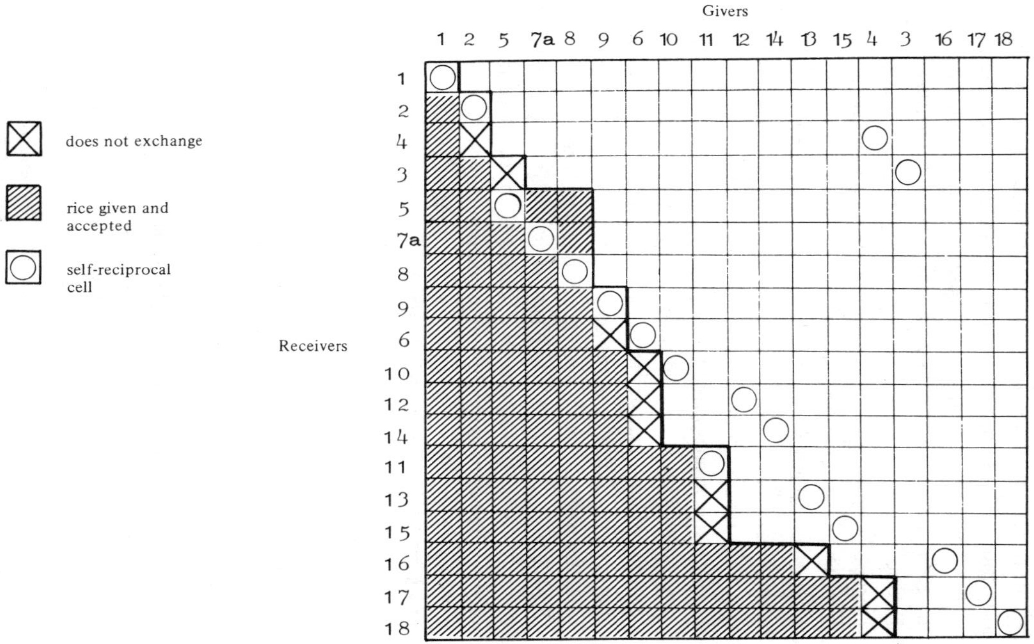

Matrix IX. Cooked rice exchange

to the lowest castes (in contrast to, say, caste 9's relative success) is not based on the failure to receive directly from those lowest castes (caste 9 does not; it would in fact be culturally unthinkable). Rather there appears to be a coalition between other upper castes (like 5 and 9) and the lowest castes such that failure to take from 5 and 9 can trigger a boycott by the lowest castes. Whatever payoff the lower castes get for such a coalition does not appear within this medium itself. (For further details see Beck 1972: 164–70.) Perhaps a full-blown game theoretic analysis considering all payoffs in all media might in fact make a lot of sense of such areas of competitive behaviour.

Turning to T-usage, we have already found the real-life analogue of one of our ideal games. This is where in the absence of a coalition, each player maximally gives (and perforce receives) T. The empirical instance is the retaliatory T-usage of castes 8, 9 and 10 to 11, and vice-versa, to be found in Matrix II and already discussed in this section. Are there also any instances where, by means of coalition, T is mutually avoided? Of course if T is avoided, given the awkwardness of perpetual pronominal avoidance between whole groups, some substitute must be found. REL could be such a substitute, and areas of REL-usage in the basic matrix (Matrix VIII above) may in fact represent precisely such coalitions over T-avoidance. We will discuss REL below in section 3.1. We must conclude, then, that there are areas of truly competitive game-like behaviour in the patterns of transactional exchange between castes in various media. But there must also be some *external* determination of rank by sanctions or payoffs in other media. This is probably true for all media.

2.7. Consensus on hierarchy

In the study of verbally expressed opinions on caste hierarchy, where a sort of opinion poll is systematically taken within a village, rather precise measures of the degree of consensus on caste ranks can be obtained. For instance Marriott is able to produce the following figures: 93% of 6,463 opinions (given by 24 informants) about the relative rank of pairs of castes chosen from the local hierarchy were in agreement in a particular North Indian village (Marriott 1968a: 138). Can we produce similar measures from our data?

It is not obvious that we can. Is it appropriate at all to talk of consensus in *behaviour* rather than in opinion? Only in this sense: the behaviour we are examining is symbolic – its 'meaning' is clearly stated in the rules of valuation. The valuation states that different modes of treating others will have different social values; and moreover that the value that an individual's act has depends critically on how the recipient acts back. If A gives a V to B, then only if B does not give V back is A higher than B. With the single exception of 11's use of T to 8, 9 and 10, there are no such symmetrical usages in our data. But this is itself a fact of interest: it means that both parties for each dyadic pattern of exchange concur in the valuation of it. We may say then that each case of V-giving records an agreement between the giver and the receiver that the giver is lower than the receiver. Similarly each case of T-giving (with the single exception mentioned above) records an agreement that the giver is higher than the receiver.

Everything that we have examined so far then is a massive set of agreements about the relative ranks of parties in particular dyads taken one at a time. But unlike opinion-poll data these judgements of relative rank are all egocentric: we cannot extract from the T/V data one caste's judgements about the relative rank of every other pair of castes. The most we can directly get is one caste's judgements about its *own* rank relative to every other caste. The maximum number of such judgements among 17 castes can only be 16 for each Ego, whereas opinions could total 272 for each Ego. So we cannot produce the same kinds of measures of relative rank as studies of local opinions.

What we can produce is collections of facts about how each caste treats each other caste (the columns in our matrices) and about how each caste is treated by all the others (the rows in our matrices). Now clearly ranks derived from receiving scores (rows) represent the collective agreement about the rank of the receiver in this medium – each caste has contributed to that overall assessment. The status of each caste's giving score is rather different: a column in one of our matrices represents that caste's view of itself, its own behavioural estimation of its rank. But note that whereas the Ts it gives are simply claims to higher status, the Vs it gives are admissions of lower status – and as such are likely to be concurrences in a consensus that the giver is lower than the receiver.

Receiving scores do then represent a general opinion about the receiving caste's rank. In so far as giving scores are isomorphic with receiving scores they represent the receiving caste's acceptance of the general opinion about its rank. We have already seen in Figure 15 that ranks as receivers in T and V (and threshold-V) were totally consistent. The 17 castes are only cut up into 9 rank-blocs, far less than the discriminations achieved in opinion polls (see for example, Marriott 1968a: Table 2; Beck 1972: Figure 4.15), but the consistency is absolute (unlike the opinion polls). It may be argued that we have here a truer picture of a consensus about rank than those derived from variable individual opinions. And the level of consensus is impressive.

2.8. Dissensus in ranking

One source of non-consensus, non-agreement and non-transitivity in the data has already been described. This was the phenomenon of countermoves, and we saw that the behaviour of caste 11 towards 8, 9 and 10 in the T-medium was best understood as an instance of competitive retaliation. But the major locus of dissensus, the only thing that stops the entire T/V data reflecting one single uniform scale of rank, is in the fact that ranks as givers are not consistent with ranks as receivers. And given the generally overwhelming pattern of consistency, this particular area of non-agreement takes on a special importance. Why does it exist, what are its sources? In this section we shall review a series of sometimes ingenious explanations in terms of rank-oriented behaviour, but despite their ingenuity we shall finally have to admit that they do not necessarily provide the correct explanation.

Let us start with the simplest of the possible explanations. We have already hinted that one reason that rank as givers is not equivalent to rank as receivers is that they are different kinds of thing. A caste's receiving scores represent the sum of other castes' opinion about its rank, whereas its giving scores represent its own view of its rank. If there is an element of competitive behaviour in transactional media then it is not surprising that there should be some discrepancy. Each caste might project a somewhat rosier image than it knows itself actually to have in the hope that others might eventually buy the rosier image.

However there are overwhelming problems with such a simple explanation. In the first place it will not work for all media. For in food transactions, for instance, in order to give successfully one must persuade the other party to accept. So no caste can simply project an optimistic image in food transactions, for others must concur in the rank claims made in order for them to take place. Yet nevertheless there are dramatic reversals of rank in food media (see Figure 16). So an account that only had application to the linguistic data and not to precisely parallel facts in the non-linguistic data would not be particularly appealing.

A second reason for rejecting this solution is that it provides no explanation for those parts of the discrepancy in ranks that come about because the *receiving* rank is higher than the giving rank. Where the discrepancy is the other way around (giving rank exceeds receiving) we can plausibly claim that a caste manipulates that rank (giving) that lies partially within its control. However there are discrepancies of the first sort also. For instance caste 5 does much better as a receiver of V than as a giver. (Admittedly these rankings are positional so that as 5 goes down in one dimension, other castes rise to fill the vacated position, so that one could explain 5's fall in terms of the others' (3 and 7a's) rise; but the question would still remain why 5 allowed its rank to lose one position downward.) Now to explain caste 5's fall in the medium it can manipulate, one would have to resort to some assumption of caste 5's *modesty*. But the whole theory only works on the contrary assumption that all castes attempt to maximize their rank.

We may now turn to the second explanation. This is Marriott's elaborate and very appealing theory of varna strategies (Marriott 1976a). It is attractive because it promises to integrate such diverse aspects of differences between castes as ideology, personality and transactional behaviour, all as concomitants of a single basic principle: the choice of an adaptive strategy in a hierarchical, partly competitive context. The basic idea is that groups operating within a set of groups, all of whom abide by the evaluations of transactions set down in our rules of valuation, have open to them a set of just four basic adaptive strategies. For a medium where giving is positively valued, like food, the strategies are these:

(a) the group can maximize status by *giving only* and not receiving ('optimal' strategy),
(b) it can assure itself of a median status by *both* giving *and* receiving ('maximal' strategy),
(c) it can assure itself of a median status by *neither* giving *nor* receiving ('minimal' strategy),
(d) it can minimize status (and perhaps maximize material benefits) by *receiving only* and not giving ('pessimal' strategy).

We can then go on to identify these strategies with the ancient varna categories. This is shown schematically in Table 6. The varna categories then are simply labels for an exhaustive set of inherently constrained adaptive strategies.

Now these patterns despite their abstraction are indeed realized (so Marriott claims) empirically in village interaction. To illustrate for our village we can refer back to Matrix IX, the matric of cooked rice exchange derived from Beck (1972: 163). Here the castes most typically associated with each strategy are shown in Table 7 (read + as maximal, – as minimal). Now in the south, as is well known, the varna categories are incomplete:

Table 6. *Marriott's varna interaction strategies*

	Givers	Receivers	Strategy
(a) Brahman	+	—	optimal
(b) Kshatriya	+	+	maximal
(c) Vaishya	—	—	minimal
(d) Sudra	—	+	pessimal

Table 7. *Examples of varna strategies in exchange of cooked rice*

Caste	Givers	Receivers
(a) 1 and 2	+	—
(b) 5, 7a, 8	+	+
(c) 3, 4	—	—
(d) 16, 17, 18	—	+

there are no true Kshatriyas by tradition, and even paradigmatic Vaishyas are not clearly identified. Nevertheless it is clear from folklore, behaviour, ethics, language usage and social structural traits that in the south the 'dominant' landowning castes, where these are not Brahmans (as they are in Tanjore), are Kshatriya-like (Beck 1972; 1973). And these rural-based power groups were in the past distinguished from their urban counterparts by the ancient terminology 'right-hand castes' versus 'left-hand castes' (Stein 1968). I propose to identify these as the South Indian correlates of Kshatriya varna and Vaishya varna respectively (although since 'left-hand' can be a term of abuse in India, it is the opposition rather than the labels that are correlated).

Now Marriott points out that if we adopt the kind of matrix that we have in fact adopted, then which 'varna strategy' (my term) each caste is playing is directly inferrable from the matrix. The relevant property of our matrix convention is the distinction between hierarchical ranks as givers and receivers, their separate representation along the two axes, and the consequent abandonment of the necessary alignment of self-reciprocal cells along the main left–right diagonal. The player with maximal transactions and the player with minimal transactions both achieve exactly the same rank. And experimentation will soon convince that using *either* maximal strategy *or* minimal strategy will *guarantee* mid-level status. They are thus rival but equally viable strategies for achieving that rank. Of course one does better to give to the greatest number of others and to receive from the least number of others: this is Marriott's 'optimal strategy' as approximated by Brahman patterns of interaction. Finally, one does worse (as far as rank is concerned) by receiving from the greatest number of others and not giving to anyone at all: this is the 'pessimal strategy' approximated by Harijan interaction patterns.

If we now construct a mini-matrix with six players, each with the following strategy sets

player 1 = (+5,0)
2 = (+3,–3)
3 = (+1,–1)
4 = (+3,–3)
5 = (+3,–3)
6 = (0,6)

then we have a playout as in the mini-matrix in Figure 17. This represents the sort of patterns associated with each varna category: player 1 plays Brahman strategy, players 2, 4 and 5 play Kshatriya strategy, player 3 plays Vaishya strategy, and player 6 plays Sudra strategy. Scores are as shown in Table 8. And the outcome really does approximate to empirical patterns observable. Now note that these patterns show up in a matrix on visual inspection: Brahman ('optimal') strategy achieves a location of the self-reciprocal cell of the optimal player at the top left of the main (left–right) diagonal, while Sudra strategy ('pessimal') achieves a location of the self-reciprocal cell in bottom right of the diagonal. For location along this diagonal indicates overall rank on both giving and receiving dimensions. But geometrical deviation of self-reciprocal cells from this main diagonal is a direct measure of the use by players of the strategies associated with the two middle varnas. The use of *maximal* (Kshatriya) strategy will cause deviation to the left of the main diagonal, while the use of *minimal* (Vaishya) strategy will cause deviation to the right of the main diagonal. So the use of particular strategies may be inferred directly from a visual appraisal of a transactional matrix. In addition, of course, one may simply count total transactions that players are involved in (as entered here in the self-reciprocal cells) in order to derive an assessment of minimal or maximal strategy use.

We may now put Marriott's theory more simply in the game theoretic terms we arrived at above. We may say that Marriott's theory amounts to the following: there are two distinct kinds of transactional behaviour (the difference between which Marriott underplays),[3] namely,

(a) rank-reflecting behaviour – the acquiescence of asymmetrical scores on the basis of external determinants,

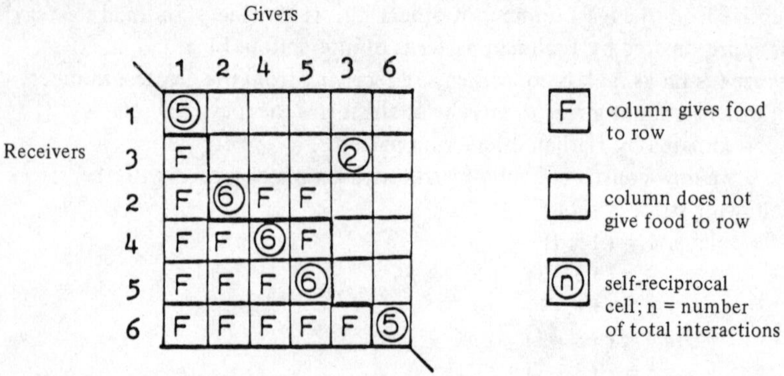

Figure 17. Mini-matrix illustrating hypothetical Varna strategies

Table 8. *Numerical interaction scores of players in Figure 17*

Player	Giving	Receiving		Net
1	+5	0	=	+5
2	+3	−3	=	0
3	+2	−2	=	0
4	+3	−3	=	0
5	+3	−3	=	0
6	0	−5	=	−5

(b) competitive zero-sum behaviour, where there are always two equally good minimax strategies (provided that necessary coalitions can be arranged) – what we have called *maximal* and *minimal*.
The type (a) is associated with the top and bottom varnas, and type (b) with the two middle varnas, where each takes a distinctive choice of the two options – options that are the only minimax strategies available in a caste system.

But to describe it as succinctly as this is not to belittle Marriott's theory, which has far reaching implications for understanding the distinctive styles of these traditional paths to Hindu prestige; it throws light on the distinctive ideologies of the Kshatriya/Vaishya opposition as well as the associated distinctive behaviour, and even makes sense of the personality-types that are associated with these two different paths (as Carstairs 1957 found, Kshatriyas are 'extrovert', instrumental exchangers, Vaishyas are 'introverts' and minimize their dealings with the outside world; see also informal remarks in Beck 1972: 10–11). But in this context the important point is that Marriott's theory provides an account of why apparent anomalies in the caste hierarchy – areas of apparent dissensus – arise: ranks as givers and ranks as receivers are often discrepant because there are highly principled strategies that castes adopt (along with the adoption of a characteristic lifestyle) which generate these discrepancies as a natural consequence.

Let us now turn to the empirical material in which these abstract patterns are embodied. Marriott stresses that castes tend to use elements from all four of these patterns (Varna strategies) but that nevertheless emphases towards one or another tend to emerge empirically: he presents data from seven villages, including Ōlappāḷaiyam (after Beck 1972: 163). Taking the full data from the last source for exchanges of cooked rice, we have the following matrix (Matrix X: the same basic data has already been presented in Matrix IX). From this matrix, derived from Beck's Figure 4.8 (Beck 1972: 163), we may extract scores by counting the number of successful gifts to other castes that each caste accumulates (positive scores), and the number of receipts received by each caste (its negative score). These scores may be added to produce a series of net scores (à la Marriott 1968a), as in Figure 18, reflecting overall rank. The scores may also be added disregarding the negative signs to produce totals of dyadic transactions (more strictly numbers of inter-caste dyads between which the transaction in question may take place from time to time) which each caste enters into; these totals are here entered into the self-reciprocal cells for each caste in the matrix for handy reference.

Viewing Matrix X diagonally (so that the main top left/bottom right diagonal is vertical), we see that castes deviate somewhat from the central ranking line formed by the main diagonal. Vertical position on this indicates approximate overall rank (on giving and receiving dimensions) however far to the left or right of it castes may be. Two castes (3 and 4) stand way out of line as minimal givers and minimal receivers, that is as *minimal strategists*. Beck describes these two castes as belonging to the left-hand bloc, but castes 7a and 6 also belong by the same criteria. Nevertheless here 3 and 4 display the classic strategy of their Vaishya-like category, while 6 and 7a happily align with right-hand castes 5, 8 and 10. Note that the net scores of 4 and 3 are 0 and –3, comparable with the rank of 10 and 11, but their total transactions (as noted within the self-reciprocals) only sum to 4 and 3 (compared to caste 10 and 11's total of 13 transactions). It is interesting to note that, as Marriott also found (1976a: 123ff.), minimizers stand out more than maximizers. Note, though, that

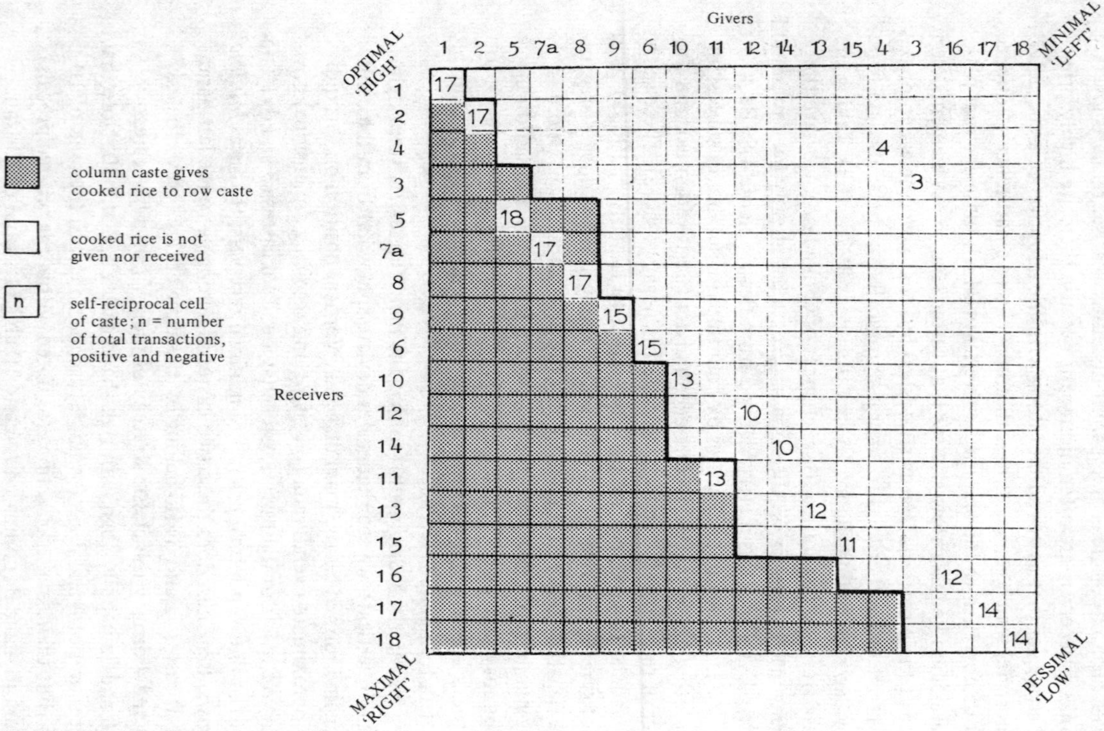

Matrix X. Varna strategies in cooked rice

Castes*	Giving scores (G)	Receiving scores (R)	Net (G plus R)
1	17	0	17
2	16	−1	15
4	2	−2	0
3	0	−3	−3
5	14	−4	10
7a	13	−4	9
8	13	−4	9
9	10	−5	5
6	9	−6	3
10	6	−7	−1
12	3	−7	−4
14	3	−7	−4
11	5	−8	−3
13	3	−9	−6
15	2	−9	−7
16	0	−12	−12
17	0	−14	−14
18	0	−14	−14

*Castes are here ordered by their rank on the receiving dimension.

Figure 18. Scores in cooked rice transactions

had we displaced caste 5 to the bottom of its rank-bloc, its maximizing role would have been diagrammatically emphasized to tell us what its total transaction sum tells us, namely that it is the greatest maximizer of all the castes. Thus in this empirical case maximizers, and to an even greater extent minimizers, are clearly locatable – and these castes correspond correctly to the varna-like categories 'left' and 'right' as predicted by Marriott's theory.

Let us now turn back to the linguistic media, and look just at the medium of V-giving and receiving. Recollect that V-giving is disvalued and corresponds to food *receiving*, so the polarity of the scoring will be reversed to continue to reflect rank. If we now look at Matrix XI (the basic facts here were presented in Matrix II and III above) and view it with the main (left–right) diagonal vertical, we find that most castes line up approximately on the now vertical diagonal that measures rank. Some castes though lie markedly to one side (a pattern we have emphasized by moving them to the end of their rank-blocs): caste 5 lies to the right with a total of ten transactions (as marked in its self-reciprocal cell), while castes 3 and 7a lie to the left of the diagonal with the smallest numbers of

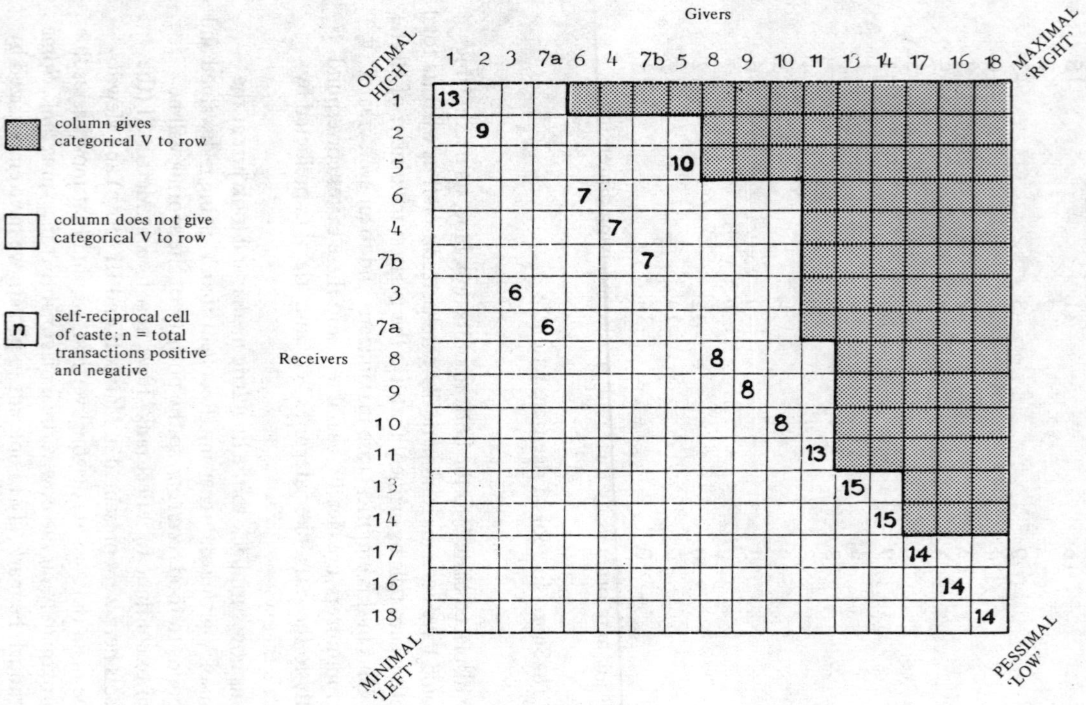

Matrix XI. Varna strategies in T/V usage

transactions in this medium, a total of six (composed of zero-givings and six receipts). Referring back to the similar matrix for cooked rice exchanges (Matrix X), we see that there 3 and 4 were in a precisely similar position to that in which 3 and 7a find themselves here in the linguistic medium; while caste 5 was there too a maximal transactor.

We now have a possible answer to our original question: why are the ranks as givers of T/V not congruent with the ranks as receivers? The possible answer is: because some castes make differential use of the two dimensions in their strategies to establish the overall rank they desire. One viable strategy is *minimal* use of both dimensions: since minimal use on one dimension will yield low scores, while minimal use on the other will yield high scores, this will guarantee a median place in the hierarchy. Another viable strategy is *maximal* use of both dimensions, which will yield high scores on one dimension and low ones on the other – again guaranteeing a median position. In V-giving 3 and 7a use minimal strategy, 5 uses maximal strategy; in food (cooked rice) 3 and 4 use the minimal strategy and 5 uses maximal strategy.

Let us deal at once with one puzzlement. We have suggested that the use of the minimal strategy is associated with the values of the left-hand bloc. Indeed there seem to be intrinsic connections between the minimal strategy and the socio-cultural traits associated with left-hand bloc membership: left-handers have relatively closed small marriage circles (associated with the patrilateral cross-cousin marriage preference in ideology) which serve to minimize the numbers of social units that are transacted with; in matters of daily interaction they are aloof and minimize their interactions with others. There is a consistent pattern here (Beck 1972: Introduction) of which Marriott's minimal strategy seems to be the core; while the other consistent ideological and organizational pattern (the right-hand model) has maximal strategy as a core. Nevertheless of the relatively high caste left-handers only castes 3, 7a and 4 seem to embrace thoroughgoing minimal strategy in interactional media. The others, castes 6 and 7b (and 4 in the linguistic media), align with the right-hand caste patterns quite closely. Why? Does this invalidate the correspondence between strategy and varna-like category?

If we turn to ethnographic observations the reasons for the 'treachery' of 6 and 7b, and sometimes 4, are fairly evident. Members of caste 6 in Ōlappāḷaiyam are the prosperous dependable carpenters and smiths for the dominant caste 5; they contrast in this with caste 3, also traditional carpenters and smiths, who do not work solidly to service village agricultural needs at all. Members of 3 tend to work on special jobs, house-building and so on, travelling far, often into urban centres. Members of 6 have large well-equipped workshops in the village and clients go to them rather than summon them. In short, members of caste 6 are integrated into the rural economy and the set of village service interdependencies: their major clients are Kavuṇṭars (caste 5) whose interactional strategies and linguistic propensities (strong tough speech with local Koṅku forms) they tend to emulate. As for members of 7b, Kavuṇṭar blood actually runs in their veins (as all acknowledge): they are compromised left-handers if anyone is. Their ideals and interactional strategies seem Kavuṇṭar-like throughout. Caste 4 on the other hand has different reasons for not rigidly maintaining left-hand ideals in linguistic media: it is represented by a single family not well established in the village (and expelled only eight years ago from another) – its members simply cannot afford to make claims to rank that might be opposed. So among the higher castes only 3 and 7a are economically and ideologically free to pursue a left-hand strategy that will isolate them from the central right-hand patterns that are buttressed by the interdependence of the rural economy.

But perhaps looking at the left-hand category as a *strategy* should banish the puzzlement in any case. It is simply not a bloc of castes at all, not a club with a set membership. Rather it is a path, or varna, one of the four basic ones that the ranking system offers. Castes can use this path or strategy if conditions make it attractive: otherwise they can choose another. And indeed ancient lists of right- and left-hand castes display a flux hardly intelligible on any other view (see Stein: 1980). In so far as castes are intrinsically urban based or rural based by the nature of their traditional occupations, there will be a tendency for these castes to provide relatively stable foci for left-hand and right-hand blocs (Ceṭṭiyār and Mutaliyār for the left, Kavuṇṭar and Nāṭār for the right perhaps). But other castes may fluctuate from one strategy to another as the demands of a particular local ranking arena (urban or rural) make appropriate.

We seem then to have arrived at a satisfactory solution to the problem of discrepancies in ranks on the two dimensions, giving and receiving. We need (on this account) to appeal to no basic principles regulating intercaste affairs except a concern with establishing rank. Then in terms of two aspects of this concern, namely (a) the symbolic expression of ranks established on the basis of external affairs, and (b) competitive rank-minimization, we seem to be able to account for the observable patterns in the matrices.

However our success is not complete. Various doubts and alternative explanations arise. In the first place, the equivalent nature of linguistic and material media is open to question: there are no abstentions from T/V media altogether on a caste-wide scale, therefore talk of 'minimal strategy' may be here misplaced. In the second place, we underplay the source and significance of coalitions, for if we turn to media other than food or V, to T in particular, we see that large-scale coalitions are involved. In the third place, the dissensus which we are trying to explain involves only a few crucial cells. In linguistic media these are only 3 and 7a's non-giving of V to 1 (in contrast to 5's giving of V to 1). If 3 and 7a gave V to 1 then they would rank equally with 5, 6, 4 and 7b, and all inconsistency in the giving and receiving of T and V (other than 11's retaliative T-giving) would be dissolved. But if we can find alternative sources for the usages in these cells Marriott's elaborate theory need not be called into play – at least not for the linguistic media.

These three points of doubt converge in the following argument. The application of Marriott's theory to the linguistic data assumes the comparability of material and linguistic media in a number of important respects. But as noted already, there are differences: here the relevant difference is that whereas in a specific food medium total withdrawal from all transactions is possible, there cannot be (or perhaps just contingently is not) any such total withdrawal by a whole caste from the T/V media as a whole. Communication must go on, and pronominal avoidance, although possible (and practised) on an individual-to-individual basis, would be cumbersome in the extreme as a caste-wide practice. But whatever the sources, it is a fact that non-use of T implies use of V or REL, non-use of V implies T or REL, and non-use of REL implies use of T or V. It follows that *minimal* strategists cannot minimize their dealings in all three of these media simultaneously: in minimizing total transactions in one medium they will end up maximizing them in another.

It does not necessarily follow from this that castes 3 and 7a's non-use of V *cannot* be seen as an application of minimal strategy, just that it *need not.* For it could be viewed as an application of the strategy in the more important of the two media. In other words 3 and 7a could be willing to increase their use (be indeed maximal transactors) in the more neutral medium of REL in order to maintain minimal strategy in the strongly valued V-medium. However, due to the necessary (or at least empirical) interdependence of T, V and REL, this is not the only possible interpretation. The other is that 3 and 7a do not use V to 1 because they positively wish to use the alternative they do in fact use, namely REL.

If we turn back to Matrix VIII (the basic matrix) we find that 1, 2, 3 and 7a symmetrically (reciprocally) exchange REL. Now we know from our discussion of the valuation of symmetrical usages above that these are potential expressions of solidarity or even intimacy. It could then be that what underlies these few crucial cells which are the source of the dissensus, is that 3 and 7a have some special relationship, some form of coalition, with castes 1 and 2. And the general importance of such coalitions may be gauged by referring again to the facts about T-giving. In the basic matrix (Matrix VIII) we see that T-giving does not fill a triangular area in the matrix in the way that V-giving does. For there is an area that extends all the way down to 7b in the receiving axis, where no T's are given at all; in fact we may say (given our definition of the 'upper castes' as the bloc from 1 through 7b) that no upper castes give T to any other upper castes. From our discussion in section 2.6 we know that a pattern of reciprocal T-avoidance will not emerge in a competitive ranking game without a coalition (whereas reciprocal *usage* of T would emerge in the same context without a coalition). If the area in question were not a competitive area, but rather a *rank-ascribed* area, then we would expect a pattern of T-usage from superiors to inferiors; and indeed in other media, like V, the 'upper castes' are cut up into two or three rank-blocs. Nevertheless what we in fact have here is an area of T-avoidance. We conclude then that some sort of coalition or alliance must underlie this abstention from T-usage among all the upper castes (and moreover that this will not readily be explained in terms of bargains made within the game – the T-medium – itself).

Now if such alliance relationships exist in any case, they would then provide an independent and alternative account of how the dissensus in giving and receiving arises. For although some slightly higher castes may make pacts with slightly lower ones (as judged by behaviour in other media), castes outside the pact may not accord the lower-rank members of the pact equal treatment with the higher ones; moreover high ranking castes outside the pact may do less well on the giving dimension than those within it (who may have secured favourable terms), although when it comes to the mass of opinion reflected in receiving scores they will remain higher in rank than some members of the pact. Thus a special pact between 3 and 7a on the one hand and 1 and 2 on the other will not necessarily prevent other castes from distinguishing between them, which in fact they do, judging 5 higher than 3 and 7a (but lower than 1 and equal to 2).

There is then the possibility of a rival explanation for the discrepancy in giving and receiving ranks in the T/V media, along the lines that the few troublesome cells involved arise not from a concern with caste ranking within the V-medium but rather from a positive preference for REL (with consequent impingements on V patterns) in accordance with quite different concerns. Let us now turn to explore these concerns. And although we will there find reasons to find this alternative explanation convincing, we should remember that we have not ruled Marriott's theory out as a possible additional and supplementary explanation. Moreover for those media like food transactions where abstentions from one medium do not automatically imply usage of another, Marriott's theory has no rival of the sort we are proposing for the T/V media. It remains, then, the more general theory.

3. INFERENCE OF ALLIANCE RELATIONS

So far we have operated as if there were only one principle that regulates inter-caste affairs, namely a concern with relative *rank*. But even within that framework we have seen that the possibility of an alternative account of dissensus in ranking presents itself, which presupposes reference to another dimension of inter-caste relations, namely *alliance* as the source of particular coalitions. We here turn to explore this second principle regulating inter-caste relations, find that its operation in the linguistic media can be shown to exist, and indicate that its importance in other media in other village studies has been underestimated or entirely overlooked. A side benefit of the analysis is the alternative account of dissensus in caste-ranking (along the lines already outlined above).

A few remarks of clarification will be useful at the outset. We understand the notion 'alliance relations' in such a way that it is *reciprocal exchange* in media that is their basic expression. This is of course a more restricted sense of the phrase than that associated with Lévi-Strauss's theory of kinship and marriage (Lévi-Strauss 1949), where asymmetric exchanges are also specifically included. It is also not always equivalent to the notion of a coalition in Game Theory, although it is so in the particular games we have looked at. The extra constraint that we incorporate into the notion of 'alliance relations' is that these should constitute relations of solidarity and rank-equalization. In our area of interest at any rate, this rules out asymmetrical exchange relations and coalitions with differential payoffs to members.

Now given our definition of 'alliance relations' as those relationships of solidarity and rank-equalization expressed in symmetrical exchange, we can say at once that in the T/V media it is only in REL-usage that 'alliance relations' manifest themselves. For we have already seen that there is no symmetrical V-exchange at all (inter-caste), and only a few cells of reciprocal T-usage (from 11 to 8, 9 and 10) which we explained (on the basis of external ethnographic evidence) in terms of retaliation in a competitive area of T-usage. REL then will be the focus of this section, although non-verbal and other verbal media will be considered. It should be remembered, though, that symmetrical exchange in a medium cannot necessarily be assumed to express solidarity or a caste neutralization: it may reflect a policy of retaliation, or it may indicate a wary admission of equality without solidarity.

A second important point to bear in mind during the following analysis is that alliance relationships as here defined will be an automatic reflex of *maximal* strategy. For if a player maximizes gifts *and* receipts then he will find himself in a situation of symmetrical exchange with other players playing the same strategy. On the other hand, alliance relations can only be purchased at a cost by minimal strategists who are trying to cut down on both outgoings and receipts. It follows from this that if only maximal strategists were to form alliance relations together, then the additional principle here being introduced would be redundant. But if erstwhile minimal strategists are to be found engaging in alliance relations, then an independent principle is necessary to the analysis and this turns out to be the case.

3.1. REL: patterns of exchange and blocs of allies

So far we have given short shrift to the third basic option in T/V usage: the use of both T and V to members of other castes depending on the relative age of speaker and addressee. The basic pattern is that older addressees get V, younger ones get T, and there is a certain range of usage one way or the other for near coevals, although V is generally preferred.

Hitherto we have treated this pattern as simply the residual category of usage, predictable from the non-usage of both categorical T and categorical V. But as we remarked earlier, this usage has more than merely residual social-semantic content: it is the basic ideal *intra*-caste usage (and indeed the ideal intra-familial usage), and its use across castes is likely to carry the connotations of these other usages. Certainly to use REL (relative age T/V) is to imply that caste as a determinant of interaction is here neutralized, in favour of seniority by age.

However we must emphasize that despite this intrinsically caste-neutralizing, solidarity-claiming valuation, REL is *not* necessarily reciprocally exchanged. There are a number of cases of REL in one direction, within a dyad, and T or V given in return. There are in fact three observable configurations (see diagram below). Whereas in (i) A apparently gives

(i)

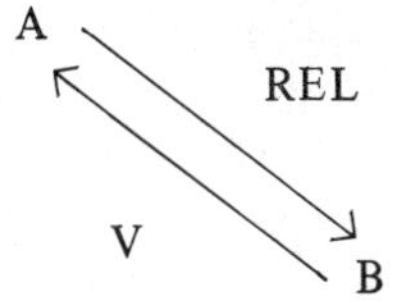

(ii)

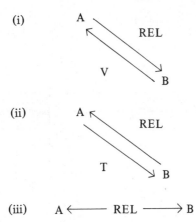

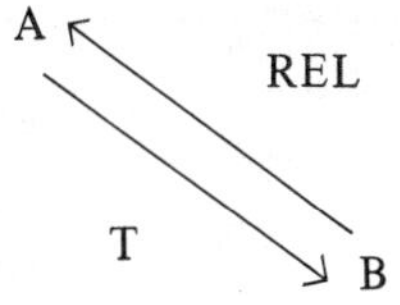

(iii) A ⟵ REL ⟶ B

REL downwards, and receives V in exchange, in (ii) B apparently gives REL upwards and receives T in return, and in (iii) A and B reciprocally (symmetrically) exchange REL. In other words if REL intrinsically neutralizes caste in one direction, a consideration of both dimensions (the reciprocals used) may reinstate caste-rank distinctions. However it remains true that the great majority (55 cases out of 77) of REL-givings are reciprocated with REL. Let us analyse the facts in detail.

Retaining the ranks established on the basis of T- and V-giving as in the basic matrix, Matrix XII presents the facts about REL-usage, distinguishing between symmetrical exchange of REL and asymmetrical usages of REL. We can see that there are six distinct areas or blocs in the matrix, of which four (with the partial exception of Bloc 6) are composed entirely of symmetrical REL-exchange, and two show REL being given in one direction only within a dyad.

Taking these two blocs of asymmetrical REL-usage first, we have Bloc 2 where caste 1 (Brahmans) use REL to castes 5, 6, 4 and 7b who reciprocate with V (as can be ascertained from the basic matrix); in short, Bloc 2 constitutes an area where our configuration (i) above prevails. The other asymmetrically exchanging REL-bloc is Bloc 4, where we find the use of REL by 8, 9 and 10 to 3, 6, 4, 7a and 7b – in this case reciprocated with T as in the configuration (ii) above. We may speculate immediately that there are fundamentally different sources for these two kinds of asymmetrical REL-usages: in the case of Bloc 2 it occurs because castes 5, 6, 4 and 7b feel obliged to express respect to caste 1, the Brahmans. In the case of Bloc 4 the asymmetry occurs because 8, 9 and 10 claim a neutralization of caste rank in favour of age – i.e. a measure of equality – a claim

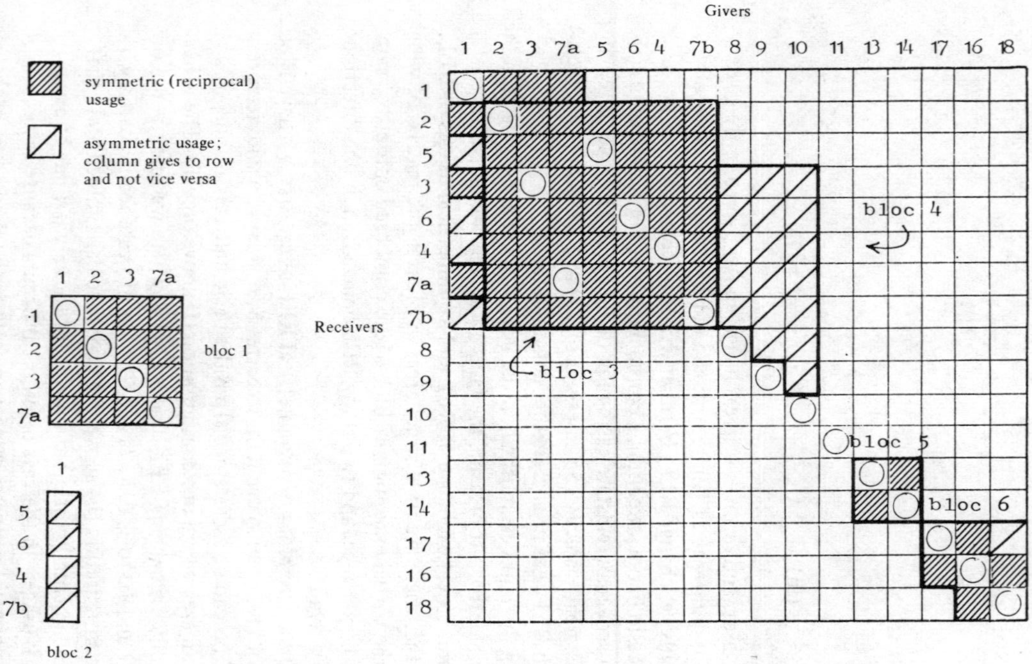

Matrix XII. Symmetrical and asymmetrical usage of REL

addressed to 3, 4, 6, 7a and 7b; this claim is roundly denied by the REL recipients who reply with categorical T.

Turning to the symmetric blocs (where REL is reciprocated between members of each dyad), we have had to extract Bloc 1 from the matrix and reassemble it to the left because the disjunction between ranks as givers and receivers (derived from the basic matrix) disperses it (note that if we here gathered them together in the matrix we would disperse Bloc 4). What we find here (in Bloc 1) is a very significant pattern of caste-neutralization among the strategic leaders of the left-hand division. What marks this bloc off from Bloc 2 is the participation of the Brahmans; or rather, the symmetric claims of caste-neutralization and solidarity that include Brahman participation.

If we allow ourselves to refer to external ethnographic facts we can confirm that this usage in Bloc 1 is not just a reflection of accidents of propinquity and familiarity between the particular families who represent these castes in the hamlet.

For instance, a Brahman who spends most of his time in an urban *agrahāram* (Brahman street) but returns to dwell in the hamlet when his rotating duty as temple priest occurs, told me the following facts. Brahmans in this area, like other castes, but unlike Brahmans in other areas of Tamilnadu, distinguish their *vīṭṭuppācai* ('house language', here Brahman caste-dialect) from the language they speak outside (standard local colloquial). Brahmans in this region have complete fluency in the local colloquial dialect, while their *vīṭṭuppācai*, the language of the *agrahāram*, on the other hand has all the features of the Brahmanical dialect of Tamil as used elsewhere in Tamilnadu (see Bright and Ramanujan 1964; Ramanujan 1968; Zvelebil 1964). Now Piḷḷais (caste 2) and Cōḻi Ācāris (caste 3) and Vaishya Ceṭṭiyārs (not represented in Ōlappāḷaiyam) are regular visitors to the *agrahāram*, according to the Brahman informant, and when there they adopt the Brahmanical dialect – or at least some lexical and morphological markers of it, so that the Brahmans do not feel constrained to code-switch into non-Brahmanical standard Koṅku colloquial. The informant claimed moreover (and I have proof of this on tape) that Brahmans exchange kin-words in extended usage to both caste 3 and caste 2 who both reciprocate (although they do not use such metaphorical kin-words to each other: see Levinson 1977: 400ff. for details). Daily interaction in Ōlappāḷaiyam between these three castes is very close; members of 2 and 3 can often be found seated on the *tiṇṇai* (verandahs) of members of caste 1 (see Beck 1972: 158–61), while the women of caste 3 do the household work (other than cooking of course) for visiting Brahman priests.

These ethnographic facts do indeed suggest that the pattern in Bloc 1 in Matrix XII is highly significant: members of the left-hand division, or those whom we may now call the more extreme minimal strategists, here celebrate their solidarity with the top member of the hierarchy by means of a symmetrical exchange of REL. This suggests that Obeyesekere's critique of Beck's interpretation of the role that Brahman and Piḷḷai play as models for the left-hand division is ill-founded: the fact is that the top-most castes and the left-hand castes are allied, and in this Beck is correct (see Obeyesekere 1975).

Now note that it is in a sense *because* of this alliance, which grants 2, 3 and 7a the privilege of REL rather than V to Brahmans, that 3 and 7a achieve their high ratings as givers of V. Whereas Kavuṇṭars (caste 5) give V to Brahmans and thereby lower their net scores in this medium, castes 3 and 7a exploit their privilege to rank higher than Kavuṇṭars in this medium. But this will gain 3 and 7a little on the receiving scale. And so we end up with that disjunction between giving and receiving ranks that occupied so much of our attention above. There we explained the disjunction as a direct outcome of 3 and 7a's use of minimal strategy in the V-medium. Now we are offering an explanation in terms of a special option open to 3 and 7a in the REL-medium, which happens to have a reflex in the V-medium – by virtue of the fact that the three linguistic media are alternates.

Now these two explanations can be complementary. In the first place they are non-contradictory and compatible so that they can both be correct simultaneously. Note that since the T/V media are an interdependent set of alternatives, Bloc 1's minimizing in one medium (V-giving) necessarily involves maximizing in at least one other (REL-giving). Secondly, the interdependence of the media requires an interdependent explanation along the following lines. Castes 3 and 7a refuse to give V where even the dominant caste (5) cannot refuse. But how can they dare to do this? Because they have neutralized the only groups with a primary right to object, namely the recipients (castes 1 and 2). Therefore by *allying* in one medium one can buy *rank* scores in another.

Let us turn now to the second bloc of symmetric exchange in Matrix XII. Bloc 3 is a much wider bloc than Bloc 1 and incorporates erstwhile maximal and minimal strategists in one great bloc of relative equality counterposed to the excluded lower castes 8 through 18. Here we have to face the fact that the motives lying behind this symmetrical usage may be different for different castes, rather than a solid bloc generated by uniform maximal strategies in this area. To see this we have to bear in mind the related facts about categorical T- and V-usage. Let us map onto our REL-usage the rankings emergent from the T and V media. Relative to this independent (or partially independent) ranking scale (immanent in the known interactional facts), we may then roughly estimate which castes are giving REL to superiors and which to inferiors. This is significant because to give REL to a superior is to cheat him of a V, while to give REL to an inferior is to extend downward generosity of an intriguing kind.

Let us take as an approximate overall index of rank on T/V criteria the *net* scores for giving and receiving V (this is simply for convenience – no fine points will be made that depend crucially on this). The scores are shown in Figure 19 (see Matrices III and IV above). Here scores for giving are added to scores for receiving to yield net scores which in turn are expressed in the linear ranking line to the right. If we add rank-cuts between 8, 9 and 10 and between 17, 16 and 18 we approximate an over-all ranking with the maximum number of cuts attested in the linguistic media (actually threshold-V-usage adds some more). We add these additional rank-cuts as dotted lines.

So if we now map this rank-order onto the central area of REL-usage we can get an idea of who is giving REL upwards and who downwards. This is visually represented in Matrix XIII, where the order of castes in the righthand column is the net rank-order in Figure 19, and where REL-cells are distinguished according to whether they are

(a) 'V-substitutes' : i.e., REL given to superiors,
(b) 'T-substitutes' : i.e., REL given to inferiors,
(c) 'REL to equals': i.e., REL given to those ranked equal in V-medium.

It is immediately evident from Matrix XIII that while all three kinds of cells are present, the majority are *not* cases of REL to equals, but are rather 'T-substitutes' or 'V-substitutes'. Giving REL to superior castes is to claim *upward solidarity* (and to cheat upper castes of a V); giving REL to inferior castes is generously to extend *downward solidarity* to them (and to abstain from giving a T). The number of castes that do each are listed in Figure 20.

Concentrating on the castes involved in the symmetrical exchange of REL in Bloc 3 of Matrix XII, on the basis of the table in Figure 20 we can say this:

(i) The castes at the top of the hierarchy display a remarkable amount of *downward generosity*, as indicated by the large numbers of inferior castes they give REL to.

(ii) Just below them this downward generosity ceases abruptly (where it ceases exactly will depend on the external ranking system used to judge

Caste	V giving (g)	V receiving (R)	Net (R+G)	Net rank order
1	0	13	13	1
2	0	9	9	2
3	0	6	6	5
7a	0	6	6	3
5	−1	9	8	7a
6	−1	6	5	6
4	−1	6	5	4
7b	−1	6	5	7b
8	−3	5	2	8
9	−3	5	2	9
10	−3	5	2	10
11	−8	5	−3	11
13	−12	3	−9	13
14	−12	3	−9	14
17	−14	0	−14	17
16	−14	0	−14	16
18	−14	0	−14	18

Figure 19. Net ranks by V-giving and receiving

which castes are inferior and superior, but by any of the available scales, by 7b generosity has ceased absolutely. In our ranking system it ceases at 7a, before 6, 4 and 7b).

(iii) As downward generosity declines, *upward claims to equality* increase, as indicated by the large numbers of superiors to whom REL is given. The lower the caste within our Bloc 3 of REL-exchanges the more castes that receive REL as a V-substitute from it. This trend continues into Bloc 4 (an area of asymmetric REL-usage) and all the way down to caste 10 where it abruptly ceases. Thus REL as a V-substitute accounts for about half of the usages in Bloc 3 and all the usages in Bloc 4 as Matrix XII makes clear.

Given the valuation of REL, REL to equals is the natural expression and recognition of social equality. REL as a V-substitute is easily understood in terms of rank-maximizing motives. But REL as a T-substitute is a different story. Whereas theories of caste-ranking prepare us for upward claims to rank, they do not in any way explain the downward generosity evinced by the use of REL to inferior castes. The question is what is it that leads all the upper castes to stand together and exchange REL, in contradistinction to the lower castes? For, referring back to Matrix XII, there is a remarkable *caesura* between the castes 1 through 7b on the one hand and 8 through 18 on the other. It is this solid use of REL within the upper

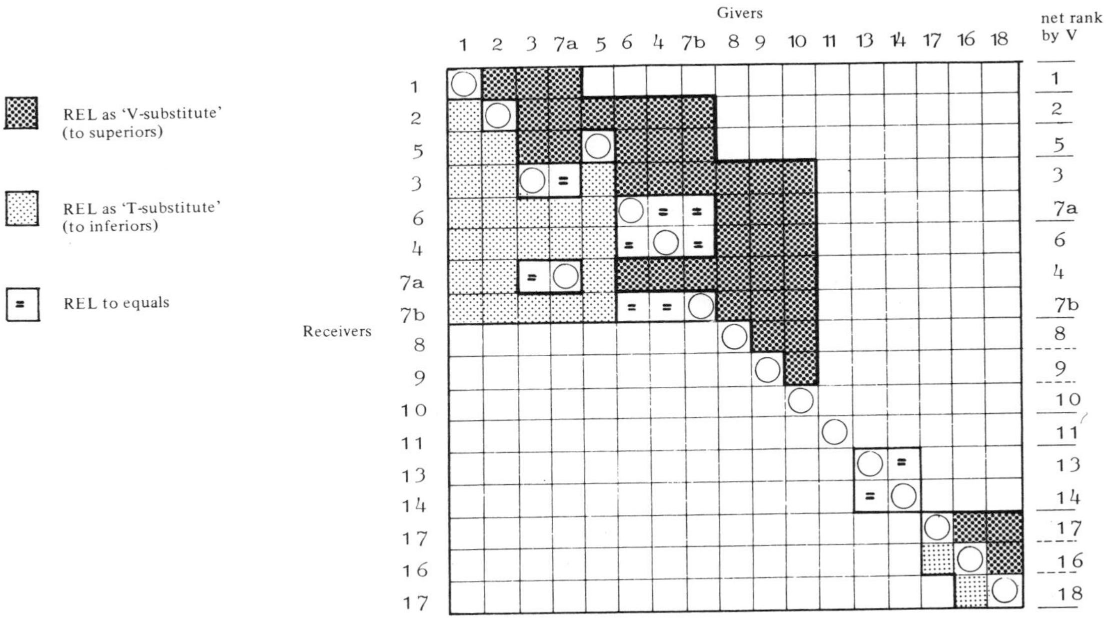

Matrix XIII. REL as T and V substitutes

Castes in net rank order	Total inferior castes given REL	Total rank equals given REL	Total superior castes given REL
1	7		0
2	6		1
5	5		1
3	3	1	3
7a	3	1	3
6	0	2	4
4	0	2	4
7b	0	2	4
8	0		5
9	0		6
10	0		7
11	0		0
13	0	1	0
14	0	1	0
17	1		1
16	1		1
18	0		2

Figure 20. REL to superiors and inferiors

castes that is responsible for the strangely truncated, table-topped matrix for T-usage that we analysed in section 2.5.

It does seem then that the study of inter-caste relations is in need of some principle complementary to rank, a principle we may call *alliance*. The principle must, like ranking, provide a motivation for behaviour and thus a set of predictable outcomes in a particular situation. But instead of upward claims to equality and downward expression of superiority, it must predict downward extensions of solidarity – not in all circumstances for then rank and alliance would be diametrically opposed (and what the one did the other would undo). And indeed in our data downward solidarity has rapid and abrupt boundaries.

We will return to the nature and distribution of alliance relations. Let us now complete the survey of the distant blocs of usage ascertainable in Matrix XII. Bloc 5 is the symmetrical exchange of REL between washerman and barber castes (castes 13 and 14 respectively). The two cells involved are also instances of REL to equals (note though that threshold-V did make some rank distinction between 13 and 14). The alliance of barber and washerman is expressed also in their exchange of kin-terms. For most purposes they form, in the eyes of villagers, a single unit of ritual and social rank, and this perhaps ensures that they form a coalition and a solidary unit as far as the linguistic media are concerned.

The last area of REL-usage, Bloc 6, is composed of interaction between Harijans. In a way this area constitutes a microcosm of the larger whole: we find here both patterns of downward generosity and upward claims as we found in Bloc 2. In Figure 20 this same resurgence of patterns found higher up in the hierarchy can be seen, after a gap (between 10 and 17) wherein little REL-usage takes place. Here both caste 17 and 16 display downward generosity to the immediate caste below. Whatever explanation will do for the phenomenon higher up in the hierarchy will do here also, and indeed will be required.

Let us look at the facts implicit in Matrix XIII in a slightly different way: let us ask what role each caste plays in the generation of the REL-patterns, and let us also make some assessment of the distribution of solidary alliance relations. We can get some measure of the 'popularity' of each caste (as far as being a desirable ally is concerned) by counting the number of REL-receipts it gets, and similarly some measure of each caste's 'outgoingness' by counting the number of RELs it gives; and then we may count those RELs that are symmetrically exchanged to get some idea of 'alliance success'. The table (Figure 21) provides this information.

Looking at the columns for REL-outgoings and receipts, we see that caste 1 gives more REL than it receives, but that this pattern is already reversed by caste 5, to receiving more than it gives. Clearly at the top of the hierarchy one can extend REL generously without fear of exploitation: recipients will continue to give V in return. But castes further down have to be more judicious for they are likely to be swamped by receipts from those below. And those below, like 8, 9 and 10, are busy exploiting REL possibilities even though they receive few in return. So we end up with caste 10's massive outgoings without a single return. In short, although a distinct alliance principle is operative in the REL-medium, it is also true that the other principle, the principle of rank or hierarchy, reimposes itself in this 'caste-neutral' medium as pressures mount to exploit the equality implications of REL in order to maximize rank.

A remarkable feature of Figure 21 is the position of caste 11, which stands absolutely outside all alliance claims, neither giving nor receiving a single REL. This fits with other ethnographic facts about caste 11; these are the Vaṭuka Nāyakkar, a left-hand caste of traditional well-diggers and house-builders. Despite having a traditional occupation no more ritually polluting than that of agriculture, they rank consistently in this local

Caste	REL-receipts	REL-outgoings	Number of castes exchanging symmetrical REL
1	3	7	3
2	7	7	7
5	7	6	6
3	10	7	7
7a	10	7	7
6	10	6	6
4	10	6	6
7b	10	6	6
8	2	5	0
9	1	6	0
10	0	7	0
11	0	0	0
13	1	1	1
14	1	1	1
17	2	1	1
15	2	2	2
18	1	2	1

Figure 21. Symmetrical exchange of REL

interaction arena just one step above (and sometimes even equal to) the washerman and barber, which are polluting occupations (for interactional ranks in many media see Beck 1972: 171, 175, 178 and Figure 16 above). Yet, as informants reported, there are other local interaction arenas about thirty miles away where members of 11 enjoy a rank close to caste 5; indeed there were even reported to be areas where some subcaste of Nāyakkar were the dominant caste. Given this it is easy to see why local Nāyakkars do not accept the superiority of castes 8, 9 and 10, a fact that showed up in the retaliative T-usage described above.

Less clear is how 8, 9 and 10 are able to maintain their superiority. The answer does seem to lie in the fact that 8, 9 and 10 are right-hand division members along with 5; and 8, 9 and 10 are bound by traditional service relations to the dominant caste 5 in a way that Nāyakkars, whose traditional skills are required only occasionally and can be imported for a particular task, are not. Even though this privileged position of 8, 9 and 10 is not reflected in the solidary extension of REL to them, they do nevertheless feel free to use REL to most upper castes. And 11 cannot do this. Indeed it is very noticeable in daily interaction that members of 11 give much more kinesic and linguistic deference to the upper castes in general than do members of 8, 9 and 10. In short, members of 11 are 'outsiders' as far as this local area is concerned, and it is their isolation from solidary relations with any other castes that shows dramatically in their zero REL-usage.

Turning to the last column of Figure 21, note that the final column tabulates the number of other castes each caste symmetrically (reciprocally) exchanges REL with. From this final column we see that the only castes that achieve a massive level of solidarity-expression are castes 2, 5, 3, 7a, 7b, 6 and 4. And although this pattern could in part be seen as upward claims to near-equal rank by the lower members of the upper castes, there still remains the irreducible and astonishing fact of the downward generosity of 2 and 5, and to a lesser extent 3 and 7a.

The significant finding of this section is, then, that there are some castes, especially 1, 2 and 5, who are downwardly generous in REL. In addition we see that these three leaders in downward generosity include the models for *both* left- and right-hand divisions, and this rules out an interpretation in terms of left-hand solidarity, even though the majority of solidarity-expressors are members of the left-hand division. But the fact that left-hand members are deeply involved also rules out an interpretation of the REL-patterns as the automatic reflexes of massive use of *maximal strategy*, for that is a pattern associated with the right-hand castes. We must conclude then that the creation of solidary inter-caste relations is an important motive in the conduct of inter-caste affairs and that consequently these will never be understood without an appeal to a principle like *alliance* that runs alongside the much better documented principle of rank or hierarchy.

A problem however remains. Why is there the dramatic cessation of REL-usage at the point in the hierarchy formed by the 7b/8 boundary? One might argue, pointing to the absence of this particular boundary in many other media (see Figure 16), that this is of no great significance. Yet other media do not have the daily repetition of transactions and the caste-wide and population-wide participation that the linguistic media do; moreover there is (as mentioned) a keen interest and awareness of what goes on in the linguistic media. We cannot then dismiss it lightly. One should, though, recall that the boundary may be a little less abrupt than here described, in that (as discussed above) there is some minor variation in thresholds for REL-usage to castes like 7b so that patterns of interaction can move towards full categorical T-usage by degrees. However these are only marginal effects: the fact is that members of the top eight castes volunteered consistently that T-usage begins with caste 8 and not before.

One possible explanation for this abrupt boundary and for the downward generosity evinced by the higher castes is that what underlies the great blocs of symmetrical REL-exchange is a concern felt by all the higher castes to erect an insurmountable barrier between the upper and lower castes. In order to effect this, the topmost castes are willing to extend their REL-usage downwards to include all those they wish to detach from the lower castes, while the latter are to be thus symbolically excluded from the brotherhood of the upper castes. Less metaphorically, this interpretation would amount to claiming that our alliance principle is nothing other than the familiar fact of coalition in a ranking game, but that the nature of the game is here a little different. In this game the topmost castes have some vested interest in the relative rank orders of those below them. This could have various sources: one might be a policy of 'divide and rule'. Another might be a concern with stability, and a desire to stop the steady upward creep of some ambitious and able group. In such a game context the topmost castes would be willing to barter downward REL in exchange for an agreement to give T to players still further down. Having then obtained the help of the middle castes in holding down the lowest, the topmost castes can then reassert their superiority over the middle castes in another medium (e.g. V-receiving).

Although such a scenario is not totally implausible, my informants never spoke that way nor I suspect ever would. I have then no way seriously to assess it. Another explanation of the caesura between upper and lower castes which suffers from the same sort of assessment problem has been given to me by Edmund Leach (personal communication). This explanation proceeds in the 'structuralist' vein, that is by assuming that there is a kind of cultural logic that guides performances, which consists of simple operations on binary sets. The argument goes like this. Dumont points out that the notion of *hierarchy* (at least as employed in Hindu materials) combines two separable ideas: rank as serial order, and the concept of serial dichotomous segmentation (where A 'encompasses' B + C, and B 'encompasses' E + F . . . etc). The classical Varna scheme is organized in terms of the second concept. The sequence of segmentations is:

(a) Twice Born *versus* Sudra,
(b) within Twice Born: Brahmans *versus* the rest,
(c) within 'the rest': Kshatriya *versus* Vaishya.

We need one other cultural presupposition: that Kshatriya alone are also somehow opposite in kind to Brahmans. Then since both Vaishya and Brahmans are opposites of Kshatriya, in a cultural 'logic' based on operations on binary sets, they must be similar to each other. Now if we introduce a caste category that is socially defined as opposite to Brahman, and opposite to Kshatriya, and is not *like* Brahman (therefore not Vaishya), it *must be* Sudra. Suppose we now identify caste 1 as Brahman, caste 5 as Kshatriya, caste 7 (both 7a and 7b) as Vaishya, then caste 8 is neither Brahman nor Kshatriya. But being assimilated to the Kshatriya style (right-hand division), it is not *like* Brahman. Therefore it must be Sudra. Hence the caesura in the hierarchy at the 7b/8 boundary coincides with the first and fundamental Twice Born *versus* Sudra dichotomy, (a) above. And that is why the abrupt cessation of REL exists.

Although the 'cultural logic' deployed in this argument may be a pretty wonky logic (failing to distinguish oppositions at various levels – hence the equation of Vaishya = Like-Brahman), that does not definitely argue against it. That could be the way it works. The attractive aspect of it is this: Vaishya is really merely a residual category of castes who are neither Brahman nor Kshatriya but are nevertheless respectable. But they are *like* Brahmans. There is therefore no category for respectable castes who are Kshatriya-like: they have to be Sudra (unrespectable). Consequently there can be no high ranking 'right-hand' castes other than the leader of the division itself (here caste 5). And this is empirically the case: 8, 9 and 10 are the next highest right-handers and they fall far behind the left-hand castes 3, 4, 6, 7a and 7b. On the face of it this is curious: how does it come about that the caste with the key command of patronage (caste 5) is unable to reward its loyal followers (8, 9 and 10) more adequately? Some explanation, perhaps along these lines of Leach's, does seem required.

3.2. Symmetrical exchange in other media

Here we briefly describe patterns of symmetrical exchange in other media. Our purpose here is simply to point out that the principle we have dubbed *alliance* plays a role in inter-caste affairs that has been overlooked or underestimated, and we do this by showing that symmetrical exchange can be found in many media. Of course, as pointed out, symmetrical exchange can have a number of different sources, of which the most obvious are the expression of equality (plus or minus solidarity) and retaliative abuse. The last is clearly not possible in media that require a separate act of acceptance in order for a transaction to take place, that is in material transfers. There are other problems of interpretation that we shall touch upon as we proceed.

Mayer seems to have been the first to encounter and describe relations of symmetrical transactional exchange: he distinguished a set of 'allied castes', grouped around the dominant caste in a Malwa village, who exchanged *kacca* food together (Mayer 1960: 33–40). Dumont hailed this, and the high rank gained by the allied castes, as 'unique' (Dumont 1970: 88). But in fact an over concern with *ranking* has led to an underestimate of the very general role that this other dimension plays in inter-caste relations. Matrix representation can help to obscure it too. For instance Beck (1972) provides matrices for cooked rice and curd exchange that hide within them a crucial area or bloc of symmetrical exchangers – our castes 5, 7a and 8. The redrawn matrix in XIV illustrates this for cooked rice exchange, and curd exchange exhibits an almost identical pattern. Another of her interactional media, informal seating on the verandah of a house shows symmetrical reciprocity on a much larger scale. This is illustrated in Matrix XV, drawn from her Figure 4.7 (Beck 1972: 161), where each superimposed square is a bloc of symmetrical exchange.

Passing on to linguistic media, Matrices XVI and XVII display some blocs of symmetrical exchange in two dishonorific media.[4] There is, perhaps not surprisingly, no symmetrical exchange of various super-honorific items, e.g. *nām* and *cāmi*, but here in the dishonorifics we find fairly extensive symmetrical exchange blocs. There are no facts that occasion surprise given our earlier findings about T/V, but there are a number that independently support those findings and are worth pointing out. Note that, in Matrix XVI, caste 3 is able to exchange reciprocally the dishonorific *ṭā* with caste 1 and 2 (provided, for all castes, the addressee is under fifteen or so in years). We see here a facet of that familiarity and caste-neutralizing solidarity between caste 1 and 3 which was one source of the dissensus on giving and receiving dimensions in the T/V data. Another repeated pattern is the retaliative symmetrical usage of *ṭā* by caste 11 to 8, 9 and 10, just as in the T-medium. A pattern that is distinctly different from that found in the T/V data is the partial inclusion of 8 and 9 into a group of upper castes (3, 4, 6, 7a, 7b) in the matter of reciprocal under-fifteen *ṭā* usage. In Matrix XVII *ppā* usage also displays some partial blurring of the 7b/8 boundary between the upper and lower castes that we were concerned with in the previous section. But this is still more apparent in the food transfers in XIV (where 5, 8 and 7a symmetrically exchange).

Since the interpretation of these facts would take us too far afield, we leave them here. Additional data and analysis concerning the use of fictive kin-terms between members of different castes reveals further complexities in inter-caste alliance behaviour, but there is not sufficient space to discuss them here (see Levinson 1977: 400–25). Nevertheless, it is clear that symmetrical exchange is a far more prevalent pattern in inter-caste interactions than seems to have been realized.

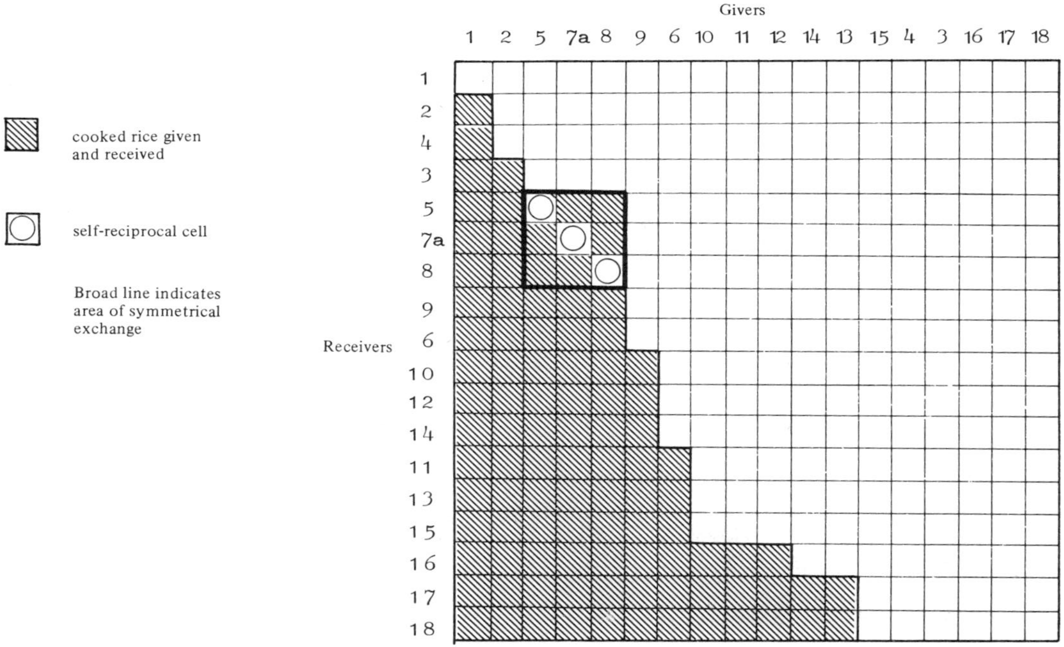

Matrix XIV. Symmetrical exchange of cooked rice

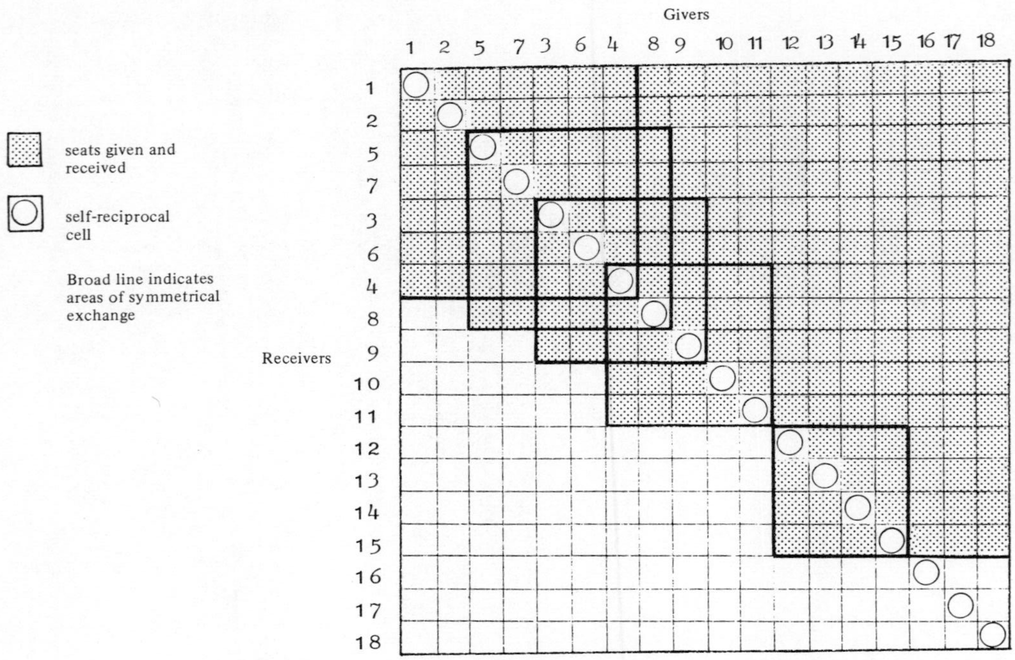

Matrix XV. Symmetrical exchange in informal seating

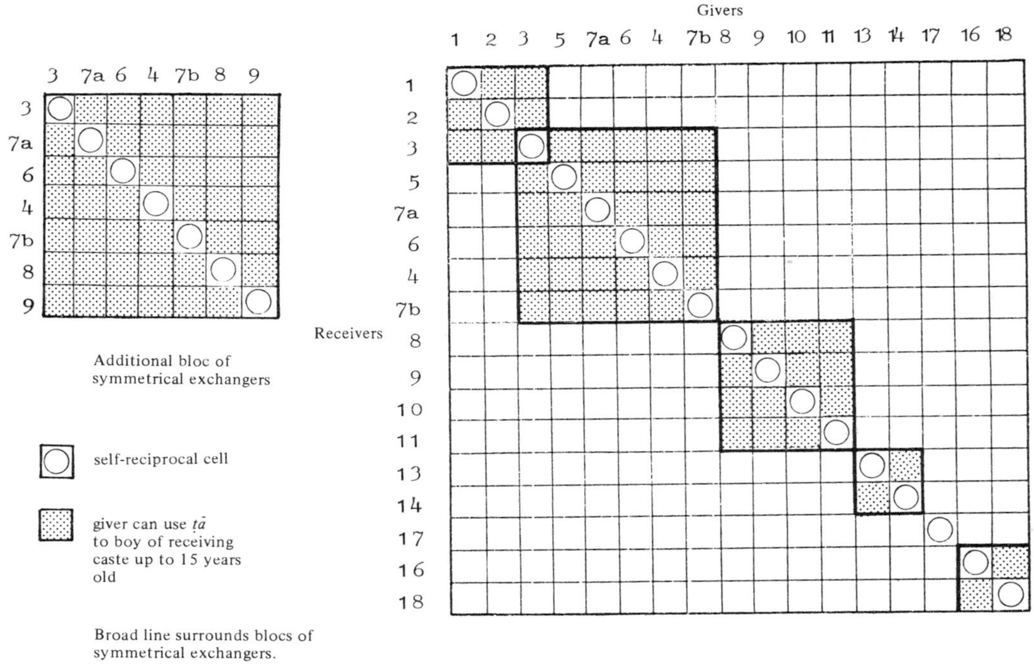

Matrix XVI. Symmetrical exchange in the dishonorific, *ṭā*

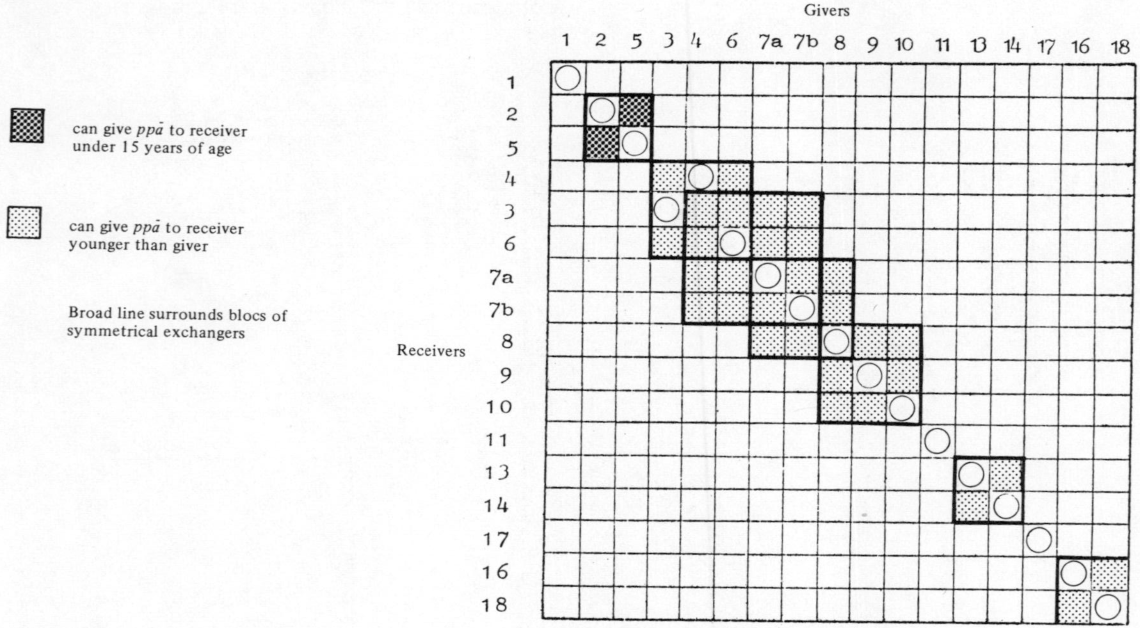

Matrix XVII. Symmetrical exchange in the dishonorific, *ppā*

4. POWER AND CLASS

So far we have almost entirely ignored the effect on honorific usage of sources of rank other than those based on caste. Our assumption has been that assessments based on caste membership are basic for members, while other sources of rank (wealth and office, for instance) are secondary, though not unimportant. One reason for treating non-caste sources of rank as secondary is that they are attributes of individuals, and exceptional in the sense that most individuals do not have attributes such as significant wealth or office.

But one non-caste-based source of rank simply cannot be dismissed in this way as secondary. This source is membership in the *periya kuṭumpams* ('big families') of caste 5, that is membership in what we have called the 'squire class' as described in section 1.1 and elsewhere. In the first place, membership in this class of wealthy landlords is not an individual attribute, but seems rather to be an attribute of a lineage segment that is handed down through the generations. Thus the children of *periya Kavuṇṭars* ('big Kavuṇṭars') are not treated like the children of a self-made wealthy landlord, but rather as the heirs to an inheritable authority. Membership is then technically inclusion in what Weber calls a status group rather than an (economic) class. And it appears to be a well-defined and closed group.

Moreover, the squire class forms a cohesive unit from an interactional point of view. Members are treated in a very special way by all other members of the village regardless of their caste. For example, if one such aristocrat is positioned by the side of a road, all passers-by must dismount and give a formal and respectful greeting. Conversely, when such aristocrats approach people, they may do so with an arrogance and boldness that takes no cognizance of higher caste rank.

Honorific usage fits this picture neatly; indeed one could pick out the class of aristocrats on those grounds alone. Thus in an analysis of the use of *nām* or 'super-V', members of the squire class of caste 5 came out as the highest ranking group on the receiving scale: castes 1, 2, 3, 4, and 6 and 7a (i.e., all the highest castes) give *nām* to such aristocrats without reciprocation. Also one caste (11) claimed to give *cāmi* (title meaning literally 'God') only to Brahmans, aristocrats and the incumbent *karṇam* of the Piḷḷai caste. But most clearly there was one title of address, *ecamāṅka*, almost (but not quite) reserved for members of the squire class. Brahmans and Piḷḷais would only use this to the highest titled members of this class, but others would use it to all male members of the squire class. Members of lowly castes (13 and 18) extend this usage to ordinary non-aristocratic members of caste 5, but even here the recipients would either be 'squires' or lesser landlord patrons for the most part.

However we have ignored the effect of such aristocrats on standard T/V usage, and taking this into account now will yield a radical revision. The facts are given in Matrix XVIII. The startling thing about this matrix is that the ritual superiority of castes 1 and 2 (in particular) is here superseded by the secular power of the great families of caste 5: both Brahmans and Pi̤l̤lais give the members of these families categorical V (the threshold here seems to be low: the addressee may be no more than fifteen years old). It is true that in turn the Brahmans receive a similar treatment from those of the squire class, but that this is a courtesy is shown by the fact that there have been aristocrats who chose not to extend it (thus the elder brother, now dead, of the head of one of the leading families is consistently said to have used T to adult Brahmans). In any case Pi̤l̤lais (caste 2) cannot expect V from aristocratic Kavuṇṭars, although the *karṇam* (village accountant, hereditary office held by head of the local family of caste 2) does seem to receive V.

The picture, then, is that everyone of all castes gives V (or super-V) to members of the squire class providing that they are fifteen years old or so (the lower the caste of the giver the lower the age of the threshold of transition from T to V). In turn, members of the squire class give T to all other castes with the single exception of the Brahmans (and they also appear to make exceptions of influential office holders like the *karṇam*).

There are only three families of this order in the revenue village, but if we take them into account we must make an important revision to the description of inter-caste T/V usage described in the sections above. Essentially, we must superimpose on that earlier picture another one, where landed power backed by traditional authority achieves a standing that is second to none and equal with the Brahmans.

A final point of some importance is the relationship of these great families to the lesser families of their own caste (caste 5). In the matrix we have not specified the T/V usage exchange by 5* (the squires) and 5 (ordinary Kavuṇṭars), because this cannot be so simply described. Typical would be the following tape-recorded usages, where a woman aged 23 and married to a squire (aged 55) addressed (i) a 45-year old member of caste 3 by T, receiving V, (ii) a 50-year old member of her own caste 5 with T, receiving V, (iii) another 45-year old male member of her own caste with T, receiving V. In the case of (iii), the addressee was employed as a bailiff, and had no land of his own, while in the case of (ii) he was a poor man

5* members of squire class

V = categorical V

T = categorical T

○ = self-reciprocal cell

Givers

Receivers	1	2	3	7a	5*	6	4	7b	8	9	10	11	13	14	17	16	18
1					V												
2					T												
5*	V	V	V	V	○	V	V	V	V	V	V	V	V	V	V	V	V
3					T												
6					T												
4					T												
7a					T												
7b					T												
8					T												
9					T												
10					T												
11					T												
13					T												
14					T												
17					T												
16					T												
18					T												

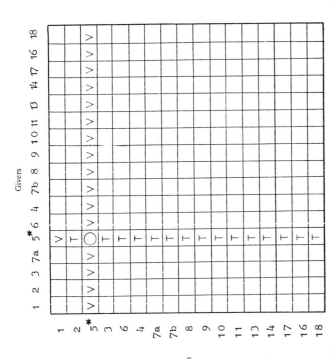

Matrix XVIII. T/V usage to and from *periya Kavuṇṭar* squires with a little land, temporarily employed. Both were therefore employees with little capital of their own.

However there is another side to the picture: members of the squire families will not use T to older men of substance of their own caste, at least not generally. To some extent this is attributable to the real or potential kinship connections between the squire families and other men of substance: the 23-year old woman mentioned above was herself, for example, from a prestigious but decayed family that is no longer of clearly squire status.

5. SOME CONCLUSIONS

We started with an initial problem that has beset the analysts of Indian society: members of the society clearly believe that in a local situation there is a well-defined caste hierarchy, but how the sociologist is to isolate this turns out to be problematic. This is also a more general sociological problem: how is the sociologist to build overall models of a social system while retaining the perspective of its members (which, after all, is a predominant factor in the system being the way it is)?

Our answer has been this. First locate some media in which all members of the society transact. Then see what social valuations are attached to particular configurations of these transactions by participants. Next exhaustively collect which configurations occur between each and every distinct category of persons in the society. Finally make inferences from this distributional map and from the valuations, to the value attached to each category of persons by each other category.

In our case the application of this method yielded some positive results. In the first case we found that the distribution of honorifics (as used across castes) provided a very fine-scale *ranking* of castes, thus providing an answer to our initial problem. The rank orders can be shown to be implicit in the materials and thus available to members, and much more discriminating than any ranking that can be derived from caste-dialects. This suggests that the emphasis on the individual speaker's dialect in current sociolinguistic theory is misplaced: far more sociological information resides in patterns of usage *between* individuals.

We were aided in our inferences by the very substantial consensus about caste rank that emerged from the materials. But the consensus was not absolute, and in seeking an explanation for divergences we were led to further inferences. We were able, for example, to explore to what extent active competition for status underlies the patterns we found, and to conclude that (contrary to some views of Indian society) competition is not always a prevalent feature. More importantly, we located an entirely different principle of inter-caste organization, *alliance*, which seems to have been ignored in most of the literature. Inter-caste relations are visibly structured on more dimensions than just that of rank.

Finally, attention to honorifics allowed us to isolate a distinct principle of power and authority that picked out a clearly defined category, the *periya Kavuṇṭars*, or squire families of caste 5. This principle crosscuts caste rank, and indeed supersedes it, and the results indicate that these families have an importance that has not been appreciated in the ethnography of the region.

All these inferences derived from the usage of honorifics amount to some substantial sociological results. Many of them could no doubt have been obtained in a more traditional manner by careful general ethnography. But an approach through language usage is at once more direct and simple, and has the great advantage of providing us insight that conforms to members' views. This *verstehen* perspective seems to be the most important contribution that sociolinguistics can make to sociology and to social anthropology.

However, language is not the only area that provides important *verstehen* insights. Marriott, working with other media of transactional exchange (food and services), had already seen the importance of interactional materials to problems in Indian sociology, and indeed we have utilized a great deal of his method here.

So it remains for us now to clarify the relation of linguistic to non-linguistic media of interaction. The relation is important because the results on different media are not entirely coincident. Fortunately, Beck (1972: 154–81) provides much data on interaction patterns in the same village in non-linguistic media, some of which is summarized in Figure 22. With reference to the figure, the linguistic media of T/V usage provide the first column, with the top column representing ranks by giving and the bottom column representing ranks by receiving, and the non-linguistic media follow. 'Seating' here indicates rank determined by the willingness to offer and accept a seat on the verandah of a house belonging to a member of another caste; 'eating leaves' represents the rank determined by willingness to 'give' the service of disposal of leaf-plates to another caste, and by the number of castes willing to do this service for each caste (determining its 'receiving' rank); 'curds' represents ranks by the giving and receiving of milk products; 'rice' by the giving and receiving of cooked rice on informal occasions. The first two non-linguistic media (seating and leaf-

	T/V	Seating	Eating leaves	Curds	Rice
Giving ranks	1	1	1	1	1
	2	2	2	2	2
	3	5	3	5	5
	7a	7a	4	7a	7a
	5	3	6	8	8
	6	6	5	9	9
	4	4	7a	6	6
	7b	8	8	10	10
	8	9	9	12	12
	9	10	10	14	14
	10	11	12	11	11
	11	12	14	13	13
	13	13	11	15	15
	14	14	13	4	4
	17	15	15	3	3
	16	16	16	16	16
	18	17	17	17	17
		18	18	18	18
Receiving ranks	1	1	1	1	1
	2	2	2	2	2
	5	5	5	5	4
	3	7a	7a	7a	3
	6	3	8	8	5
	4	6	9	9	7a
	7a	4	6	6	8
	7b	8	10	4	9
	8	9	3	3	6
	9	10	4	10	10
	10	11	12	12	12
	11	12	14	14	14
	13	13	11	11	11
	14	14	13	13	13
	17	15	15	15	15
	16	16	16	16	16
	18	17	17	17	17
		18	18	18	18

Figure 22. Ranks in linguistic and non-linguistic media

removal) have the same valuation as V-exchange, while the second two (rice and curds) have the same valuation as T-exchange. A point of difference between Beck's ranks and ours is the different inventory of castes: she includes caste 12 and 15 excluded in our discussion, and does not distinguish 7b; but comparison is not seriously affected.

Now the most remarkable thing about behaviour in these different transactional media is the fundamental similarity in the rules of valuation and the patterns of ranking that emerge. These results hold out great promise for some *general theory of transactions*, or principles of interaction. We have already hazarded some guesses at why the principles should be the way they appear to be, and concluded that, *pace* Marriott (1968a, 1976a), the reasons do not appear to be peculiarities of Hindu culture but rather general properties of interaction systems. Specifically, we suggested that the valuations have a natural source along the following lines. Taking the reciprocal exchange of intimate material (food, T-pronoun) as a basic and natural symbol of solidarity, the one-way transfer of intimate material can be shown to have a natural interpretation as a symbol of asymmetric rank. The universal principle seems to be that the higher one's rank the more privacy, the greater the inviolability of one's preserve, while the lower one's rank the greater access others have to one's preserve. So one-way intimacy establishes a rank disparity. And this explains the universal facts about the use of T as both a pronoun of solidarity and of superiority, and the use of food both as a symbol of equality (commensality) and as a symbol of dominance (the feast provided for the servants).

However, differences of rank on the different media do emerge and these need to be explained. Beck suggests two theories. One, somewhat lame but no doubt in part correct, is that different media measure different criteria of rank: so, for example, behaviour in offering and receiving seating is essentially about power and material status, while the exchange of cooked rice is essentially about ritual status (Beck 1972: 162). The other theory, which I shall call the *conversion theory*, is adumbrated thus:

> it is my impression that when changes in ranking occur, they occur first in informal seating arrangements and only later in the realm of informal food exchange. Once these informal changes become generally accepted, they will be ratified at a formal feast. Thus we see a possible ordered progression of any particular innovation through several contexts and media (Beck 1972: 172).

In other words, actual rank is first established and recognized in everyday interactional media, and this rank then slowly passes through more ritualized, conscious and carefully guarded media. For a caste trying to maximize its rank, then, the optimal strategy is to *convert* rank recognized on the highly unstable and ephemeral media of everyday interaction to the stabilized ritual media resistant to change. In this way it can gain a measure of security for its achieved rank. Covert in this theory is the Durkheimian view of ritual as a celebration of existing social structures, and the notion that some media of interaction are more ritualized than others. Both of these premises seem well founded in this context.

In relation to these two theories the linguistic media play a special role. With respect to the first theory, the special property of the linguistic media is that they are *not* tied to any particular dimensions of social rank. We can show this by demonstrating, as we have above, that honorifics are sensitive both to overall caste rank, alliances between castes in the ranking arena, and to rank based on traditional power and authority. The linguistic media seem to be sensitive to virtually all social dimensions at once.

With respect to the conversion theory, the linguistic media again play a special role. For they are *par excellence* the media of everyday ordinary interaction. Linguistic media are one of the few areas where it is not possible in practice to abstain, with the result that we have universal exchange between all parties. Moreover, nearly all parties are aware of the details of this exchange, which contrasts with the details in other media. This follows from the public and endlessly replicated transactions in linguistic media. It seems likely then that the linguistic media are *the* primary arena in which actual overall caste ranks are achieved and recognized. Other daily interactional media like kinesic display, seating and touching (during delousing sessions, which occur across castes) would also have a primary significance, but they occur less often, less universally between all parties, or have less clear rank implications (valuations), and would thus be of less interest both to members and ethnographers.

If the conversion theory is correct in essentials, we could expect there to be some lag in the recognition in ritual media of ranks newly achieved in the everyday media. Some confirmation of this can be gained from charting the fortunes of castes 3 and 4. Returning to Figure 22, these castes have a high rank in the linguistic media, and also in the other everyday medium of seating. Their rank begins to be less certain in the more pollution/purity sensitive medium of eating-leaf removal, and has a positive fall in curd exchange transactions. And this low rank does not rise significantly in informal rice exchange, perhaps the most sensitive ritual medium. A reasonable interpretation of this is that castes 3 and 4 have in fact established a high overall rank for themselves in everyday interaction, but are now experiencing the built-in resistance and lag in the ritual or purity-related media where acceptance of high rank would be more permanent. And certainly caste 4 does seem to be in general in the region attempting systematically to up-grade its status (Den Ouden 1969).

We may conclude with the observation that the linguistic media, as represented by our honorifics, do seem to provide the most direct access to indigenous views of the overall general rank of local castes. They do so because they are media unattached to any particular social dimensions (secular or religious rank, for instance), and constitute everyday *de facto* recognition of the actual state of affairs. They are, moreover, media in which all parties exchange, with usages that are generally known to all parties, and where the valuations are particularly clear and can be non-circularly assigned. In short the study of language usage between castes seems to be amongst the very most important sources of information on the nature of the caste system.[5]

Caste and politics in India since 1947

Geoffrey Hawthorn

> The science of history proceeds no doubt as the detailed criticism of sociological generalisations . . . of generalisations so rudimentary and so little analysed that they constitute primitive archetypal images lurking in the background of the historian's consciousness rather than a formed system of ideas. In South Asian studies such images are the simple dichotomies of East and West, tradition and modernity, continuity and change, status and contract, feudalism and capitalism, caste and class . . . In the present age, the historian must content himself with the role of humble camp follower to the sociologist . . . But like the sweeper in my regiment who carried the thunder-box of the sahibs through the Arakan campaign there is the hope that in the end it is he and not they who will be awarded the decoration.
> (Stokes 1978: 19, 289)

Many have claimed that Indian society is in good part constituted by ideas and relations of caste. Many have claimed that Indian politics are too. I shall argue that an influential version of the first claim rests on a series of theoretical mistakes and that a simple version of the second, accepting the most basic of these mistakes and taking a foreshortened view of the facts, is even when corrected at best very partially true.

I

The belief that Indian society is at least in part constituted by ideas and relations of 'caste' rests on two other beliefs, each more general than this and each apparently opposed to the other. The first is that all societies can be seen to be set on the same course, that each occupies a point on a continuum that stretches from Stokes' 'East' to his 'West', from 'tradition' to 'modernity', from 'status' to 'contract', from 'feudalism' or an 'Asiatic mode' to 'capitalism'.[1] The second is that a society must be seen in and on its own terms, through its own distinctive, constitutive categories. A certain kind of comparative sociology, it is true, the kind implied most especially in Marx but also in Max Weber and Barrington Moore (Marx and Engels n.d.; Lichtheim 1963; Weber 1958; Moore 1966, 1978: 55–64), holds only the first and rejects the second. A certain kind of social anthropology holds only the second and rejects the first. But each can also serve the other. The first argument usually concedes that societies like those in South Asia are very different from those in Europe and North America. It is a short step from this to the view that their own categories must at least in part be used to show how. The second argument sees societies as so different that comparison must lie in the contrast of ideal types rather than the assessment of the values of common variables. And it is a short step from this back to the use of more inclusive and cross-culturally generalizable categories of analysis. In Louis Dumont's influential account of caste, the two kinds of argument combine. 'On the one hand', he argues, 'it is the indigenous theory which provides us with the name . . . On the other hand, in so far as we are able to detect in the facts a dimension other than that contained in indigenous consciousness, this is thanks to comparison, thanks first and foremost to the implicit and inevitable comparison with our own society' (1970: 36–7).

In some cases, the terms that emerge from any such comparison are, as Stokes says, 'so rudimentary and so little analysed' that they amount to little more than 'primitive archetypal images'. In other cases, they are so elaborate as actually and often indeed deliberately to circumscribe and confine debate. This is so with caste (as it is also of course with some Marxist concepts of class) and again nowhere more so than in Dumont.[2] Caste, he suggests, is a 'single principle' which encompasses all relations, even when they seem to oppose it (1970: 78, 212–13). It is an ideological 'structure' whose elements are exhaustively constituted by the relations between them. It consists of 'the specialisation and inter-dependence' of abstract elements within a 'hierarchical whole' (1970: 65–6, 92, *passim*). Equality is set over against hierarchy, power against virtue, and pollution against purity. If it is changing, then it is changing to a different but equally exhaustive ideology of another sort, the only other sort that Dumont admits, 'to a modern . . . a totalitarian mentality'. All men are being recreated equal in the name of a freedom that denies itself. 'Egalitarianism, leaving the limited zone', the zone of power, 'in which it is well tolerated, causes a profound modification and [in the Durkheimian sense] brings the threat of religious totalitarianism' (1970: 231). This contrast between hierarchy and equality is quite deliberately grounded in a 'primitive archetypal image' in the early modern European mind. Dumont's two exclusive and exhaustive ideologies are identical to the two by which, for example, Hegel argued that European political thought had become constrained at the beginning of the nineteenth century (Taylor

1975: 403–21). But one does not need Hegel's arguments to see why Dumont's characterization will not do. It starts from a false premise, misuses evidence, and in practice threatens to confine and distort the facts.

Dumont concedes that although the ideology of caste is 'an encompassing conscious form' it is not consciously held in all its aspects by anyone but him. He takes 'the liberty of completing and systematising the indigenous or orthogenic theory of caste – not without employing empirical aspects in a secondary capacity – by postulating that men in a society behave in a coherent and rational manner, especially in such an important matter, and that it is possible to recover the simple principle of their thought' (1970: 37). One might forgive the lapse into 'behave'. It is clear that it is not what men do that primarily interests him, and even if it were, he could not consistently take it as evidence for what they think, even or especially if they do not all or each fully know what they think. One cannot so readily forgive the postulate itself. This is exactly what it claims to be, an assumption of an exhaustive and accessible rationality of a kind long familiar in French sociological writing and characteristic of the diffuse Cartesianism that pervades a great deal of French thought. However, one should be sceptical of its truth, particularly if one accepts that there is a necessary indeterminacy in translation and that, by virtue of their being constituted by a particular interpretation, even agents' own interpretations are not privileged and incontestable. These are arguments which can each be made against Descartes himself (Williams 1978: 297–303) and which make one sceptical of the possibility of arriving at any determinate truth about beliefs. One has thus to accept that a postulate of accessible Hindu rationality such as Dumont's is at the very best a provisional interpretation, tentative and under-determined.

Dumont does recognize this, although not for the reasons I have given. Hence his 'liberty' with the evidence that he uses 'in a secondary capacity'. Yet it is by no means clear that the liberty he does take is defensible. He refers to the classic texts on *artha* and *dharma*. He claims to find in them a single principle, the subordination of power to purity, of *artha* to *dharma*, of king to priest. Hence his view of the 'encompassing' status of the distinction or (as he chooses to call it) the 'opposition' between purity and pollution. His account of what the texts say about the relations between power and purity, *artha* and *dharma*, Kshatriya and Brahman, between what he calls 'power' and 'hierarchy', is curiously thin (1970: 71–2; but see the new appendix, 1979: 351–75). But this apart, his reading of them is very much open to question. There is no doubt that these texts, like all (or nearly all) texts of political theory in any society at any time, were attempts to provide a more or less principled criticism or defence of a more or less practically immediate problem and its possible solutions. Like others, it would be surprising if they were within and between themselves perfectly consistent, or were even intended to be. Other commentators have indeed stressed their ambiguity (for example, Basham 1963: 11–23; Tambiah 1976: 19–31). Even if one accepts that Kautilya's famous *Arthashastra* is indeed exceptional,[3] the fact remains that it was written and noticed and cannot except by fiat be removed from the classical corpus; the fact remains that it is only by deciding in advance, as Dumont does, that there must be a fundamentally consistent view, that one can insist on the priority of the dharmashastric over the arthashastric. There may of course be differences of degree between the texts so wide as to lead one (as Tambiah is led in his comparison of Hindu and Buddhist views of kingship) to conclude a difference almost of kind. But to decide that the dharmashastric contains the real, or true, or fundamental Hindu view of the relations between power and virtue is exactly analogous to, and as pointless as, deciding that the many pieces of conventional advice to princes in later Renaissance Italy contain the real or true or fundamental view of these relations and that Machiavelli can be set aside (Skinner 1978: 113–38). On the scale that Dumont attempts, it is indeed analogous to and as pointless as deciding that Plato rather than Machiavelli contains the real or true or fundamental view of these relations in Europe as a whole. It is probably even more pointless, for almost all agree on the extraordinary flexibility of Hinduism, on its capacity to absorb and thus to justify an extremely wide range of more or less principled actions for different actors in different situations. Dumont, in short, starts selectively to reinterpret classical texts whose meaning he thereby narrows and which together and even separately give no absolutely clear and unambiguous account of the relations between power and virtue. He then asserts that this interpretation is itself a 'conscious form', available to modern agents whose beliefs and actions it can describe and explain.

Nevertheless, caste is part of the language of life in India, and one has to decide how to see it. Even if Dumont's own characterization is tendentious and narrow, his insistence on the distinction between its 'structure' (the traditionally fluid, holistic, and relational logic of segmentation and opposition of caste categories within a larger system of castes) and its 'substance' (the tangible social organization of individual caste groups directed to questions of political and economic welfare and asserting claims to unique, fixed, intrinsic, almost racial, caste identity) may be of use. Others tacitly agree. Bailey, for example, arguing against Dumont and those like Leach (1960) with a similarly narrow view, has suggested four 'referents'; *varnas*, *jātis*, 'caste categories', and 'caste associations' (1963). Béteille has resisted this, pointing to 'the fact that caste is a segmentary system', which 'means (and has always meant) that people view themselves as belonging to units of different orders in different contexts' (1969: 150). Yet elsewhere, Béteille has himself argued in the opposite direction, not only for a clear analytical view of caste, a clear definition, but also for a connection between this and a clear analytical view of 'class'. 'Relations', such as relations of caste, 'are structured in terms of certain basic principles and it is material interest which provides structure to the relations between classes'. 'Louis Dumont has examined Indian society in terms of its structure of ideas . . . There should be some place by the side of this for a sociology of interests' (1974: 54–5). Inequalities everywhere reduce to practical inequalities of money and power, of 'organisation', and to principled inequalities of 'evaluation', of which caste is one expression (Béteille 1977). Local languages of inequality in India, as elsewhere, can ultimately be mapped into these two (Béteille 1974: 117–41).

Such suggestions, of course, are clear and simple and consistent with the familiar distinction, Max Weber's distinction, between 'class' and 'status' and with Weber's view that 'power' is to be seen as an ability to pursue an interest in either or both. Even Dumont, who at one point argues that caste is not merely an exceptional form of status, being 'primarily a religious matter', eventually lapses (1970: 24–7, 212–13).[4] Yet there seems no good reason to accept that money and status are the two irreducible human interests, or at least, the two irreducible interests informing social life. It seems at least as reasonable to accept that men may also want justice, or mutual understanding, or power for its own sake, or, like Dumont, consistency, and that none of these or any other is non-vacuously reducible. We are committed to interpretation.[5]

My argument against Dumont is thus both particular and general. In particular, there seems no good reason to accept his postulate of a single accessible Indic rationality and so no good reason to accept that he uses his chosen evidence correctly. In general, there seems no good reason to accept that *any* postulate about human interests is incontestably correct and so no good reason determinately to characterize any motive, action or identity. To try to escape from this indeterminacy into a distinction between 'structure' and 'substance', idea and reality, the analytical and the empirical, between what we may believe something to be and how it may appear, is thus an illusion. It either restates a belief in what is really the case or commits the empiricist mistake of supposing that analytical categories themselves carry no commitment to the real nature of the phenomena they are intended to distinguish and denote. These are strong conclusions. In the light of standard practice in the social sciences, they are also eccentric. As Dunn puts it, most human scientists who have supposed any generalizable knowledge at all to be possible have more or less deliberately sought 'to render human performance in an idiom in which replicability and inter-observer reliability are at a premium' (1978: 150); and they have then more or less explicitly suggested that such renderings are renderings of reality. Unlike, say, most historians, they have therefore committed themselves through this series of philosophical mistakes to some version or other of the thesis that *plus ça change plus c'est la même chose*.

The implications of these conclusions clearly vary according to the kind of belief or action one is trying to explain. Hermeneutic fastidiousness may matter less for some kinds than for others. But it is difficult to see where it could matter more than in identifying and trying to explain the intrusions of caste into politics or of politics into caste. If groups identify themselves for the purposes of political action as *jātis* or *varnas* (or, respecting Bailey's somewhat untidy distinctions, if they identify themselves with the name of a *jāti* or a *varna*) and if they seem to be acting merely for reasons of status, the grounds for suspecting such intrusions are clear. But if they do not identify themselves in this way or do not claim to be acting for this kind of reason, it does not follow that the grounds do not exist. However one chooses oneself to characterize the springs of their actions, the fact remains that there is always room for doubt. Men speak for themselves, but neither we nor they can incontestably be presumed to *know* what they are doing.

II

Nevertheless, political scientists have presumed to know about the intrusions of caste into politics and of politics into caste. The more confident among them have tended to argue with or to a view of 'political modernisation'. They have seen India as more or less steadily set on a natural progression away from 'tradition'. Kothari, for instance, one of the most conspicuous of these and the one who has done more than any other to try to draw this argument together, detected three stages in the progression in the first twenty years of independence. In the first stage, the struggle for power was limited to the entrenched and ascendant castes. There was 'polarisation'. In the second, competition developed within these castes. There was 'factionalism'. In the third, the lower castes have been 'mobilised' and shifting interests and identities have replaced steady ones. There has been true 'modernisation'. 'It is not politics that gets caste-ridden; it is caste that gets politicised' (1970b: 14–20).[6]

By 1970 such a scheme certainly seemed to begin to make sense of the facts. The socialist Asoka Mehta's observation in the early 1950s that 'as the franchise is widened, each social group and sub-group within the generally immobile Hindu society struggles for predominance or at least for a share in the loaves and fishes of offices and jobs' (quoted by Fürer-Haimendorf 1963: 63) has been widely endorsed in later studies of state politics in India in the first decade or so after Independence, by Harrison for Andhra Pradesh (1956; 1960), by Hardgrave and Rudolphs for the Nadars in southern Madras (1969; 1967: 36–49), by the Rudolphs for the Vanniyars in northern Madras (1967: 49–61), and by Bailey for Orissa (1960: 191). All reveal that it was those who aspired to power, rather than those who already had it, who in dispute deliberately drew the lines as lines of caste. Elliot's observation for Andhra, that 'throughout the state it is remarkable that the politicians with the strongest caste orientation are of middle peasant rather than notable status' (1970: 155), seems to have been more generally true.[7] The status of Kshatriya *varna*, for example, the status of warrior and king, the overtly political status, was claimed by Coorgs in Mysore, Jats in Rajasthan and Punjab, Marathas in Maharashtra, Kammas and Reddis in Andhra, Ahirs, Kurmis and Koeris in Bihar and Uttar Pradesh, Bariyas in Gujarat and Nadars and Vanniyars in Tamil Nad (Kothari and Maru 1970: 96; Hardgrave 1969: 110; Béteille 1970: 262). Observers agreed that 'where it once exercised social control at the level of functionally integrated villages, caste now' reinforced 'economic and political conflict' (Harrison 1960: 101), that it had become 'the unit in which men associate for competition against others' (Morris-Jones 1964: 65–6). Few doubted that in this, the first of Kothari's three stages of 'modernisation', it had quickly become a force if not in itself a focus of political conflict. Horizontal alliances, whether in the name of a *varna* or merely of a local *jāti*, were seen to be common (Béteille 1970: 261–2; Kothari and Maru 1970: 72). 'Competition for power and office', Béteille remarked in 1964, 'requires a certain aggregation of segments. The thousands of minimal segments in a given region cannot compete individually in the struggle for power. When they come together they follow alignments inherent in the traditional structure of caste. That is why the larger segments which compete for power today regard themselves as castes or *jātis* and are so regarded by others' (1969: 151). The interests in these struggles, however, as many hinted, were not merely or even mainly interests of what might be described as 'status'. Some groups, it is true, started to wear the sacred thread, but this, like the names they used for themselves, was a symbol, a declaration of another kind of intent. Nevertheless, few who looked at these struggles in the states paid much attention to what the other intents might be, or asked themselves why these symbols were the ones that were used.

It is more difficult to reconcile the literature to the second of Kothari's three stages. Hardgrave, for example, reflecting on his study of Nadars in Tamil Nad but generalizing to the whole of India, took the view that such horizontal alliances followed rather than preceded factionalism within a caste (1969: 103) and Harrison predicted a progressive (but in his view morally regressive) intensification of caste contests. But Elliot, reassessing the course of the fight for supremacy between Kammas and Reddis and Congress and the Communists in Andhra, disagreed. 'In areas where there is a dominant caste, the process of vertical [rather than horizontal] mobilisation often enhances its political power. Where this has occurred, vertical mobilisation under dominant caste leadership may be an alternative means to modernisation' (1970: 131). It looked as though the move from the first stage, as Kothari defined it, to the second was more conditional than he allowed. It is certainly difficult to agree that factionalism has been a passing phase.

There was no doubt though that the move to the third stage was a strictly conditional one. Kothari saw it as following from the 'mobilisation' of lower castes. But it is not clear what this means. The Naxalites certainly managed to mobilize some Scheduled Castes and Tribes in Andhra, Bengal and Orissa. This, however, is not what Kothari can have had in mind. Jagjivan Ram's long unassailable position in Union politics depended upon his being seen as representing the Scheduled Castes. But he can hardly be said to have mobilized them. And there is evidence that even at the reputed height of political involvement from below, at the time of the 1977 elections, the lowest castes and the groups below them were not only not mobilized but did not even have a very clear conception of what mobilization itself would mean (Schlesinger 1977: 630). If, however, Kothari's 'lower castes' in any place only have to be lower than what has come to be called the 'dominant' caste (Srinivas 1959; Bailey 1963), and if merely one such 'low caste' is sufficient, then his point is trivial. On this argument, for a variety of interests and symbols to become important, and for caste alone to cease to be important, politics have simply to cease to be the province of one caste alone. And that seems indistinguishable from the condition of the move to the first of the three stages. Other observers have been more specific and more plausible. Brass, for example, one of the very few who have consistently denied the causal importance of caste in at least the politics of the north, suggesting what he at one point describes as 'the independence of political leadership' there 'from social forces' (1974: 397), argued that where there is no external threat, where there is 'consensus on ideological issues' and where there is no authoritative leadership, there will be highly unstable alliances (1965: 232), and that the same pattern will result when 'social mobilisation outpaces assimilation and, conversely, that assimilation will occur when social change in a cultural group is slow enough for its members to be absorbed gradually into another, dominant cultural group' (1974: 422). These two arguments are consistent or can be made so. They suggest that the manipulation of caste identities (and communal identities under other descriptions) in politics is a temporary affair, likely only under conditions of rapid change – of what he calls 'unevenness in development' (1974: 419). Most remarkably, in this literature the arguments put a good deal of weight on the discretion and causal force of politicians themselves. Mayer, whose interest has been in urban politics rather than those of the States, and who mentioned Brass with approval (1967: 129), was similarly sceptical. Even where there was a 'dominant' caste in the part of Madhya Pradesh in which he worked, the issues of dispute, the lines of cleavage and alliance and the mobilization of support as often as not crossed caste lines. 'Factions tend to span a number of castes, and caste membership is one among several criteria of selection of municipal candidates. The need to have new candidates, uncontaminated by the mistakes of their predecessors, is at least as important as caste, as may also be class or profession' (1967: 130; see also 1963: 119).

Kothari's scheme, therefore, seems somewhat wanting. It presumes the existence of castes. In at least the first of his three stages, they are in his view real corporate groups deliberately acting as *jātis* or as the instantiation of a *varna*. It presumes a set chronology. And even if only by default, it presumes in this chronology the unfolding of a natural course of political development, a course of 'modernisation', in which it is accepted that 'political parties, especially in developing societies, are dependent forces, which at best reflect and at worst exacerbate existing cleavages' (Brass 1974: 431) and that the cleavages which appear at the start of 'development' are above all the 'primordial' ties, as Geertz (1963) called them, of kin, community and (in India) caste, cleavages which are supposedly uncharacteristic of and inimical to the rapid and secure establishment of civil society, but cleavages which will gradually fade to become merely the names of groups and interests of other kinds. None of these presumptions will do. Castes are not fixed entities and so are real in many senses and in none. Kothari's chronology fits the facts only to the extent that there has until very recently been a decline in horizontal alliances. And there is no reason to suppose the cause of political change to be natural, the expression of a preordained and unconditional progression. It has to be explained.

III

The conditions of political development in India are many and various. But three, which are related, stand out and still obtain to explain the changes that have taken place in the mutual intrusions of caste and politics in India since Independence. The first of these is the way in which the British constituted the grounds for political dispute before 1947. The second is the way in which Congress was forced to and at the same time wished to redefine them from then until its first defeat in 1977. The third is the way in which that defeat allowed, if it did not force, parts of the Janata coalition to redefine them yet again.

If one takes the view that India is emerging from 'tradition' to 'modernity' and the view, fostered and indeed sincerely held by many Englishmen in the colonial period, that England, even nineteenth-century England, was a 'modern' society, it is perfectly natural to see the effect of the colonization as a move 'from Indian status to British contract' (Cohn 1961). But the truth was not so simple. There were, of course, liberal Englishmen, convinced that the necessary conditions of social and political and (in agriculture, at least) economic progress consisted in a free market in land and the establishment of an independent and responsible landlord class. These men accordingly sought to replace customary allocations and administrations of land by more modern, market principles, to establish titles of ownership and to settle a large degree of responsibility on the landlords (Ambirajan 1978). And they did introduce a good deal of contract law. The corollary of their intent, however, was quite the opposite, that unless and until such changes were made, Indian society would continue as they thought it had always been, an inert and complex hierarchy of mutually excluding groups, pervaded by beliefs of an unequivocally ancient and uncivil kind. To defend 'modernity' required them to exaggerate 'tradition'. But there were also Englishmen, more numerous and certainly more consequential in the administration of the country, who by conviction and administrative convenience actually reinforced this 'tradition'.

> The civil law, for example, made ascriptive . . . identity relevant to many crucial issues of litigation. Over matters of inheritance, family law, social status, rights to worship . . . Indians did not stand before the law as equal individuals. They stood as members of prescriptive communities each of which had its own rights, practices, differences and deferences. Not even at the level of theory did Indian jurisprudence move radically from principles of status to principles of contract under the colonial regime. Legally-defined ethnic groupings became operational categories in the Indian social process where, in many cases, they had not been before. The attempt to make censuses of caste and language groups also 'objectified' these and helped to make the status of the whole caste, or the level of development of the whole language group, the touchstone of social success or failure (Washbrook 1979: 29–30).

Contemporaries remarked on it. 'The last few years', wrote one, 'and especially the occasion of the present census, have witnessed an extraordinary revival of the caste spirit in certain aspects. For numerous caste *Sabhas* have sprung up, each keen to assert the dignity of the social group it represents' (Census of India 1911, Vol. XII Part I: 178, quoted by Fürer-Haimendorf 1963: 56; see also Census of India 1921, Vol. V Part I: 346). With the extension of these legally-defined identities into the criminal law, the education code, the famine code, bureaucratic patronage and the developing institutions of self-government, and with their promotion by Indians themselves (in the south, it seems, especially by those who had been to Oxford), such identities, of ethnicity, caste and language, became rhetorically more evident and practically more consequential. 'One of the most amazing features of India under the Raj was the apparent plasticity of its political organisations. The British had only to think of a political category, however unrelated to society outside, and somebody would come forward to fill it.' 'Madras political society', for example, responded to its government at the turn of the century 'by producing caste associations in the image of the caste categories' (Washbrook 1975: 184–5, 187, 194). Englishmen of all sorts, in short, reinforced and to a considerable degree actually created 'tradition'. And in so doing, they helped to exacerbate that lack of consensus which Brass describes as an obstacle to 'modern' politics and so perpetuated and actually created a society which was not only not 'traditional' (however much it may have given later anthropologists an idea of what 'tradition' might have been) but which also, in lacking consensus, lacked precisely what 'tradition' is supposed to consist in.[8] To put it too simply, too crudely, but not inaccurately, where in the pre-colonial period caste status had been relative, a matter of achievement in interaction and dispute, it later became absolute, a matter of formal ascription before such interaction or dispute.

The liberal theorists of 'modernisation' are the indirect intellectual descendants of the more progressive members of the British Raj. They too are anxious for a properly civil society and in their anxiety suppose that this is held back by a deep and long-lasting 'tradition', the only possible obstacle to a self-evidently rational and thus natural progression. Hence their question, implicit in Kothari's remark that 'it is not politics that gets caste-ridden' but 'caste that gets politicised', of how and why the process has not been swifter and more sure, of how and why caste in this liberal sense of what it is to be 'politicised' has not become more so. But the deliberately political exacerbation and even creation of this 'tradition' in the colonial period suggests that this is not the right question, that what one might more reasonably ask is why caste has since 1947 been 'politicised', in this sense, as much as it has. For far from it being natural to assume that in a newly independent India it would soon cease to be a basis for political claims, the fact that it had become more so under the British and the fact that analogous distinctions, of race, of ethnicity and of language have become the currency of claim and contest in other newly independent societies suddenly presented with a universal suffrage and the associated rhetoric of liberal democracy, the fact conceded, as I have said, by theorists of 'modernisation' themselves, would lead one to *expect* that Indian politics since 1947, despite the constitutional prohibition, would have been suffused with both the ideology and what Dumont calls the 'substance' of caste. If, as Béteille plausibly puts it, 'conflict over material interests is universal, and therefore cannot by itself account for the specific forms in which tensions appear in particular societies', and if 'in order to understand these, one has also to take into account certain irreducible historical and cultural patterns by which each society is characterised and differentiated from others' (1969: 55–6), the question is why have Indian politics between 1947 and 1977 been relatively so *free* of such ideology and substance?

The answer lies in the second of the three conditions of the course of political change in India, in the constraints on Congress after Independence and in its political ambitions. The most decisive of these constraints was universal suffrage and the associated proclamation of a formal equality of status, confused, if not qualified, by a commitment to positive discrimination in favour of the Backward Classes. The most decisive ambition was simply to limit the possibility of any other effective party. In the 1920s, 1930s and early 1940s Congress was a largely urban association. It had virtually no rural base. Committed, however, to a full extension of the franchise and understandably determined to inhibit opposition, it had after 1947 to make sure of votes from the countryside. It thus agreed to continue the division of responsibility created by the Montagu-Chelmsford reforms in 1919 whereby the states and not the centre were to be responsible for determining the levels of agricultural taxation. The understanding was that those who would benefit, men with control over land, would deliver the votes in the general elections. This reinforced the power of what had in the colonial period already become apparent as a political class in the countryside (Musgrave 1972; Stokes 1978: 43; Washbrook 1973). The interest of this class now lay in preventing horizontal alliances that could cut across the vertical hold that it had down into the villages. Elliot was only partly right when she said that 'in areas where there is a dominant caste, vertical mobilisation under dominant caste leadership may be an alternate means to modernisation'. For any caste which wanted power, it was the only means. The horizontal alliances in the years immediately after 1947, Kothari's 'polarisations', were fights to secure it. What they produced was a reinforced dominance. But this was a dominance of caste only because of the pre-existing connection between the power of caste and the power of land. By virtue of both kinds of power, the political class was able to deliver the votes. Carter, describing south-western Maharashtra in the 1960s, revealed that 'economic relations' were 'the main structural basis of vertical political alliances' and that although the political class did overwhelmingly consist of relatively high-caste *vatandar* Marathas, they allowed 'themselves to be limited in their choice of allies by considerations of caste and kinship at their own risk' (1974: 122, 159). It was a political class created as such from above, the composition of which was dictated by the pre-existing pattern of political, economic and symbolic stratification and one consequence of which is the formation of a clearly economic class. In a nice reversal of another supposed progression, a politically caused class *for* itself became in the colonial period and even more after independence an economic class *in* itself. And it remains very powerful, the crucial connection between state and citizen.

Accepting this, it might still be said that its power depends upon the symbolic force of degradation down through the hierarchy of castes to untouchable groups at the bottom, and that in this way and to this extent caste is still politically important. I would argue that it is not, or at least, that it is not crucially so. For paternalism and patronage, 'clientist' politics, are common where universal or nearly universal suffrage has been imposed on a society in which a considerable range and proportion of goods is provided by the centre, and even if the patrons in some of these societies are not able to impose their will through an ideology as convenient as that of caste in India, few have to contend, as in India, with an indigenous (rather than merely acquired and necessarily flimsy) countervailing ideology of equality (Gellner and Waterbury 1977: 63, 162, 202, 237–8 and *passim*; Parry 1974). Indeed, horizontal alliances of anything resembling 'status' or 'class' have in the later 1950s, 1960s and early 1970s been *less* common in India than in some other industrializing but still largely agrarian societies. This makes it clear that such differences have less to do with variations in the type and degree of stratification in such countries than with the fact that independent India, unlike say, Brazil, has to 1977 been a society in which one political party has dominated politics and successfully (if not always honestly) claimed to accommodate almost all identifiable interests, a fact (the contrast is again most clear in Latin America) which is itself largely explained by the way in which and the time at which it achieved political independence. Hence the consensus that Brass described in Uttar Pradesh and the Punjab. It was the consensus of a politically imposed 'modernity'.

There is nothing novel in the conclusion that the purportedly natural progressions of a theory of the 'modernisation' of politics misdescribe and fail to explain. There may even be nothing novel in the conclusion that there is almost always a choice of political identities in any at least nominally democratic society. But for sociologists affected by the view that interests, identities and ideologies are always interests, identities and ideologies of 'class' or 'status', and for anthropologists affected by the view that interests, identities and ideologies in India are always interests, identities and ideologies of 'class' or 'caste', there is perhaps point, if not novelty, in the conclusions that neither is incontestably right and that even if they were such reductions do not themselves explain. The explanations lie rather in the constitution of political dispute in the country and its structural conditions. Atavistic categories of caste became the currency of dispute in the later nineteenth century largely by British decision and largely (although by no means entirely) disappeared after independence. From being a way in which men could legitimately and effectively press claims of legal right, economic status and political power, they quickly faded as the pattern of power, rather than of interests, became such that it could not profitably be used. 'With the advent of independence, separatism' of *this* kind 'as a political device lost its value (Zelliot 1970: 54). But the one tendency is no more 'modern' than the other.

IV

Nevertheless, there is no good reason to suppose that caste in any sense has finally ceased to intrude into politics in India. One condition of its revival indeed might be thought to be the development of a more explicit politics of 'class'. In other now more pervasively industrial societies, the politics of class, the uses of the term in political claims and in justifications and definitions of political divisions, seem to be directly related to the force of the pre-industrial status orders. Such politics are more evident, for example, in Italy than they are in Britain, more evident in Britain than in Sweden, more evident in Sweden than in the United States.[9] Béteille's point, that 'conflict over material interests is universal, and therefore cannot by itself account for the specific forms in which tensions appear in particular societies', is right. But it is not only 'certain irreducible historical and cultural patterns by which each society is characterised and differentiated from others' which can. If India moves towards a two-party or many-party politics, a politics in which the parties in some sense claim and are seen to claim to represent different class interests, the 'tensions', the lines that are drawn, may certainly reflect not only these interests but also that anger and resentment at social exclusion so frequently produced by caste. Some see signs of such tension in the countryside although not, yet, in the towns (Breman 1974: 241–60; compare, for another rural area, Djurfeldt and Lindberg 1975: 172, and for a city, Holmström 1976: 136–47). But for it to become more widespread and to be reflected in any enduring division of parties at the centre, the established alliance between urban and rural interests and the control over voters in the villages will both have to break. For the first to happen, the long-standing dispute between interests such as those in the Planning Commission, in growth led by productive industry, and those in parts of Congress, much of the Janata coalition between 1977 and 1980 and almost all of the State governments, in a more moderate growth led by agriculture, will almost certainly have to be resolved in favour of industry. Then India will have embarked on the course pursued, for example, by Brazil since 1964, a course which requires holding down urban and rural wages and the cost of wage goods, in order to encourage overseas investment and a high rate of capital formation. But at this point, the future becomes wholly obscure, since the experience not only of Brazil and of other countries in Latin America but also of many in Africa and elsewhere suggests that this is a course which, in requiring measures to deflect opposition and to guarantee order, inhibits democracy itself.[10] For the second to happen, all parties will have deliberately to abandon their own local political classes.

There are few signs of either possibility now. A different condition, the third of the three which together do much to explain the different kinds and degrees of the intrusion of caste into politics in India and one which promises (or threatens) once again to increase this intrusion, is much more likely and already clear. It is the resentment of the Backward Classes at the success of the positive discrimination in favour of the Scheduled Castes and the use, even the encouragement, of this resentment by politicians wanting to establish a base under strictly political conditions in which their using it is both permissible and likely to be effective. In 1965, Béteille predicted that those members of the Backward Classes who were not members of Scheduled Castes or Scheduled Tribes would become increasingly disaffected with the positive discriminations of Congress in favour of the Harijans, the Scheduled Castes, and 'would make increasing use of political action to bargain for a better position in society' (1969: 134, 142).[11] Béteille made his prediction in the political conditions of the early years of independence, looking back at the decade in which horizontal alliances had been more common. Now, under quite different conditions, it seems as though he might be right. Brought to power by other more immediate disaffections, the Janata coalition permitted if it did not actually encourage this particular disaffection. The coalition was fragile enough, uncertain enough, to make it possible for those bidding for power within it to do so with a reasonable chance of success, and the ideology of at least some of its constituent parties, the Jan Sangh and the B.L.D., for example, allowed them to do so by appealing against material and educational disadvantages in the name of caste. There is no doubt that this is the most effective way in which to make the appeal. Other criteria, of occupation, for instance, of income or of education, are not only not agreed but also have the disadvantage of including some members of the Scheduled Castes and of excluding some of the men who themselves wish to make political capital out of the appeal. It is not, therefore, an appeal of 'status'. It actually requires those who are making it publicly to humble themselves. It is an appeal of economic and political interests which is most effectively made in the name of caste but an appeal which is only very weakly explained by the very existence and persistence of caste, or of

Bailey's 'caste categories'. It is an appeal which is more directly caused by social changes which have been taking place or been seen to have been taking place since the early 1950s and which is legitimated and so facilitated by the constitutional recognition of the Backward Classes and the change in Union government. The 'modernisation' of Indian politics is taking another perverse turn.

NOTES

Caste conundrums: Views of caste in a Sinhalese Catholic fishing village

This paper is based on fieldwork carried out in Sri Lanka between 1969 and 1971, and in 1974. It was financed by the British SSRC, the Smuts Memorial Fund, and the Esperanza Trust. I should like to acknowledge the help and encouragement I have received at various times from E. Nissan, G. Obeyesekere, J.P. Parry and D. Winslow.

1 Except for Father Rastoldo, all names in this paper are pseudonyms, as is the name of the village in question.
2 The terms mentioned here are general throughout Sinhalese Sri Lanka – and elsewhere, as in Wellagoda, they are basically ambiguous. See Leach 1961, Obeyesekere 1967, Yalman 1967 etc.
3 Dumont's writings on this subject are both familiar and voluminous. See in particular Dumont 1970; Dumont and Pocock 1959.
4 The most complete discussion of *killa* in Sri Lanka is, unfortunately, not yet published. See Winslow 1980.
5 In low-country Sri Lanka, it seems fairly clear that the situation is generally much as I have described it in Wellagoda. In the Kandyan areas, my own experience has been that Yalman's stress on female purity is greatly overdone. In a village north of Matale I found a similar unwillingness on the part of informants to associate caste with pollution, purity etc.
6 Again, the unilaterality of caste, and the fixing of one's caste position at birth seems to be general throughout low-country Sri Lanka. Even in the Kandyan hills, things may not always be as Yalman portrays them. For instance, Gombrich presents a case of inter-caste marriage where the woman was of higher caste than the man, yet, 'as far as I know (she) was (not) considered to have lost caste' (Gombrich 1971: 302). My own experience in up-country Sri Lanka supports Gombrich's comments.
7 One is reminded here of Dumont's comments concerning the 'substantialization' of caste in modern times in India. See Dumont 1970: 222. (Also Lévi-Strauss 1966.)
8 One priest I met in 1977 had returned to Sri Lanka for a holiday from the United States (Coney Island to be exact). Completely unsolicited he told me that the Goyigama, unlike the Karāva, were 'snakes in the

grass', smooth operators whose words you could never trust. Needless to say, he was a Karāva.

9 For scholars, perhaps I should say a little about these terms. *Avassa* simply means 'own'. *Vasagama* literally refers to 'dwelling village' although in this part of Sri Lanka *vasagama* names relatively rarely refer to place. *Pelantiya* is perhaps most closely related to caste implications. The dictionary gloss is 'family, lineage, line'. Obeyesekere (1967) gives a fascinating discussion of how *pelantiya* names are used in another part of Sri Lanka.

10 *Pelantiya* names are related to caste only in that one can tell from them what caste(s) a person does *not* belong to. Thus anyone called Fernando could not be a Goyigama but could be a Karāva, Radā, Hunu, Durava etc.

11 The most exhaustive elaboration of these themes is contained in Raghavan's eulogistic story of the Karāva. See Raghavan 1961 especially Chapter 5. Another interesting source is the journal, *Kurukshetra*.

12 These *kulam* names link up with nicknames, a nickname often being an elaboration of a *kulam* name. Villagers hypothesized that *kulam* names were originally nicknames and I know of a few instances where nicknames have been inherited by a son from a father.

13 On the use of the term *kulam* elsewhere, see Béteille 1965; Tambiah 1968: 218.

14 Again *Kurukshetra* and Raghavan's book on the Karāva show this tendency at work, albeit at a very different social level.

15 Professor Obeyesekere tells me that the prototype of this myth is to be found in the Buddhist 'Book of Origins'.

16 In this context one is reminded of Hocart's discussion of *kuṭimai* or servant castes. See Hocart 1950: 7.

17 Fittingly, money tends to be associated with women in Wellagoda. Self-conscious 'traditionalist' males deny any knowledge of household finances and, if possible, never carry any money.

18 There is a proverb in Sinhala which runs, *salli deviyange malli*: 'money is the younger brother of the gods'. But in Wellagoda people would laugh and say that money was now the gods' elder brother.

19 I found it impossible to produce any matrix analysis concerning the ranking of castes.

20 Despite Father Don Peter's comments (1978: 273–9) I would argue that Catholicism has in general hardened rather than mitigated caste barriers.

21 Yet I have heard it said that Christ belonged to David's *gotra*.

22 I realize this is a somewhat cursory treatment of caste and Catholicism. I hope to produce a separate treatment of the topic in the near future.

23 In fact he didn't give his eldest daughter (the only one married by 1977) to a Rodiya. She married a wealthy and well-respected Karāva.

24 For the record, perhaps I should say that Hocart's representation of caste seems infinitely preferable to Yalman's for what I know of the interior of Sri Lanka.

Mukkuvar vannimai: Tamil caste and matriclan ideology in Batticaloa, Sri Lanka

Initial fieldwork in the Batticaloa region was carried out for 18 months in 1969–71 while I was a doctoral candidate at the University of Chicago. Financial support for this research was provided by NIMH Pre-doctoral Fellowship No. MH38122 and NIMH Research Grant No. MH11765 awarded by the U.S. Public Health Service. Additional shorter (4 to 6 month) periods of fieldwork were undertaken in the same region in 1975 and in 1978, while on leave from teaching duties at Cambridge University. This recent research was funded by British SSRC Research Grants No. HR3276 and HR5549, and also by grants from the Smuts Memorial Fund and the University of Cambridge Travelling Expenses Fund. I am indebted to all the people of Batticaloa who assisted me in this research, and especially to K. Mahesvaralingam, Nilam Hamead, K. Kanthanathan, and V. Ratnam.

1 It has been pointed out that Dumont's formulations were less 'dualistic' in his earlier writings (Marriott 1976b: 190–2).
2 David (1977: 182) states that 'the classificatory term for the high castes (*uyirnda cātihul*) [sic] derives from the term for spirit (*uyir*)', and he cites this as evidence for the belief that 'spirit resides in the blood'. This is surely a lexical error deriving from the mis-transcription of colloquial dialect. The derivation of the expression is from *uyar*, meaning 'to rise, to become high' (Winslow 1862: 137), hence the phrase *uyarnta cātikaḷ* (lit. 'high castes'). This expression is common also in Batticaloa, where it is sometimes colloquially pronounced '*ucanta cāti*'. See section 3.1.
3 The term 'Moor' dates from the Portuguese period (1505–1658 A.D.), but it has remained the official designation of the native Muslim population of the island for Census and other purposes. In the Batticaloa region they are all Sunni Muslims of the Shāfi legal school. The Tamil name for this community is *Cōnakar*, but in the present climate of pan-Islamic consciousness many prefer to be known simply as 'Muslims'.
4 The largest concentration of Christians is in the town of Batticaloa itself, where Roman Catholics, many of them Portuguese Burghers (*Paraṅkiyar*), are a very strong community. Methodists and Anglicans have established smaller congregations there. There are modest Christian groups in all of the major towns along the east coast, plus some tiny Christian groups inland. Roman Catholics are by far the largest denomination.
5 Starting in the early years of Independence (post-1947), the government of Sri Lanka sponsored a large-scale irrigation and land-settlement project in the Gal Oya Valley, approximately 15 or 20 miles inland from the Tamil and Moorish settlements along the coast. This has made some new lands available to Tamil and Moorish cultivators, but it has also brought an influx of landless Sinhalese

colonists to what was formerly a sparsely populated area to the west (Farmer 1957). There has been very little mixing of the Tamil and Sinhalese populations and a good deal of communal friction. There is archaeological evidence of ancient Buddhist settlements in the Batticaloa region, but most of the present Sinhalese population is of recent origin.

6 To the casual observer, there is a great deal of physical resemblance between the Moors and the Tamils. This is acknowledged as the result of prior intermarriage. Some of the Moors, however, do have more noticeable Arab features.

7 Until a few years ago, when local Muslim reformers decided that it was un-Islamic and undesirable to employ Paraiyars to provide music at mosque festivals, weddings, and circumcisions, these Drummers gained a substantial income from the Moorish sector. In other settlements in the region, either Paraiyars or higher-status Naṭṭuvar Musicians are still employed by Moors.

8 The excluded local groups are (A) the Portuguese Burghers (*Paraṅkiyar*), who are identified as Christian mixed-breeds linked to the European race (*Veḷḷaikkārar*, 'White Men'); (B) the Kaṭaiyar Lime-burners, who are Christian newcomers during the past 40 years; (C) the Cakkiliyar Sweepers, who are seen as a tiny number of very recent 'Indian' newcomers; and (D) the Kuravar Gypsies, who are seen as forest-dwelling newly-Christianized semi-tribals. There are also settlements of other castes in other parts of the region which are only partially familiar to informants in Akkaraipattu: namely Kōvilār Temple Servants (ranked just beneath Mukkuvar), Karaiyār Fishermen (ranked roughly on a par with Taṭṭār Smiths), and Cīrpātam Cultivators (sometimes associated with Karaiyārs). For additional details on these groups see McGilvray 1974.

9 The term *kaṭṭuppāṭu* in Batticaloa is not used to characterize the relationship between castes. It is, however, heard in the context of ritual rules and devotional austerities, where it means 'restriction' in the general sense of the term.

10 As this inference is based on data gathered in a survey questionnaire, it is possible that some of the trend is an artifact of a tendency to think of the spouse's matrilateral kinship connection, e.g., MBD, rather than a patrilateral connection which might be equally valid, e.g., FZD. This could arise in the numerous instances when MB and FZ (real or classificatory) are husband and wife. A genealogical examination of each response to this question was not possible.

11 The rates of *kuṭi* exogamy revealed in samples of marriages from each caste are as follows: Vēḷāḷar + Kurukkaḷ + Mukkuvar – 97% (N = 261), Taṭṭār – 100% (N = 59), Cāṇṭār – 100% (N = 44), Vaṇṇār – 74% (N = 46), Nāvitar – 39% (N = 43), Paraiyar – 81% (N = 58).

12 Offspring, regardless of sex, bear the personal name of their father, followed by their own sex-marked personal name, which is often chosen with the aid of astrological signs. There is some genealogical

evidence of the Tamil custom of repeating names in alternate generations, but the practice seems much rarer in the present day.

13 See note 42.

14 Yalman recorded references to traditional marriage relationships between matriclans in Tambiluvil, but he did not appreciate the implication of isogamy which these expressions convey. His informants seem to have said nothing about the formal non-marriageable relationships between clans which are logically entailed (Yalman 1967: 289, 326).

15 The views represented are primarily those of high caste Hindu males. A quarter (9/35) of these informants, including the only two Moors, were full or part-time non-Western curing practitioners; a handful (4/35) were Vīracaiva Kurukkaḷ temple priests, and a similar number (6/35) were low caste informants (1 Taṭṭār, 1 Vaṇṇār, 4 Paṟaiyars). Not every informant could answer all of the specialized questions I asked, but the sample consisted of the most knowledgeable people in these areas of enquiry. The data they supplied have the characteristic strengths and weaknesses of all intensive first-hand fieldwork material, but I think the most important potential sources of bias have been mentioned.

16 It was interesting to observe some of the minor confrontations between traditional medical systems and Western medicine which arose during the research. There are a number of government hospitals in the region, as well as some Western-trained private practitioners, and Western medical concepts have entered the popular culture. There was an awkward moment during one interview on the topic of the beneficial effects of 'forceful' circulation of the blood. Someone present asked why, if this were true, so many older people today were said to die of 'high blood pressure'.

17 This was a source of initial embarrassment to some local curing practitioners and other informants who had acquired a degree of awareness of Western theories of reproduction and who were afraid to contradict my presumed beliefs. Several informants knew that the testicles were considered to be very important in Western medicine, but all were relieved not to be held accountable for their function.

18 Both among Kandyan Sinhalese (Yalman 1967: 137) and among Koṇṭaikkaṭṭi Vēḷāḷars in Tamilnadu (Barnett 1976: 146) it is reported that repeated sexual intercourse is recommended during pregnancy to supply additional semen which will nourish or strengthen the foetus.

19 Tangible evidence of the prior existence of this opening is seen in the fontanelle, the soft spot every newborn baby has at the top of the cranium.

20 The similarity between seminal fluids and breast milk in this respect is reflected in the fact that one of the rarer terms for male semen is *kāmappāl*, 'milk of lust'.

21 Some informants say that, just as a man's blood (semen) goes into the woman's body during sex, so some of the woman's blood (female

semen) enters the man through his penis. This can have a beneficial effect upon the man if the woman is young and vigorous herself. Copulation between an elderly man and a very young woman has a potential payoff for the man in terms of his bodily reinvigoration, but, because of the simultaneous expenditure of the old man's weak and scarce blood, it is recognized to be a very risky business. This set of beliefs about reciprocal transfer of blood between sex partners seems more widespread among the Sinhalese population of the island (Kemper 1979: 489). Family planning officials in Colombo told me that some young Sinhalese men had objected strongly to the use of the condom because it threatened to block the reverse flow of beneficial female semen into their own bodies. The inverse of this belief is reflected in the Tamilnadu Koṇṭaikkaṭṭi Vēḷāḷars' concern that polluted blood might enter a man's penis and mix with his own blood during intercourse with a low caste woman (Barnett 1976: 144).

22 In most ordinary marriages, the groom is rarely a 'stranger' in the sense of someone unknown, since he is usually a local person, frequently a cross-cousin of some sort. It is in wealthy, high-status families that the groom is most likely to be a true stranger to the bride's household, since these marriages are arranged to a greater extent according to a calculus of wealth, education, and occupational status, as opposed to kinship ties.

23 There is explicit evidence that Tamil kinship ideas in south India sometimes recognize the concept of 'share' (*paṅku*) or 'sharer' (*paṅkāḷi*) of patrilineal descent and inheritance (Beck 1972: 217; Barnett 1970: 58; 1976: 140–1). In his 'cultural account' of Jaffna Tamil kinship categories, David (1973a) divides the kinship domain under three headings, defining *cakōtarar* as 'sharers of natural bodily substance', *campantikkārar* as 'uniters of n.b.s.', and *cakalar* as 'non-uniters of n.b.s.', although these designations appear to have nothing to do with the etymology or denotative meaning of these words in Tamil. There is no way to know how Jaffna kinsmen really think about each other from an analysis which is framed in such alien jargon, nor is it possible to understand how these abstractions were generated. The only actual use of the Tamil word 'sharer' (*paṅkāḷi*) in Jaffna is said to be in the domain of inheritance, where it overlaps with David's category of 'non-sharing non-uniters', leaving the argument truly opaque.

24 One of the frequently mentioned ailments of the blood is *kotippu* ('boiling'), which is described as a kind of over-heated state of the blood which generates internal pressure leading to the rupture of blood vessels and haemorrhage. Today it is sometimes linked to the Western diagnosis of 'heart attack', which is assumed to consist of a physical bursting of the heart under the intense pressure of the 'boiling' blood.

25 Several informants argued against the idea of intrinsic differences in the blood of different castes and matriclans by reasoning that, if such differences existed, medications supplied either by traditional curing

practitioners or by the government hospital would necessarily affect patients of different castes differently. The fact that medication (for a given ailment) was uniform supported the contention that blood was uniform.

26 States of pollution, ordinary purity, and enhanced purity are distinguished respectively among Havik Brahmans as *muṭṭucheṭṭu*, *mailigē*, and *maḍi* (Harper 1964: 152); among Coorgs as *polē*, *mailigē*, and *maḍi* (Srinivas 1952: Ch. 4), and among KV's as *tiṭṭu*, *satāranam*, and *maḍi* (Barnett 1976: 143).

27 The general word for ritual pollution among the Moors is *muḻukku*, which is apparently derived from the same verb, *muḻuka*, 'to bathe completely'.

28 The explanation of alleged sex-specific differences in the spread of death pollution was linked to the theory that the sex of the child is determined by the relative amounts of maternal semen versus paternal semen which is deposited in the womb. This theory, which was adduced by only two informants, fits nicely with the idea that pollution is transmitted through shared bodily substance. It predicts that pollution will predominate on the father's side of the family if the deceased is a male, and on the mother's side if the deceased is a female. It was a surprisingly consistent interpretation of conception and pollution, but it was also highly idiosyncratic from the standpoint of the survey findings.

29 In areas of very strong Mukkuvar dominance, particularly in Manmunai Pattu, the more literary form is often heard, i.e., Muṟkukar or 'Mukkukar', meaning the 'foremost Kukans'. This literary fōrm is given as the authentic name of the caste in the regional traditions of the *Maṭṭakkaḷappu Mānmiyam* (Nadarajah 1962), which also refers to the caste as Kukan Kulam. All of these titles represent claims of caste descent from the mythological Guha (T. *Kukan*), loyal ferryman of Lord Rama, whose noble qualities are particularly eulogized in the Rāmāyana of Kamban (Rajagopalachari 1961). This is not a unique puranic charter: it is shared by the Valan fishing caste of Kerala, the Maṟavar warriors of Ramnad, and the Sembadavan fishing caste of Tamilnadu (Anantha Krishna Iyer 1909 vol. I: 232; Thurston 1909 vol. V: 24; vol. VI: 352).

30 Mukkuvars in Batticaloa emphatically deny any connection between themselves and the 'Mukkiyar' fishing castes of Jaffna, and there appears to be no communication between these two groups today. However, there are legends in Jaffna that the Batticaloa Mukkuvars represent the descendants of fishermen expelled from Jaffna for defiling a temple with fish (Brito 1879).

31 There is considerable controversy over the interpretation of this alleged Kalinga ancestry (see Indrapala 1965: 246, for a summary of the arguments). It is, however, a living tradition in Batticaloa, where one of the foremost Mukkuvar matriclans is Kāliṅkā kuṭi.

32 H.W. Tambiah (1954: 89) has argued that the Vēḷāḷars of Batticaloa were distinguished from the Mukkuvars and the rest of the population

of the region by the fact that they followed the Thesawalamai legal code of Jaffna. His evidence for this is found in a few ambiguous passages in the Sir Alexander Johnston Papers (Public Record Office, London) which seem scarcely able to bear such a positive interpretation. I know of no ethnographic evidence to corroborate his view.

33 Vegetarianism is acknowledged to be an ideal form of behaviour for anyone who wishes to attain enhanced piety and spirituality, and some individuals do limit themselves to a vegetarian diet (*Caiva cāppāṭu*, 'Saivite food'). As a caste-wide rule of conduct, however, neither the Vēḷāḷars nor any other caste, except the Vīracaiva Kurukkaḷs, enforce vegetarianism. It is much more common as a special religious austerity during periods of religious observance. Even among Vīracaiva Kurukkaḷs, vegetarianism may be limited primarily to active temple priests, who are the only persons who wear the personal lingam at the present time.

34 Tēcāntara Kurukkaḷs are said to regard 'Akōrāmāyā Tēvar' as their ancestral preceptor, while Caṅkamar Kurukkaḷs claim 'Paṇṭitārccuna Tēvar' or 'Paṇṭiyāttiriyāyā Tēvar' as their ancestral preceptor. These would correspond to Ekoramarādhya and Panditarādhya respectively, two of the standard Lingāyat sages (Anantha Krishna Iyer 1931 vol. IV: 114). *Mallikārccuna* (Mallikarjuna) is the form in which Civa is worshipped at the Vīracaiva centre known commonly as Sri Saila in the Kurnool District of Andhra Pradesh (Shree Kumaraswamiji 1956: 99; Narahari Gopalakristnamah Chetty 1886: 182; Ramanujan 1973: 47).

35 The phrase 'Guru-Linga-Jangama' is a motto which commemorates the three cornerstones of Vīracaiva doctrine: the religious preceptor, the iconic lingam stone, and the Jangama or priest (McCormack 1959: 119; Thurston 1909 vol. IV: 272). The term Makēsvara is a Saivite title sometimes applied to the Jangama priest (Enthoven 1922 vol. II: 355).

36 The term *vamicam* corresponds to the Sinhalese *wamsa* (Yalman 1967: 138), to the Bengali *baṅśa* or *bongso* (Davis 1976: 14; Fruzzetti & Östör 1976), and to cognate terms in other Indian languages which typically refer to patrilineally defined social units. However, the term is used in this instance to refer to a set of matrilineal descent units. The term also is used to refer to matrilineally defined groups among the North Kerala Nayars (Gough 1961: 388).

37 Brahman priests from Jaffna are presently employed in a number of larger urban temples in the vicinity of Batticaloa and Kalmunai towns, as well as at the ancient 'regional temple' of Tirukkōvil.

38 It should be emphasized that the histories, legends, and formulations of ancient customs contained in the *Maṭṭakkaḷappu Mānmiyam* are still part of the fragmentary oral culture of Batticaloa. Informants volunteered recitations from parts of this corpus before I was even aware of its existence. The common term for any discrete palmyra leaf inscription is *ēṭu*, while texts pertaining to historical tradition and custom are known by the general term *kalveṭṭu* ('stone inscription'),

although this is merely a metaphorical term. The *Maṭṭakkaḷappu Māṉmiyam* contains a number of these separately known *kalveṭṭus* but there are others which exist outside this compendium (e.g. Raghavan 1953).

39 According to Gunasingam (1974), there is epigraphical evidence of only two royally-endowed Brahman caste settlements (*brahmadeya*) in Sri Lanka during the Cōḷa period, one of which seems to have been located in the Trincomalee District at Kantalai. It appears to have been a sizeable settlement which conformed to the pattern of Brahman settlements in South India during that period (Stein 1968), and it was patronized by Sinhalese kings of Polonnaruwa after the demise of Cōḷa power in the island. There is no evidence of any such Brahman settlement having been founded in the Batticaloa region.

40 Several people had heard of an additional document, the *Mukkuvar ērpāṭu* ('Mukkuvar enactments'), but I was never able to locate it.

41 There are only three examples of collective management of agricultural lands on a matrilineal basis about which I have much information: (A) There was traditional cultivation of lands belonging to the Kokkaṭṭiccōlai Civa temple by members of two specific Vēḷāḷar caste *kuṭis* from the village of Paḷukāmam. This is discussed in section 5.9. (B) There is a more complex system of management of temple lands in the Cīrpātam caste village of Turainīlāvaṇai, whereby members of 13 recognized kuṭis are annually allocated the 88 standard shares of land in accordance with some principle of rotation. This allocation is in the hands of a special committee of land administrators (*Kāṇi Aṭappan*) who are in turn accountable to the 13 kuṭi representatives who constitute the temple committee. This is an indirect management system which involves many kuṭis, not just one, in the cultivation of temple lands. Court records over the past 25 years indicate that the probity of the special committee of *Kāṇi Aṭappans* has not been above question. (C) Four generations ago, a Vīracaiva Kurukkaḷ priest in Akkaraipattu, who had no children of his own, bequeathed about 50 acres of paddy land to his sisters and to his sisters' female descendants. His intention, according to informants, was to provide an endowment to be managed jointly and to be shared by succeeding generations of women of his priestly matriline. Today only 12 acres can be cultivated, due to unforeseen inundation from new irrigation projects. These 12 acres are presently leased to local Moors, and the revenue is shared by the living descendants. Joint management in this case involves a specific branch of the founder's matriclan, rather than the matriclan as a whole.

In addition to these three examples, there is fragmentary evidence of the existence of some joint kuṭi lands (*kuṭi paṅku kāṇi*) in both Moorish as well as Tamil areas, but no one was able to locate them for me. The principle of *taṭṭumāṟu*, or rotating shares of land within a larger tract, is an old type of land tenure which has almost disappeared. Informants were not sure whether traditionally the shareholders within a given tract would have been members of a single kuṭi. In the few existing instances of *taṭṭumāṟu* in the Kokkaṭṭiccōlai area, the shareholders are said to be members of many different *kuṭis*. For other accounts of shareholding and joint cultivation see Leach 1961 and Obeyesekere 1967.

42 The expression *urimaip pen* may also mean a man's 'rightful marriage partner' in many Tamil areas (Beck 1972: 237; David 1973a: n. 15; for Sinhalese equivalent see Yalman 1967: 113n.), but this usage was not noted in Batticaloa.

43 My high caste Tamil landlord in Akkaraipattu, a man of the prestigious Maḻuvaracan kuṭi, summed up his disdain for the modern arrogation of *varicai* honours by saying, 'Only the little people bother with it nowadays'.

44 Stirrat (1975a: 592) reports another unilinear deviation from the model of bilaterally-ascribed caste in a Catholic Karāva caste fishing village in the bilingual (Sinhalese/Tamil) zone near Chilaw on the west coast of the island. There, however, the rule of caste ascription is strictly patrilineal. A patrilineal emphasis is reported in Beck's Koṅku data (1972: 235).

45 In the past there seems to have been a distinction between the ritual duties of the two main Kurukkaḷ matriclans (see section 5.3). There is still today a pattern of Kōvilār caste temple duties which allocates specific tasks to certain matrilines within the caste. Moorish matriclan names include several titles referring to occupational categories, e.g. Ōṭāvi (carpenter) or Levvai (Lebbe, leader of mosque prayers), but these names bear no present relation to actual occupation.

46 Tamils in the Batticaloa region do not seem to bother with elaborate comparisons of the horoscopes of proposed marriage partners, in contrast with Sinhalese concern for these matters (Kemper 1979).

47 As an ideal characterization, marriage between Kurukkaḷs and Vēḷāḷars is said to be more common than marriage between Kurukkaḷs and Mukkuvars, but there is no empirical evidence for this in Akkaraipattu. In the Vēḷāḷar-dominated village of Tambiluvil, Kurukkaḷs seem to have married spouses of the highest ranking Vēḷāḷar clans no more than 25% of the time (Hiatt 1973: 248), yet Kurukkaḷ informants often told me that a Vēḷāḷar spouse was a very respectable 'second best'. The Vēḷāḷars in Tambiluvil, at any rate, often speak of the Kurukkaḷs as members of their caste, but they rank them below the most prestigious pair of Vēḷāḷar *kuṭis*.

48 Yalman (1960; 1967: 142) has discussed the importance of the possession and manipulation of hereditary names and titles in Sinhalese society. The manner in which even a conventional naming rule (e.g. patronymic) can encourage the development of a 'pseudo-unilineal' ideology with no empirical basis has been illustrated by Leach (1973), using material from the genealogies of eminent English Quaker families of the 19th century.

49 There are a number of functional similarities between this ritual and the annual Äsala Perahära in Kandy, which 'enacted' the constitution of the Kandyan kingdom in visible form through a series of dramatic

processions associated with the sacred Tooth Relic of the Buddha. Also like the Kokkaṭṭiccōlai temple, the Temple of the Tooth is organized around the distinction between the ritual duties of an 'inner group' (*ätul kaṭṭalē*) of Goygama caste servants who assist the officiating Bhikkus and an 'outer group' (*piṭa kaṭṭalē*) of secular temple administrators. The chief of the 'inner group' is the Kāriya Karavana Rāla, who is also in charge of the temple store-room and who seems to occupy a role similar in many ways to that of the Vēḷāḷar temple chief at Kokkatticcōlai (Hocart 1931: 8–15; Seneviratne 1978: 26–37). The historical traditions of Batticaloa refer occasionally to the role of the Kandyan king as a patron of major temples, and it seems likely that there would have been some sharing of ritual conventions between the two regions.

50 Recent years have witnessed the development of patterns of sponsorship by new categories of participants, e.g. civil servants employed in government offices in the Akkaraipattu area. This corresponds to a trend noted also in Tamilnadu (Appadurai and Breckenridge 1976: 203–4).

51 Much more historical information is needed, however, before all the puzzles are solved. There remains the fact that the Timilar caste, which tradition recounts was driven out of the Batticaloa region in a war with the Mukkuvars, and which is found today in the vicinity of Verugal and Toppūr south of Trincomalee, follows a pattern of matrilineal clan organization substantially similar to that of the Mukkuvars, Vēḷāḷars, and other Hindu castes of present day Batticaloa.

52 Aside from the Vīracaiva Kurukkaḷs, the only group which appears to be unique to Batticaloa is the Cīrpātam caste (Raghavan 1953; 1971: 109–12).

Caste rank and verbal interaction in western Tamilnadu

This paper is based on Chapter 4 of my doctoral dissertation (Levinson 1977), where much further pertinent material can be found. The acknowledgements made there carry over to this paper, but I must specifically thank Brenda Beck for inviting me into her research locale, E. Annamalai for detailed linguistic help, John Gumperz for guiding the course of the research, O.K. Suntaram and family for embracing me within their family, and Suntaram, Baskaran, Balu, Subramaniam and Gopal for their field assistance, given with little or no remuneration. I am much indebted for significant corrections or additions suggested by E. Annamalai, Brenda Beck, Penelope Brown, John Gumperz, Edmund Leach, and Dennis McGilvray. Fieldwork was in part funded by the University of California, Berkeley, and the facilities of the Central Institute of Indian Languages at Mysore were generously put at my disposal. Colin Duly very kindly and patiently redrew the matrices. Finally, the editor of this volume put an immense amount of work into improving a rambling manuscript, and without his help this paper would never have appeared.

1 See, however, the work done independently by Den Ouden (1975).

2 There is a slight discrepancy between the caste inventory used by Beck and the one in Table 1.1. As noted, I have recognized a subcaste, 7b, related to her 7 (which is here labelled 7a). Beck also took into consideration castes 12 (a subcaste of washermen) and 15 (a subcaste of barbers), which I have omitted because they did not occur in the hamlet of study or its immediate environs. But castes 12 and 15 would almost certainly pattern very closely to the linguistic behaviour of castes 13 and 14 (the washermen and barbers included in this study), so little important comparative material is lost.

3 To be more precise, Marriott underplays rank-reflecting behaviour. As we saw, fully competitive behaviour simply cannot generate hierarchy, so his 'optimal' and 'pessimal' strategies are not, in terms of the theory of games, viable strategies at all (since the first requires prior acquiescence by others, and the second prior admission of defeat by self). In contrast, Marriott's 'maximal' and 'minimal' strategies are true game-theoretic minimax strategies, and it is this aspect of his theory that is the important contribution. It is thus only the two middle varnas that systematically treat transactional media as competitive games.

4 These matrices are extracts from the full matrices of dishonorific usage, just indicating areas of symmetrical exchange. They specifically do not include the full range of usage, which patterns very roughly like the area in Matrix VIII formed by adding the areas of relative age T/V to the area of T-giving (see Levinson 1977: 298, 304).

5 Curiously, perhaps, the study of intra-caste language usage also yields fundamental insights into the nature of the caste system. This is because, just as Beck (1972) found that the internal customs and social organization of castes were related systematically to their place in the caste system, so the detailed facts of honorific and dishonorific usage within castes (and thus between real or putative kinsmen) are finely attuned to both caste rank and left/right division membership. The implication is that the caste system does not just operate to organize the external affairs of an endogamous group, but penetrates deeply into its internal organization, affecting the very character of the most intimate social relationships, as expressed by the solidarity of T-exchange (typical of lower castes) or by the inequality of asymmetrical T/V exchange (typical of upper castes). See Levinson 1977: 503–89 for details. The caste system is not just a heap, not even a hierarchically structured heap, of unitary caste cultures, as early descriptions of Indian society (preoccupied with historical visions of castes as accreted strata) suggested. The culture and structure of each caste can only be understood by reference to its place in a many-dimensional caste system, within which its own internal organization can be seen to be in patterned opposition to that of its structural counterparts in the system.

Caste and politics in India since 1947

This paper owes a very great deal to conversations with André Béteille. But even his exceptional patience, knowledge and good judgement cannot extend to a responsibility for what it contains. I am also grateful to John Dunn, Edmund Leites, Mary Katzenstein, Dennis McGilvray, and John Thompson for their comments.

1 The 'Asiatic' mode has been and remains the least plausible even of these. Soviet scholars abandoned it in 1931 (Clarkson 1979: 202).
2 Dumont has himself reviewed and replied to the criticisms of his thesis in a new preface to a new edition of *Homo Hierarchicus* which I read after I had written this paper (1979: i–xl). He distinguishes these criticisms in the following way: as criticisms of his insistence on the encompassing power of hierarchy which come not from anthropology or Indology but from 'modern ideology' in general (vii–viii); criticisms of what is taken to be his hostility to materialist explanations (iii); criticisms from what he calls 'empiricism' of his indifference to much ethnography, his connections between precepts in old texts and practices in modern society, his emphasis on the constitutive importance of ideas and his analytical dissociation of 'infrastructures' from 'superstructures' (ix–xxv); and criticisms of detail (xxxiii–xxxix). Several of my own criticisms coincide with these. My central objection, however, owes nothing to political radicalism, analytical materialism, Marxism or 'empiricism'; it comes from a particular view of what 'interpretation' can and should be. In another recent essay which I did not read until I had finished this paper, Dumont makes his theoretical convictions clearer, in at least two respects, than he has done before. He explains that his emphasis on the importance of hierarchy in India is in part intended to restore a true sociological perspective to all societies (1978: 94–5). Modern 'individualism' and 'egalitarianism', as he thinks of them, are in his view an historical aberration and a real, that is to say distorting, 'ideology'. He also explains that the modern or early modern thinker who saw this most clearly and gives us the best perspective on it is Leibniz (1978: 90–1). It is interesting to see what this commits Dumont to. Leibniz argued in roughly the following way. All worlds are inhabited by individuals or singular things. Each individual is defined by its concept. This consists of a set of attributes exclusively satisfied by it and exhaustively constituting it. Only it satisfies them and it satisfies them all. Attributes are either 'simple' or 'complex'. Simple attributes are primitive and 'positive'. They are what we normally understand by 'properties'. Complex attributes are negative or conjunctive. They are properties too, but of a quite different kind, qualities and quantities that the individual has, not intrinsically, but through his relations with all other individuals at all points in space and all points in time, past, present and future. Individual concepts are 'compossible' if they are capable of being

realized together. Compossibility is a logical matter and an empirical one, a matter of logical consistency and empirical compatibility. Any world, therefore, including the actual world, this world, is a set of compossible individuals or singular things which by virtue of their attributes are peculiar to one world. Leibniz is accordingly committed to what might now be called the most uncompromising 'holism'. So, one presumes, is Dumont. It is, of course, a metaphysical commitment in the literal sense. And quite apart from that, it is at variance with the Enlightenment assumption, roughly speaking, that relations in the world may or may *not* be necessary, although it is not at variance with some other almost equally strong holisms that come, *via* Spinoza and Marx, from Paris. I take my characterization of Leibniz not from Dumont himself but from *Theodicy*, paras. 1, 2, 7, 8, 9, 10, 34, 37, 42, 52, 58, 174, 225, 291, 310, 311, 349, 360 and 367, *Discourse on Metaphysics*, paras. 8, 9 and 13, *Monadology*, paras. 33, 37 and 38, the letter of 12 April 1686 to von Hessen-Rheinfels and the remarks on a letter from Arnaud written in May 1686. These can all be traced in standard editions.

3 Kautilya's *Arthashastra* is a text in which, as Drekmeier puts it, there is not 'a thorough going divorce of politics and ethics' (quoted by Tambiah 1976: 29) and in which ethics are not therefore grounded in *dharma* alone.

4 Max Weber argued that it was not primarily a religious matter. For the view that it is, very close to Dumont, see Stern (1971).

5 In an extended and exceptionally subtle defence of this view, on which I depend, Dunn (1978) suggests that we might begin with the question of what the putative truths of the human sciences are truths about. His answer (in what he describes as a 'shop-soiled but still serviceable phrase') is ' "real living men", past present and future, or more broadly human acts taken under intentional descriptions'. His reasons for this are both pragmatic and moral. If we abandon such descriptions, we are likely both to make predictive mistakes and to do the 'data', our subjects, an injustice. But since neither they nor we can in any proper sense *know* what they mean in these intentions (there is no acceptable theory of meaning) we cannot completely suspend disbelief and so may, with delicacy and discretion, supplement (but not replace) their accounts. The commitment to interpretation and the impossibility of a 'cumulative, convergent, self-vindicating . . . science of man' (Williams 1978: 302) are very plain. One should be clear, however, that the case for interpretation does not depend upon the kind of assumption that Dunn makes about the distinctively intentional or reflective character of human performances. It does not depend upon any assumption at all about these performances. It is, indeed, compatible with the most remorseless behavioural materialism. For an argument, and an excellent review of the whole issue, see Rorty 1979: especially 343–56.

6 The Rudolphs (1967) and Kothari's collection (1970b) each contain reasonably full reviews of the connections between caste and politics

as they were seen up to the late 1960s, and Kothari (1970a) is a more general account of Indian politics in the liberal pluralist manner. Carter (1974) contains one of the best of more recent reviews.

7 Not surprisingly, there is at least one report of a once-dominant group making such an appeal as it fell (Béteille 1970: 272). Marxists and those affected by *marxisant* analysis (such as Wolf and Alavi) have seen the agitation of 'middle peasants' as economically caused and potentially revolutionary. For a brief but critical review of this argument, its presuppositions and its truth (for South Asia), see Stokes (1978: 283ff.).

8 The Rudolphs are unique in the literature in political science in taking account both of the legal changes in the colonial period and of the evidence of what used to be called 'political behaviour' after independence. Whether this account, at variance with my own, is a plausible one may be judged from my own sources and from Fox's very critical review (1970).

9 But of course, 'the complexities of political response in Europe would warn of the difficulty of constructing some handy ready-reckoner on which the student of Indian political history could happily rely' (Stokes 1978: 288).

10 As President (formerly General) Branco of Brazil put it in a speech at the National War College there in 1967, nicely reflecting American theories of a modernized liberal pluralist policy, 'For a society to be democratic, it must have free expression for disagreement; for it to be viable, it is necessary that the areas of agreement outweigh those of disagreement' (quoted by Flynn 1978: 513 n. 25).

11 An indication of the success of these discriminations, 75 district collectors are now reported to be Harijans.

BIBLIOGRAPHY

Abeyasinghe, T.B.H. (1966). *Portuguese Rule in Ceylon 1594–1612.* Colombo: Lake House.

Aiyappan, A. (1944). *Iravas and Culture Change.* Bulletin of the Madras Government Museum n.s., General Section, vol. 5, no. 1.

Ambirajan, S. (1978). *Classical Political Economy and British Policy in India.* Cambridge University Press.

Anantha Krishna Iyer, L.K. (1909). *The Cochin Tribes and Castes*, vol. I. Madras: Higginbotham & Co.

(1912). Idem, vol. II.

(1931). *The Mysore Tribes and Castes*, vol. IV. Mysore: Mysore University.

Anonymous (n.d.). *Mukkuvarin Cātivaḻamai* (Caste Customs of the Mukkuvars). A Tamil ms in the Public Record Office, London. CO-54/123, pp. 186–7.

Appadurai, Arjun and Carol Appadurai Breckenridge (1976). 'The South Indian Temple: Authority, Honour and Redistribution', *Contributions to Indian Sociology* n.s. 10: 187–211.

Bailey, F.G. (1960). *Tribe, Caste and Nation.* Manchester University Press.

(1963). 'Closed Social Stratification in India', *European Journal of Sociology* 5: 130–4.

Baker, C.J. and D.A. Washbrook (1975). *South India: Political Institutions and Political Change, 1880–1940.* Delhi: Macmillan of India.

Banks, Michael Y. (1957). 'The Social Organization of the Jaffna Tamils of North Ceylon, with Special Reference to Kinship, Marriage and Inheritance'. Unpublished Ph.D. thesis, University of Cambridge.

(1960). 'Caste in Jaffna', in E.R. Leach, ed. (1960).

Barnett, Stephen A. (1970). 'The Structural Position of a South Indian Caste: Koṇṭaikkaṭṭi Vēḷāḷars in Tamilnadu'. Unpublished Ph.D. thesis, University of Chicago.

(1973a). 'The Process of Withdrawal in a South Indian Caste', in Milton Singer, ed., *Entrepreneurship and Modernization of Occupational Cultures in South Asia.* Durham, N.C.: Duke University Program in Comparative Studies on Southern Asia, Monograph 12.

(1973b). 'Urban Is as Urban Does: Two Incidents on One Street in Madras City, South India', *Urban Anthropology* 2: 129–60.

(1975). 'Approaches to Changes in Caste Ideology in South India', in

Burton Stein, ed., *Essays on South India.* Honolulu: University Press of Hawaii.

(1976). 'Cocoanuts and Gold: Relational Identity in a South Indian Caste', *Contributions to Indian Sociology* n.s. 10: 133–56.

Barnett, Stephen A., Lina Fruzzetti, and Ákos Östör (1976). 'Hierarchy Purified: Notes on Dumont and His Critics', *Journal of Asian Studies* 35: 627–46.

(1977). 'On a Comparative Sociology of India: A Reply to Marriott', *Journal of Asian Studies* 36: 599–601.

Barth, Fredrik (1960). 'The System of Social Stratification in Swat, North Pakistan', in E.R. Leach, ed. (1960).

Basham, A.L. (1963). 'Some Fundamental Political Ideas of Ancient India', in C.H. Philips, ed., *Politics and Society in India.* London: Allen & Unwin.

Beck, Brenda E.F. (1972). *Peasant Society in Koṅku: A Study of Right and Left Subcastes in South India.* Vancouver: University of British Columbia Press.

(1973). 'The Right–Left Division of S. Indian Society', in R. Needham, ed., *Right and Left.* University of Chicago Press.

Béteille, André (1964). 'A Note on the Referents of Caste', *European Journal of Sociology* 5: 130–4.

(1965). *Caste, Class, and Power: Changing Patterns of Stratification in a Tanjore Village.* University of California Press.

(1969). *Castes: Old and New.* Bombay: Asia Publishing House.

(1970). 'Caste and Political Group Formation in Tamilnad', in Kothari, ed. (1970b).

(1974). *Six Essays in Comparative Sociology.* Delhi: Oxford University Press.

(1977). *Inequality among Men.* Oxford: Blackwell.

Bloch, Maurice (1977). 'The Past and the Present in the Present', *Man* n.s. 12: 278–92.

Brass, Paul R. (1965). *Factional Politics in an Indian State.* University of California Press.

(1974). *Language, Religion and Politics in North India.* Cambridge University Press.

Breman, Jan (1974). *Patronage and Exploitation: Changing Agrarian Relations in South Gujarat.* University of California Press.

Bright, William and A.K. Ramanujan (1964). 'Sociolinguistic Variation and Linguistic Change', in Horace G. Lunt, ed., *Proceedings of the Ninth International Congress of Linguists.* The Hague: Mouton.

Brito, Christopher (1876). *The Mukkuva Law, or the Rules of Succession among the Mukkuvars of Ceylon.* Colombo: H.D. Gabriel.

(1879). *The Yalpana-Vaipava-Malai, or the History of the Kingdom of Jaffna.* Colombo.

Brown, Penelope and Stephen C. Levinson (1978). 'Universals in Language Usage: Politeness Phenomena', in Esther N. Goody, ed., *Questions and Politeness: Strategies in Social Interaction.* Cambridge Papers in Social Anthropology 8. Cambridge University Press.

Brown, R. and A. Gilman (1960). 'The Pronouns of Power and Solidatiry', in Thomas A. Sebeok, ed., *Style in Language.* Cambridge MA: MIT Press.

Burnand, Jacob (1794). *Memorial Compiled by Mr. Jacob Burnand, Late Chief of Batticaloa, for his Successor, Mr. Johannes Philippus Wambeek.* Trans. unknown, ms in Colombo Museum Library, Sri Lanka. For more information on other copies of this document, see T. Nadaraja (1966).

Canagaratnam, S.O. (1921). *Monograph of the Batticaloa District of the Eastern Province, Ceylon.* Colombo: H.R. Cottle, Government Printer.

Caraka (1949). *The Caraka Samhita.* Jamnagar: Shree Gulabkunverba Ayurvedic Society.

Carstairs, G. Morris (1957). *The Twice Born: A Study of a Community of High Caste Hindus.* London: Hogarth Press.

Carter, Anthony T. (1974). *Elite Politics in Rural India: Political Stratification in Western Maharashtra.* Cambridge University Press.

Casie Chitty, Simon (1834). *The Ceylon Gazetteer.* Ceylon: Cotta Church Mission Press.

Clarkson, Stephen (1979). *The Soviet Theory of Development: India and the Third World in Marxist-Leninist Scholarship.* London: Macmillan.

Cohn, Bernard S. (1961). 'From Indian Status to British Contract', *Journal of Economic History* 21: 613–28.

(1967). 'Regions Subjective and Objective: Their Relation to the Study of Modern Indian History and Society', in Robert I. Crane, ed., *Regions and Regionalism in South Asian Studies: An Exploratory Study.* Durham NC: Duke University Program in Comparative Studies on Southern Asia, Monograph 5.

(1971). *India: The Social Anthropology of a Civilization.* Englewood Cliffs NJ: Prentice-Hall.

Cronin, Vincent (1959). *A Pearl to India: The Life of Roberto de Nobili.* New York: Dutton.

David, Kenneth (1972). 'The Bound and the Unbound: Variations in Social and Cultural Structure in Rural Jaffna, Ceylon'. Unpublished Ph.D. thesis, University of Chicago.

(1973a). 'Until Marriage Do Us Part: A Cultural Account of Jaffna Tamil Categories for Kinsmen', *Man* n.s. 8: 521–35.

(1973b). 'Spatial Organization and Normative Schemes in Jaffna, Northern Sri Lanka', *Modern Ceylon Studies* 4: 21–52.

(1974). 'And Never the Twain Shall Meet? Mediating the Structural Approaches to Caste Ranking', in Harry M. Buck and Glenn E. Yocum, eds., *Structural Approaches to South India Studies.* Chambersburg PA: Wilson Books.

(1977). 'Hierarchy and Equivalence in Jaffna, North Ceylon: Normative Codes as Mediator', in Kenneth David, ed., *The New Wind: Changing Identities in South Asia.* The Hague & Paris: Mouton.

Davis, Marvin (1976). 'A Philosophy of Hindu Rank from Rural West Bengal', *Journal of Asian Studies* 36: 5–24.

Denham, E.B. (1912). *Ceylon at the Census of 1911.* Colombo: H.C. Cottle, Government Printer.

Den Ouden, J.H.B. (1969). 'The Komutti Chettiyar: Position and Change of Position of a Merchant Caste in a South Indian Village', *Tropical Man* 2: 45–59.

(1975). *De Onaanraakbaren van Konkunad.* Wageningen: H. Veenman & Zonen B.V.

De Silva, C.R. (1972). *The Portuguese in Ceylon, 1617–1638.* Colombo: Cave & Co.

Djurfeldt, G. and S. Lindberg (1975). *Behind Poverty: The Social Formation in a Tamil Village.* Lund: Scandinavian Institute of Asian Studies.

Don Peter, W.A. (1978). *Education in Sri Lanka under the Portuguese.* Colombo: Catholic Press.

Dube, Leela (1978). 'The Seed and the Earth: Symbolism of Human Reproduction in India'. Paper presented at the Tenth International Congress of Anthropological and Ethnological Sciences. New Delhi, December 1978.

Dubois, Abbé J.A. (1906). *Hindu Manners, Customs and Ceremonies.* H.K. Beauchamp, trans., 3rd edition. Oxford: Clarendon Press.

Dumont, Louis (1970). *Homo Hierarchicus: The Caste System and its Implications.* Mark Sainsbury, trans. London: Weidenfeld & Nicolson. Also University of Chicago Press.

(1978). 'La Communauté Anthropologique et l'Idéologie', *L'Homme* 18: 83–110.

(1979). *Homo Hierarchicus: le Système des Castes et ses Implications.* Paris: Gallimard (Collection Tel).

Dumont, Louis and David F. Pocock (1959). 'Pure and Impure', *Contributions to Indian Sociology* 3: 9–39.

Dunn, John (1978). 'Practising History and Social Science on "realist" Assumptions', in Christopher Hookway and Philip Pettit, eds., *Action and Interpretation: Studies in the Philosophy of the Social Sciences.* Cambridge University Press.

Elliot, Carolyn M. (1970). 'Caste and Faction among the Dominant Caste: the Reddis and Kammas of Andhra', in Kothari, ed. (1970b).

Enthoven, Reginald E. (1922). *The Tribes and Castes of Bombay*, vol. II. Bombay: Government Central Press.

Farmer, B.H. (1957). *Pioneer Peasant Colonization in Ceylon.* Oxford University Press.

Ferro-Luzzi, G.E. (1976). 'Indian Christians and Pollution', *Man* n.s. 11: 591–2.

Flynn, Peter (1978). *Brazil: A Political Analysis.* London: Benn.

Fox, Richard G. (1970). 'Avatars of Indian Research', *Comparative Studies in Society and History* 12: 59–72.

Freed, Stanley A. (1963). 'An Objective Method for Determining the Collective Caste Hierarchy of an Indian Village', *American Anthropologist* 65: 879–91.

Fruzzetti, Lina and Ákos Östör (1976). 'Seed and Earth: A Cultural

Analysis of Kinship in a Bengali Town', *Contributions to Indian Sociology* n.s. 10: 97–132.
Fuller, C.J. (1975). 'Kerala Christians and the Caste System', *Man* n.s. 10: 53–70.
(1976). *The Nayars Today*. Cambridge University Press.
(1977). 'Indian Christians: Pollution and Origins', *Man* n.s. 12: 528–9.
Fürer-Haimendorf, Christoph von (1963). 'Caste and Politics in South Asia', in C.H. Philips, ed., *Politics and Society in India*. London: Allen & Unwin.
Geertz, Clifford (1963). 'The Integrative Revolution: Primordial Sentiments and Civil Politics in the New States', in Clifford Geertz, ed, *Old Societies and New States*. New York: Free Press.
(1964). 'Ideology as a Cultural System', in David Apter, ed., *Ideology and Discontent*. New York: Free Press.
(1973). 'Thick Description: Toward an Interpretive Theoryof Culture', in Clifford Geertz, *The Interpretation of Cultures*. New York: Basic Books.
Gellner, Ernest and John Waterbury, eds. (1977). *Patrons and Clients in Mediterranean Societies*. London: Duckworth.
Gerth, H.H. and C. Wright Mills, trans. and eds. (1958). *From Max Weber: Essays in Sociology*. New York: Galaxy Books, Oxford University Press.
Gombrich, Richard F. (1971). *Precept and Practice: Traditional Buddhism in the Rural Highlands of Ceylon*. Oxford University Press.
Goody, Jack (1968). 'Introduction', in Jack Goody, ed., *Literacy in Traditional Societies*. Cambridge University Press.
(1973). 'Bridewealth and Dowry in Africa and Eurasia', in Jack Goody and S.J. Tambiah, *Bridewealth and Dowry*. Cambridge Papers in Social Anthropology 7. Cambridge University Press.
Goody, Jack and Ian Watt (1963). 'The Consequences of Literacy', *Comparative Studies in Society and History* 5: 304–45.
Gough, Kathleen (1959). 'Cults of the Dead among the Nayars', in Milton Singer, ed., *Traditional India: Structure and Change*. Biographical and Special Series X. Philadelphia: American Folklore Society.
(1961). 'Nayar: Central Kerala', 'Nayar: North Kerala', 'Tiyyar: North Kerala', and 'Mappilla: North Kerala', in David M. Schneider and Kathleen Gough, eds. (1961).
Gunasingam, S. (1974). 'Two Inscriptions of Cola Ilankesvara Deva', *Trincomalee Inscriptions Series*, no. 1. Peradeniya: University of Sri Lanka.
Hardgrave, Robert L. Jr. (1969). *The Nadars of Tamil Nad: The Political Culture of a Community in Change*. University of California Press.
Harper, Edward B. (1964). 'Ritual Pollution as an Integrator of Caste and Religion', *Journal of Asian Studies* 2: 151–97.
Harris, Marvin (1968). *The Rise of Anthropological Theory: A History of Theories of Culture*. New York: Thomas Y. Crowell.
Harrison, Selig S. (1956). 'Caste and the Andhra Communists', *American Political Science Review* 50: 378–404.
(1960). *India: The Most Dangerous Decades*. Princeton University Press.

Hiatt, Lester R. (1973). 'The Pattini Cult of Ceylon: A Tamil Perspective', *Social Compass* 10: 231–49.

Hiebert, Paul G. (1969). 'Caste and Personal Rank in an Indian Village: An Extension in Techniques', *American Anthropologist* 71: 434–53.

(1971). *Kondura: Structure and Integration in a South Indian Village.* Minneapolis: University of Minnesota Press.

Hocart, A.M. (1931). *The Temple of the Tooth in Kandy.* Memoirs of the Archaeological Survey of Ceylon, vol. IV. London: Luzac & Co.

(1950). *Caste: A Comparative Study.* London: Methuen & Co.

Holmström, Mark (1976). *South Indian Factory Workers.* Cambridge University Press.

Inden, Ronald B. (1976). *Marriage and Rank in Bengali Culture: A History of Caste and Clan in Middle Period Bengal.* University of California Press.

Inden, Ronald B. and Ralph Nicholas (1977). *Kinship in Bengali Culture.* University of Chicago Press.

Indrapala, K. (1965). 'Dravidian Settlements in Ceylon and the Beginnings of the Kingdom of Jaffna'. Unpublished Ph.D. thesis, University of London.

Kandiah, V.C. (1964). *Maṭṭakkaḷapput Tamiḻakam* (Tamil Homeland of Batticaloa). Jaffna: Īḻakēcari Ponnaiyā Ninaivu Veḷiyīṭṭu Manṟam (I. Ponniah Memorial Publication Association).

Kemper, Stephen E.G. (1979). 'Sinhalese Astrology, South Asian Caste Systems, and the Notion of Individuality', *Journal of Asian Studies* 38: 477–97.

Kothari, Rajni (1970a). *Politics in India.* Boston: Little Brown.

(1970b), ed., *Caste in Indian Politics.* Delhi: Orient Longman.

Kothari, Rajni and Rushikesh Maru (1970). 'Federating for Political Interests: The Kshatriyas of Gujarat', in Rajni Kothari, ed. (1970b).

Laberge, S. (1976). 'Changement dans l'Usage des Clitiques Sujets dans le Français Montrealais'. Unpublished Ph.D. thesis, Université de Montreal.

Leach, Edmund R. (1960). 'Introduction: What Should We Mean by Caste?' in E.R. Leach, ed., *Aspects of Caste in South India, Ceylon and North-West Pakistan.* Cambridge Papers in Social Anthropology 2. Cambridge University Press.

(1961). *Pul Eliya, A Village in Ceylon.* Cambridge University Press.

(1973). 'Complementary Filiation and Bilateral Kinship', in Jack Goody, ed., *The Character of Kinship.* Cambridge University Press.

Levinson, Stephen C. (1977). 'Social Deixis in a Tamil Village'. Unpublished Ph.D. thesis, University of California, Berkeley.

(1978). 'Sociolinguistic Universals'. Unpublished manuscript, Cambridge University.

(1979). 'Pragmatics and Social Deixis', in C. Chiarello *et al.*, eds., *Proceedings of the Fifth Annual Meeting of the Berkeley Linguistic Society.* Berkeley: Berkeley Linguistic Society.

Lévi-Strauss, Claude (1949). *Les Structures Élémentaires de la Parenté.* Paris: Presses Universitaires de France.

(1966). *The Savage Mind.* London: Weidenfeld & Nicolson.
Lichtheim, George (1963). 'Marx and "the Asiatic Mode of Production" ', *Far Eastern Affairs* 3: 86–112.
Liyanagamage, Amaradasa (1968). *The Decline of Polonnaruwa and the Rise of Dambadeniya (ca. 1180–1270 A.D.).* Colombo: Department of Cultural Affairs.
Luce, R.D. and H. Raiffa (1957). *Games and Decisions.* New York: John Wiley & Sons.
Lynch, Owen M. (1977). 'Method and Theory in the Sociology of Louis Dumont: A Reply', in Kenneth David, ed., *The New Wind: Changing Identities in South Asia.* The Hague & Paris: Mouton.
Mahar, Pauline M. (1959). 'A Multiple Scaling Technique for Caste Ranking', *Man in India* 39: 127–47.
Maloney, Clarence (1975). 'Religious Beliefs and Social Hierarchy in Tamil Nadu, India', *American Ethnologist* 2: 169–91.
Manu (1886). *The Laws of Manu*, trans. Georg Bühler. Volume XXV of F. Max Muller, ed., *The Sacred Books of the East.* Oxford: Clarendon Press.
Marriott, McKim (1955). 'Little Communities in an Indigenous Civilization', in McKim Marriott, ed., *Village India: Studies in the Little Community.* University of Chicago Press.
(1959). 'Interactional and Attributional Theories of Caste Ranking', *Man in India* 39: 92–107.
(1960). *Caste Ranking and Community Structure in Five Regions of India and Pakistan.* Poona: Deccan College Monograph Series 23.
(1968a). 'Caste Ranking and Food Transactions: A Matrix Analysis', in Milton Singer and Bernard S. Cohn, eds., *Structure and Change in Indian Society*. Chicago: Aldine.
(1968b). 'Multiple Reference in Indian Caste Systems', in James Silverberg, ed., *Social Mobility in the Caste Systems in India: An Interdisciplinary Symposium.* Comparative Studies in Society and History, Supplement 3. The Hague: Mouton.
(1976a). 'Hindu Transactions: Diversity without Dualism', in Bruce Kapferer, ed., *Transactions and Meaning: Directions in the Anthropology of Exchange and Symbolic Behavior.* ASA Essays in Social Anthropology 1. Philadelphia: ISHI.
(1976b). 'Interpreting Indian Society: A Monistic Alternative to Dumont's Dualism', *Journal of Asian Studies* 36: 189–95.
Marriott, McKim and Ronald B. Inden (1974). 'Caste Systems', *Encyclopaedia Britannica*, 15th Edition, vol. III: 982–91.
(1977). 'Toward an Ethnosociology of South Asian Caste Systems', in Kenneth David, ed., *The New Wind: Changing Identities in South Asia.* The Hague & Paris: Mouton.
Marx, Karl and Frederick Engels (n.d.). *On Colonialism.* Moscow: Foreign Languages Publishing House.
Mathur, K.S. (1964). *Caste and Ritual in a Malwa Village.* Bombay: Asia Publishing House.

Mayer, Adrian C. (1960). *Caste and Kinship in Central India: A Village and its Region.* University of California Press.

(1963). 'Municipal Elections: A Central Indian Case Study', in C.H. Philips, ed., *Politics and Society in India*. London: Allen & Unwin.

(1967). 'Caste and Local Politics in India', in Philip Mason, ed., *India and Ceylon: Unity and Diversity*. London: Oxford University Press.

McCormack, William (1959). 'The Forms of Communication in Virasaiva Religion', in Milton Singer, ed., *Traditional India: Structure and Change.* Biographical and Special Series X. Philadelphia: American Folklore Society.

McGilvray, Dennis B. (1973). 'Caste and Matriclan Structure in Sri Lanka: A Preliminary Report on Fieldwork in Akkaraipattu', *Modern Ceylon Studies* 4: 5–20.

(1974). 'Tamils and Moors: Caste and Matriclan Structure in Eastern Sri Lanka'. Unpublished Ph.D. thesis, University of Chicago.

(1976). 'Caste, Matri-kinship, and Bodily Substance in Eastern Sri Lanka', *Papers Presented to the Fifth European Conference on Modern South Asian Studies.* Leiden.

(1982a). 'Sexual Power and Fertility in Sri Lanka: Batticaloa Tamils and Moors', in Carol P. MacCormack, ed., *Ethnography of Fertility and Birth.* London: Academic Press.

(1982b). 'Dutch Burghers and Portuguese Mechanics: Eurasian Ethnicity in Sri Lanka', *Comparative Studies in Society and History* 24: 235–63.

(in press). 'Paraiyar Drummers of Sri Lanka: Consensus and Constraint in an Untouchable Caste', *American Ethnologist.*

Meillassoux, Claude (1973). 'Are There Castes in India?', *Economy and Society* 2: 89–111.

Mencher, Joan P. (1974). 'The Caste System Upside Down, or the Not-So-Mysterious East', *Current Anthropology* 15: 469–93.

Miller, G. (1956). 'The Magical Number Seven Plus or Minus Two: Some Limits on our Capacity for Processing Information', *Psychological Review* 63: 81–97.

Moffatt, Michael (1979). *An Untouchable Community in South India: Structure and Consensus*. Princeton University Press.

Moore, Barrington (1966). *Social Origins of Dictatorship and Democracy*. Boston: Beacon Press.

(1978). *Injustice: The Social Bases of Obedience and Revolt.* London: Macmillan.

Morgenstern, A. (1968). 'Game Theory: Theoretical Aspects', in David Sills, ed., *International Encyclopedia of the Social Sciences*, vol. VI: 62–8.

Morris-Jones, W.H. (1964). *The Government and Politics of India.* London: Hutchinson.

Musgrave, P.J. (1972). 'Landlords and Lords of the Land: Estate Management and Social Control in Uttar Pradesh 1860–1920', *Modern Asian Studies* 6: 257–75.

Nadaraja, Tambyah (1966). 'New Light on Cleghorn's Minute on Justice and Revenue', *Journal of the Royal Asiatic Society, Ceylon Branch* n.s. 10: 1–28.

(1972). *The Legal System of Ceylon in its Historical Setting.* Leiden: E.J. Brill.

Nadarajah, F.X.C., ed. (1962). *Maṭṭakkaḷappu Mānmiyan* (The Glory of Batticaloa). Colombo: Kalā Nilayam.

Narahari Gopalakristnamah Chetty (1886). *A Manual of the Kurnool District.* Madras: Government Press.

Obeyesekere, Gananath (1967). *Land Tenure in Village Ceylon.* Cambridge University Press.

(1975). 'The Right-Left Subcastes in South India: A Critique', *Man* n.s. 10: 462–4.

(1976). 'The Impact of Āyurvedic Ideas on the Culture and the Individual in Sri Lanka', in Charles Leslie, ed., *Asian Medical Systems: A Comparative Study*. University of California Press.

O'Flaherty, Wendy D. (1969). 'Asceticism and Sexuality in the Mythology of Śiva', *History of Religions* 8: 300–37 and 9: 1–41.

Orenstein, Henry (1965). *Gaon: Conflict and Cohesion in an Indian Village.* Princeton University Press.

Parry, Jonathan P. (1974). 'Egalitarian Values in a Hierarchical Society', *South Asian Review* 7: 95–121.

Parvathamma, C. (1971). *Politics and Religion: A Study of Historical Interaction between Socio-political Relationships in a Mysore Village.* New Delhi: Sterling.

Percival, Robert (1805). *An Account of the Island of Ceylon.* London: C. & R. Baldwin.

Pfaffenberger, Bryan L. (1977). 'Pilgrimage and Traditional Authority in Tamil Sri Lanka'. Unpublished Ph.D. thesis, University of California, Berkeley.

Pieris, Ralph (1956). *Sinhalese Social Organization.* Colombo: Ceylon University Press Board.

Pitt-Rivers, Julian (1972). 'On the Word "Caste" ', in Thomas Beidelman, ed., *The Translation of Culture.* London: Tavistock.

Pocock, D.F. (1972). *Kanbi and Patidar.* Oxford: Clarendon Press.

Raghavan, M.D. (1953). 'A Kalvettu of the Seerpadam of the Eastern Province', Ethnological Survey of Ceylon 7, *Spolia Zeylanica* 27: 187–93.

(1961). *The Karāva of Ceylon.* Colombo: K.V.G. De Silva.

(1971). *Tamil Culture in Ceylon: A General Introduction.* Colombo: Kalai Nilayam.

Rajagopalachari, C. (1961). *The Ayodhya Canto of the Ramayana as told by Kamban.* London: Allen & Unwin.

Ramanujan, A.K. (1968). 'The Structure of Variation: A Study in Caste Dialects', in Milton Singer and Bernard S. Cohn, eds., *Structure and Change in Indian Society.* Chicago: Aldine.

(1973). *Speaking of Śiva.* Harmondsworth: Penguin Books.

Redfield, Robert (1956). *Peasant Society and Culture.* University of Chicago Press.
Reisman, K. (1974). 'Contrapuntal Conversations in an Antiguan Village', in Richard Bauman and Joel Sherzer, eds., *Explorations in the Ethnography of Speaking.* Cambridge University Press.
Roberts, Michael (1969). 'The Rise of the Karāvas', *Ceylon Studies Seminar* 1968–69 Series, no. 5. Peradeniya, Sri Lanka.
Rorty, Richard (1979). *Philosophy and the Mirror of Nature.* Princeton University Press.
Rudolph, Lloyd I. and Susanne Hoeber Rudolph (1967). *The Modernity of Tradition: Political Development in India.* University of Chicago Press.
Ryan, Bryce (1950). 'Socio-Cultural Regions of Ceylon', *Rural Sociology* 15: 3–19.
(1953). *Caste in Modern Ceylon: The Sinhalese System in Transition.* New Brunswick: Rutgers University Press.
Ryan, Kathleen S. (1980). 'Pollution in Practice: Ritual, Structure, and Change in Tamil Sri Lanka'. Unpublished Ph.D. thesis, Cornell University.
Sacks, H., E.A. Schegloff and G. Jefferson (1974). 'A Simplest Systematics for the Organization of Turn-Taking for Conversation', *Language* 50: 696–735.
Schiffer, S.R. (1972). *Meaning.* Oxford University Press.
Schlesinger, Lee I. (1977). 'The Emergency in an Indian Village', *Asian Survey* 17: 627–47.
Schneider, David M. (1961). 'The Distinctive Features of Matrilineal Descent Groups', in David M. Schneider and Kathleen Gough, eds. (1961).
(1968). *American Kinship: A Cultural Account.* Englewood Cliffs, N.J.: Prentice-Hall.
Schneider, David M. and Kathleen Gough, eds. (1961). *Matrilineal Kinship.* University of California Press.
Seneviratne, H.L. (1978). *Rituals of the Kandyan State.* Cambridge Studies in Social Anthropology 22. Cambridge University Press.
Sharma, Ursula (1973). 'Theodicy and the Doctrine of Karma', *Man* n.s. 8: 347–64.
Shree Kumaraswamiji (1956). 'Virasaivism' in Haridas Bhattacharya, ed., *The Cultural Heritage of India*, vol. IV. Calcutta: Ramakrishna Mission Institute of Culture.
Singer, Milton (1972). *When a Great Tradition Modernizes: An Anthropological Approach to Indian Civilization.* New York: Praeger.
Skinner, Quentin (1978). *The Foundations of Modern Political Thought. I: The Renaissance.* Cambridge University Press.
Srinivas, M.N. (1952). *Religion and Society among the Coorgs of South India.* New York: Asia Publishing House.
(1959). 'The Dominant Caste in Rampura', *American Anthropologist* 61: 1–16.

Stein, Burton (1968). 'Brahman and Peasant in Early South Indian History', *Adyar Library Bulletin* (1967–8) 31 & 32: 229–69.
(1969). 'Integration of the Agrarian System of South India', in Robert E. Frykenberg, ed., *Land Control and Social Structure in Indian History*. University of Wisconsin Press.
(1975). 'The State and the Agrarian Order in Medieval South India', in Burton Stein, ed., *Essays on South India.* Asian Studies at Hawaii 15. Honolulu: University Press of Hawaii.
(1978) ed., *South Indian Temples: An Analytical Reconstruction.* New Delhi: Vikas.
(1980). *Peasant State and Society in Medieval South India*. Delhi: Oxford University Press.
Stern, Henri (1971). 'Religion et Société en Inde selon Max Weber: Analyse Critique de *Hindouisme et Buddhisme*', *Informations sur les Sciences Sociales* 10: 69–112.
Stevenson, H.N.C. (1954). 'Status Evaluation in the Hindu Caste System', *Journal of the Royal Anthropological Institute* 84: 45–65.
Stirrat, R.L. (1975a). 'Compadrazgo in Catholic Sri Lanka', *Man* n.s. 10: 589–606.
(1975b). 'The Social Organisation of Production in a Sinhalese Fishing Village', *Modern Ceylon Studies* 6: 140–62.
(1977). 'Dravidian and Non-Dravidian Kinship Terminologies in Sri Lanka', *Contributions to Indian Sociology* n.s. 11: 271–93.
Stokes, Eric (1978). *The Peasant and the Raj: Studies in Agrarian Society and Peasant Rebellion in Colonial India.* Cambridge University Press.
Tambiah, H.W. (1950). *The Laws and Customs of the Tamils of Jaffna.* Colombo: The Times of Ceylon.
(1954). *The Laws and Customs of the Tamils of Ceylon.* Ceylon: Tamil Cultural Society of Ceylon.
(1968). *Sinhala Laws and Customs.* Colombo: Lake House.
Tambiah, Stanley J. (1973a). 'Dowry and Bridewealth and the Property Rights of Women in South Asia', in Jack Goody and S.J. Tambiah, *Bridewealth and Dowry.* Cambridge Papers in Social Anthropology 7. Cambridge University Press.
(1973b). 'From Varna to Caste through Mixed Unions', in Jack Goody, ed., *The Character of Kinship.* Cambridge University Press.
(1976). *World Conqueror and World Renouncer: A Study of Buddhism and Polity in Thailand*. Cambridge Studies in Social Anthropology 15. Cambridge University Press.
Taylor, Charles (1975). *Hegel.* Cambridge University Press.
Tennent, James Emerson (1850). *Christianity in Ceylon.* London: John Murray.
Thurston, Edgar (1909). *Castes and Tribes of Southern India.* 7 vols. Madras: Government Press.
Wadley, Susan S. (1975). *Shakti: Power in the Conceptual Structure of Karimpur Religion.* University of Chicago Studies in Anthropology, Series in Social, Cultural, and Linguistic Anthropology 2. University of Chicago Department of Anthropology.

Washbrook, David (1973). 'Country Politics: Madras 1880 to 1930', *Modern Asian Studies* 7: 475–531.
(1975). 'The Development of Caste Organisation in South India 1880 to 1925', in Christopher J. Baker and David Washbrook, eds. (1975).
(1979). 'Indigenous Racial Ideologies in Colonial India 1860–1940'. Unpublished paper, University of Warwick.
Weber, Max (1958). *The Religion of India: The Sociology of Hinduism and Buddhism.* Hans H. Gerth and Don Martindale, trans. and eds. New York: Free Press.
Williams, Bernard (1978). *Descartes.* Harmondsworth: Penguin Books.
Winslow, Deborah (1980). 'Rituals of First Menstruation in Sri Lanka', *Man* n.s. 15: 603–25.
Winslow, Rev. Miron (1862). *A Comprehensive Tamil and English Dictionary of High and Low Tamil.* Madras: American Mission Press.
Yalman, Nur (1960). 'The Flexibility of Caste Principles in a Kandyan Community', in E.R. Leach, ed., *Aspects of Caste in South India, Ceylon and North-West Pakistan.* Cambridge Papers in Social Anthropology 2. Cambridge University Press.
(1962). 'The Structure of the Sinhalese Kindred: A Re-examination of the Dravidian Terminology', *American Anthropologist* 64: 548–75.
(1963). 'On the Purity of Women in the Castes of Malabar and Ceylon', *Journal of the Royal Anthropological Institute* 93: 25–58.
(1967). *Under the Bo Tree: Studies in Caste, Kinship, and Marriage in the Interior of Ceylon.* University of California Press.
(1969). 'The Semantics of Kinship in South India and Ceylon', in Thomas A. Sebeok, ed., *Current Trends in Linguistics*, vol. V, Linguistics in South Asia. The Hague: Mouton.
Zelliot, Eleanor (1970). 'Learning the Use of Political Means: The Mahars of Maharashtra', in Rajni Kothari, ed. (1970b).
Zvelebil, Kamil (1964). 'The Spoken Language of Tamilnad', *Archiv Orientální* 32: 237–65.
(1966). 'Some Features of Ceylon Tamil', *Indo-Iranian Journal* 9: 113–38.

INDEX

Abeyesinghe, T.B.H., 9
Ahir caste, 210
Aiyankar caste, 102n.(a), 107
Aiyappan, A., 45
Aiyar caste, 102–3, 104–5, 107, 113–14, 125, 127, 177, 179–80, 195–6
Akkaraipattu, 40–6, 84–6, 229 n.31, 230 n.43, 231 n.50
Alexander Johnston Papers, 68, 227 n.32
alliance between castes, 6, 84–6, 108, 174–95, 199, 202, 212; upper versus lower caste blocs, 41–3, 74–9, 84–6, 114, 187–94
Ambirajan, S., 213
Anantha Krishna Iyer, L.K., 59, 67, 227 n.29, 228 n.34
Appadurai, A. & C.B., 71, 231 n.50
artha, 206–7, 234 n.3
artisan castes, *see* Coli Acari; Konku Acari; Tattar; Wellagoda
'Asiatic' mode of production, 204, 233 n. 1
aṭimai castes, 43

Baedahala caste, 14, 18, 22, 30
Bailey, F.G., 207, 210–11
Baker, C.J., & D. Washbrook, 71
Banks, M.Y., 3, 38, 43, 53, 55, 88
barber castes, *see* Konku Navitar; Navitar; Panikki
Bariya caste, 210
Barnett, S.A., 36, 38, 57, 60, 88, 90, 95, 225 n.18 & 21, 226 n.23, 227 n.26
Barnett, S.A., L. Fruzzetti & O. Östör, 38
Barth, F., 13
Basham, A.L., 207
Batticaloa, 40–8, 59, 65–7, 227 n.31; Brahman castes, 63–4, 66–7; Christian groups, 40–1, 44, 223 n.4, 224 n.8; Tamil dialect, 87; Tamil names, 224 n.12; *see also* Akkaraipattu; conception; kingly ideology; Kokkatticcolai; land tenure; Palukamam; purity and pollution; Tambiluvil & Tirukkovil; Velalars
Beck, B.E.F., 3, 55, 100–1, 104–5, 113–14, 119, 121, 123, 129, 142–3, 148, 151, 154, 158, 160–1, 163–4, 167, 171, 179–80, 186, 190, 199–201, 226 n.23, 230 n.42, 232 n.2 & 5
Benedict, R., 96
Bengal: conception theories, 37–8, 51; kinship, 37–8, 48, 94, 228 n.36; marriage, 57, 91; purity and pollution, 38
Béteille, A., 11, 43, 208, 210, 215, 218–19, 222 n.13, 235 n.7
bio-moral substance, *see* ethnosociology
Blau, P., 149
Bloch, Maurice, 32
Brahman castes, 39, 60; in Batticaloa, 63–4, 66–7; *see also* Aiyankar; Aiyar; Havik Brahmans
Brass, P., 212, 214, 217
Brazil, 217–19, 235 n.10
Breman, J., 218
Bright, W., & A.K. Ramanujan, 179
British colonial policy, 6–7, 213–15, 217; *see also* inheritance; land tenure
Brito, C., 68, 71, 227 n.30
Brown, P., & S.C. Levinson, 109, 122, 124
Brown, R., & A. Gilman, 109, 120, 124
Buddhists, Sinhalese, 41
Burghers of Sri Lanka, 41, 44, 224 n.4 & 8

Farmer, B.H., 223 n.5
Ferro-Luzzi, G.E., 14
fisher castes, 67, 227 n.29; *see also* Karava; Karaiyar; Mukkuvars in Puttalam
fishing, 9–10; *see also* fisher castes
Flynn, P., 235 n.10
food transactions, 3, 91, 116–19, 121–3, 143–5, 149, 154–6, 190, 199, 200–2
Fox, R.G., 235 n.8
Freed, S.A., 42n, 124
Fruzzetti, L., & O. Östör, 38, 51, 57, 90, 95, 228 n.36
Fuller, C.J., 13–14, 24
Fürer-Haimendorf, C. von, 210, 214

Game theory, 155–60, 165–6, 173–5, 188, 232 n.3; passive score-board versus competitive game, 149–60
Geertz, C., 97, 212
Gellner, E., & J. Waterbury, 217
Gombrich, R.F., 221 n.6
Goody, J.R., 43, 97
Goody, J.R., & I. Watt, 97
Gough, K., 14, 45, 55, 228 n.36
Goyigama caste, 8, 10–11, 15–16, 18, 22–4, 26, 28, 221 n.8, 230 n.49
Gunasingham, S., 229 n.39

Hardgrave, R.L., 210–11
Harijans in Kannapuram, 102–4, 108, 165, 185
Harper, E.B., 227 n.26
Harris, M., 98
Harrison, S.S., 210–11
Havik Brahmans, 55, 227 n.26
Hegel, G.W.F., 205–6
Hiatt, L.R., 47, 82–4, 230 n.47
Hiebert, P.G., 42n, 112, 124
Hinduism, *see artha*; *dharma*; *karma*; reincarnation; Saivite invasion; temple(s); Viracaivism
Hocart, A.M., 11, 18, 31, 35, 72, 88, 222 n.16 & 24, 230 n.49
Holmstrom, M., 218
Homans, G.C., 149
honour, social, marks of, 3–4, 18–19, 35, 43, 45–6, 48, 66, 70–3, 77, 79–87, 90, 104, 106, 230 n.43
Hunu caste, 10, 18–19, 222 n.10

Ideologies, caste, 1–7, 34–5, 98–9; historical context, 95–7; *see also* Dumont; kingly ideology; purity and pollution; social science
Inden, R.B., 37, 93
Inden, R.B., & R. Nicholas, 37, 57, 94
Indrapala, K., 59, 67, 227 n.31
inheritance: in Jaffna, 226 n.23; joint estates, 70, 229 n.41; Mukkuvar Law, 68–76, 230 n.42; Thesawalamai Law, 69, 227 n.32; *see also* British colonial policy; land tenure; marriage (dowry)
interaction patterns: audience effects on behaviour, 153; boycotts, 150–2; male/female, 123, 140; methods of study, 5–6, 99, 111–49, 198; office of village accountant, 196; polyvocal symbolism of rank, 3–5, 93, 118–19, 201–3; power versus solidarity, 109, 120–1, 174–5, 189, 201; retaliative behaviour, 124, 150–2, 186–9; scaling methods, 112, 124–49; touching and kinesic display, 202; types of media, 122–3, 157, 172–3, 189, 199–203; *see also* food; game theory; inter-caste relationships; language; Marriott; seating; service; varna (transactional strategies); verbal interaction
inter-caste relationships: conflict between castes, 22–3, 80–2, 221 n8; *see also* alliance; interaction
intra-caste divisions: *lokuru minissu* in Wellagoda, 28–9; Sinhalese names and titles, 4, 16–18, 23, 222 n.9, 10, 12 & 13, 230 n.48; Tamil and Moorish matriclans, 46–8, 74–9; *see also* kinship

Jaffna, 21, 43, 54, 57, 59, 87–9, 91, 223 n.2, 227 n.30, 228 n.37; bound castes, 43, 224 n.8; conception theories, 38, 53; inheritance, 226 n.23; kinship, 38, 48, 54, 226 n.23; purity and pollution, 38, 55
jajmani system, 101
Jat caste, 210

Kaikkolar Mutaliyar caste, 101–3, 172
Kalinga, 44, 59, 227 n.31

Schiffer, S.R., 124
Schlesinger, L.I., 211
Schneider, D.M., 36–9, 74, 96
seating, 3, 154–5, 179, 190, 192, 199, 200–2
Seneviratne, H.L., 230 n.49
service transactions, 3, 119–23, 154–5, 199–200, 202
Sharma, U., 93
Shree Kumaraswamiji, 228 n.34
Singer, M., 97
Skinner, Q., 207
social science, philosophy of, 204–9, 234 n.5
sociology, French, 206
sociology of knowledge, 97
Srinivas, M.N., 211, 227 n.26
Stein, B., 60, 71–2, 105–7, 164, 229 n.39
Stern, H., 234 n.4
Stevenson, H.N.C., 37, 125
Stirrat, R.L., 10, 16, 26, 33, 230 n.44
Stokes, E., 204–5, 216, 235 n.7 & 9
substance and code, *see* ethnosociology
succession to office, 59–61, 68–87, 92

Tambiah, H.W., 69, 222 n.13, 227 n.32
Tambiah, S.J., 36, 69, 99, 206, 234 n.3
Tambiluvil and Tirukkovil, 82–4, 228 n.37, 230 n.47
Tamilnadu, 38, 43, 60, 87–8, 230 n.44; conception theories, 38, 225 n.18; kinship, 38, 226 n.23; purity and pollution, 38, 225 n.21, 227 n.26; transubstantiation of bride, 57, 91; Velalars in, 60, 88; *see also* left-hand castes; neutral division; right-hand castes
Tamils: Indian Tamils in Sri Lanka, 28; Tamil and Moorish matri-clans, 46–8, 74–9; Tamil names in Batticaloa, 224 n.12
Tattar caste, 41–3, 45, 54, 62, 66, 73, 87, 224 n.8, 225 n.15
Taylor, C., 205–6
temple(s), Hindu: caste temples, 79–84, 87, 105; management, 6, 45, 79, 82, 85, 229 n.41; as model of caste society, 4, 71–3, 78, 80, 90, 93; regional (*tēcattukōvils*), 65, 71–3, 90, 228 n.37; ritual, 6, 45, 60, 62–7, 70–3, 75, 78–87, 91, 93, 230 n.49, 231 n.50; service, 45, 60–2, 65–7, 93, 230 n.49; *see also* religion
Tennent, J.E., 9
Thesawalamai Law, 69, 227 n.32
Thurston, E., 59–61, 67, 227 n.29, 228 n.35
Timilar caste, 231 n.51
Tiyyar caste, 45
Trincomalee, 231 n.51
Turainilavanai, 229 n.41

Unilineal descent, 4, 38–40, 46–7, 95, 230 n.48
Untouchable castes, *see* low caste groupings

Vaishya Cettiyar caste, 179
Vannar caste, 41–3, 54, 61–2, 73, 85, 225 n.15
Vanniyar caste, 210
Varna, 1–2, 37, 94–5, 99, 106, 150, 163–75, 188–9, 206, 210, 212; Brahman, 4, 36, 63–4, 66–7, 88–9, 91, 97, 99, 101, 106, 228 n.37, 229 n.39; Kshatriya, 17–18, 22, 36, 60, 66, 88–9, 104, 222 n.11 & 14; transactional strategies, 6, 90, 94, 163–76, 180, 232 n.3; *see also* Dumont; Marriott
Vatuka Nayakkar caste, 102–3, 107, 185–7
Vatuka Vannar caste, 102–3, 107, 127, 184–6, 232 n.3
vegetarianism, 106, 125, 228 n.33
Velalars: in Batticaloa, 42, 45, 60–2, 64–7, 75–87, 93, 227 n.32, 228 n.33, 229 n.41, 230 n.47 & 49, 231 n.51; Karaikkal & Marunkar, 62; in Tamilnadu, 60, 88; in Wellagoda, 21; *see also* Kontaikkatti Velalar
verbal interaction, 3, 98–203, 231–2; class and, 142–3; relative age and (REL), 6, 111, 113–14, 121, 139–43, 151, 160, 173, 175–89, 196; *see also* language
Viracaiva Kurukkal caste, 35, 42, 45, 56, 60, 62–4, 66, 76–7, 79, 83, 86–7, 89, 92, 225 n.15, 228 n.33–6, 229 n.41, 230 n.45 & 47
Viracaivism (Lingayat sect), 62–4, 67, 92; *see also* Viracaiva Kurukkal